PEGGY AND ME

Also by Miranda Hart

Is It Just Me?

The Best of Miranda

PEGGY
AND ME

MIRANDA HART

**HODDER &
STOUGHTON**

First published in Great Britain in 2016 by
Hodder & Stoughton
An Hachette UK company

1

A CIP catalogue record for this title is
available from the British Library

Hardback ISBN 9781444769128
Trade Paperback ISBN 9781444769135
eBook ISBN 9781444769166

Typeset in Sabon MT by Palimpsest Book Production Ltd,
Falkirk, Stirlingshire

Printed and bound by Clays Ltd, St Ives plc

Hodder & Stoughton policy is to use papers that are natural, renewable
and recyclable products and made from wood grown in sustainable forests.
The logging and manufacturing processes are expected to conform to
the environmental regulations of the country of origin.

Hodder & Stoughton Ltd
Carmelite House
50 Victoria Embankment
London EC4Y 0DZ

www.hodder.co.uk

To Peggy

And to my fellow dog lovers and
their canine companions

CONTENTS

CHAPTER 0

Because no one reads an Introduction

Right, here goes, the first sentence of my new book. Ooh, look at that, done. Tick. Though I feel weary already. You see, I have already written this book. This book was finished. It's now summer 2016 and I finished this book on 12 October 2013. Yes indeed I shall explain forthwith.

That happy Saturday October morning I was going to have one more read through over the weekend before emailing my literary agent a copy on Monday. I was so thrilled it had come together. I had been thinking about the book since the beginning of that year, brainstormed the concept and subject areas in April (pushing myself to do so having just recovered from a knee operation, so keen was I) and wrote it on and off throughout the year. I also had a stand-up show to write and try out; was filming *Call the Midwife* and *Gangsta Granny*; and wrote and performed Maracattack, a comedy fitness DVD (I presume Team GB are currently using it to train for the Olympics). So it had been a full year, particularly as I had been travelling during the first two months on a self-imposed sabbatical and had the aforementioned unexpected knee operation on my return, so I had squeezed it all into a shorter timescale. But I had done it. And, most thrilling of all, I had really enjoyed it. I look back at a few sporadic diary ramblings and there are a number of repeated entries. 'Surprised to be really enjoying writing *Peggy and Me*.' 'Perhaps I don't hate writing after all.' 'I think I have finally found the kind of writing I love to do.' It was true. I did principally enjoy it and, after the initial and inevitable writer fears – mantras including: 'I simply have nothing to say'/'I'm going to win a prize – for the worst book ever published in the history of books'/'Is it possible to be too tall to write a book? If it is, then I'm definitely too tall'/'What if it doesn't sell a single copy and all the books get pulped? And if that happens do I get charged for the pulping? How much does pulping cost? I CAN'T AFFORD THE PULPING!' – after all that, I let go and found it an intimate and relaxing process. I wrote it as if telling one lovely person who was interested in my musings due to their being as pet obsessed as I (I had faith I would sell at least *one* copy, and hello to you and thanks for buying – shall we go out for dinner? Though you can pay – I've only sold one copy of my book and there may be pulping costs); and I ended up being relatively satisfied with it. I told my agent there would be something wrong with the world if I won a Nobel Peace Prize on account of this publication, but hopefully a few readers – or should I say, a truly exceptional, discerning, one-of-a-kind, take-me-out-for-dinner-please reader like yourself – might just like it.

On that Saturday in 2013, I was getting ready to go to my nephew's sixth birthday party and then on to a small surprise fortieth dinner party for an old university friend. As I was leaving the house I first looked at my dog. She gave me the classic 'please don't leave me here alone' eyes. The eyes that somehow manage to convey deep vulnerability and sorrow but also a distinct undercurrent of threat. The eyes which say: 'If you leave me here alone I will, within five minutes, expire from longing and grief like a little Victorian orphan. But on the way out I might somehow find the energy to destroy your curtains. Just saying.' I had no choice but to take her with me. I explained to her that my friends might not want her in their house so she might have to stay put in the car. She always looks as if she completely understands when I talk to her. Or, at the very least, her intense look suggests she would *love* to understand and would absolutely enrol in an 'English For Dogs' course at the City Lit if they saw fit to start offering such a thing (those who run evening classes can have that idea on me). So, the dog was coming with. Next, I looked at my computer. I considered taking it with me so I could start the final read of the book sitting in the car between my two parties. But quickly dismissed the notion as ridiculous, namely because I really should give myself time off, to avoid any kind of creative exhaustion through striving. Note to self: working is good, striving equals bad. I must learn to trust that things, as they always do, come together. Decision made, I was going to have a lovely day off away from the screen. However, as I opened the front door to leave I was stopped in my tracks. I looked back at the laptop on the kitchen table and a voice said, as clear as day, 'Take the laptop.' I just assumed it to be that stressy unnecessary voice of mine. You know, the kind of voice that says you should worry, even though you unplugged the toaster and put it in the fridge for safekeeping, in case it might escape and plug itself back in and toast everything you love. Not the sensible useful voice that might remind me to put the birthday present in my bag or check my teeth for spinach or my skirt lest half of it be tucked into my (probably spotty) pants. So I ignored it and drove off, looking forward to delving into a children's party – always brilliant to have a licence to pretend you are playing games for the children's sake when actually you really miss dunking your head in a bucket of water to retrieve an apple or eating a bar of chocolate with a knife and fork whilst wearing a woolly hat and gloves (actually my preferred method of chocolate-eating; it adds an element of jeopardy absent from most snacks).

I returned about midnight after a fun-fuelled day, albeit

slightly weary on a significant sugar down – I won six packets
of Haribo from Pass the Parcel, which is easily done if your
opponents are small children and you simply refuse to pass
them the parcel, claiming you are teaching them a lesson in
the value of patience and the essential unfairness of life – and
as I approached the house I noticed the sitting-room window
facing on to the road was ajar. I definitely shut it because
the sensible useful voice reminded me to. 'Oh no, I bet I have
been burgled' interrupted the stressy – nay by now, downright
panicky – voice. The front door was still locked. Phew, it's
fine. I unlocked the door. Chaos. Utter chaos. I stood motion-
less. Winded. The place had been tipped upside down. I *had*
been burgled.

I rushed around assessing what valuables might have gone.
The TV was there, my DVDs, photographs, a few other
electricals all there. Hang on, iPad gone – damn. I went
upstairs. Everything had been carelessly and violently
searched. My possessions strewn like a landfill site. All clothes
were still there. Passport still there. Jewellery – all gone.
Damn. Mind you, I don't think I own a piece worth more
than 150 quid. To me a significant amount to spend on a
necklace or a watch, but I knew the police wouldn't be interested and call my loot small fry. As I continued to scurry
around, darting from one displaced drawer to the next, alert
and terrified like a sort of oversized meerkat, I felt one positive thought calm me briefly. I realized I didn't own anything
valuable whatsoever. I felt rather proud of this. I know I am
'meant' to be interested in finery of every kind, 'oh yes, I got
this blazer for a snip at three grand at Chaz's boutique in
Shoreditch', 'yup this is a five hundred quid kitchen gadget
endorsed by Gwinee P which will juice anything I put in it
whilst chanting motivational yogic slogans', but if I have any

available funds for extravagant moments, I will immediately think of where in the world I could go, what fun experiences I could partake in and what friends I could take with me. Tea at the Ritz anyone? Thames boat trip? Salzburg *Sound of Music* Sing-a-Long minibus tour? Such fun. I will also, at the risk of portraying myself as some kind of saint, consider a charity I could donate to. I want to spend on people and experiences where I can. To me that has always made more sense than having 'things'. And I vowed to make sure that was always the case.

I had a final think. Was there anything that was really valuable? My grandmother's necklace. Oh, it so reminds me of her and I really loved it. She only died last year, and I hadn't worn it yet. I was saving it to wear to an event where feeling her calming presence would be 'just the ticket' as she would have said. I meerkat-ed (that should definitely be a verb) to the drawer. Nothing but an empty necklace box. Damn, dash and damn again. Oh now that is sad; I am cross now. Was that it? And then an arresting shudder. I hadn't looked at the kitchen table for the laptop. Oh no, please no, not the laptop. I ran downstairs. Just a laptop stand and portable keyboard. No laptop. DAMN, DAMN, DAMN, DAMN, DAMN, DAMN!

As I was jumping up and down in my kitchen, close to tears, the police made their way in. If I hadn't been so distracted by the circumstances I would have apologized and made some excuse as to why I was stomping and stropping and jumping like a child: 'Sorry, officer, I was just rehearsing for a new fitness DVD, The Angry Toddler Workout. Scream and thrash your way to abs.' But I went straight into a tirade of laptop loss, much to their bemusement. 'You see it's about a dog, officer.' 'Sorry, madam?' 'A very cute dog . . . ' 'Calm

down, madam, what are you saying?' 'The book, my book
. . . about a dog and my time with her and . . . it's taken me
most of the year . . . and I was going to take it . . . I confused
the sensible instinctive caring voice for the panicky stressy
voice . . . oh officer . . . ' 'Madam, calm down . . . ' 'Stop
calling me madam, it's making me feel like a brothel owner
. . . you know the stressy voice you ignore, well, the voice
said take the laptop . . . and actually I see now it was a kind
God-like voice trying to get me to take it . . . it knew this
was going to happen. OFFICER, YOU HAVE TO GET MY
LAPTOP BACK – IT'S ABOUT MY DOG!' Shaking him
and biffing him on the shoulders was probably not a good
idea. Neither was my final parting shot, 'Sorry, officer, sorry,
I don't know why I was treating you like a lover who had
jilted me . . . ' 'What?' 'I was just saying it was as if you and
I were lovers . . . Ha ha . . . me and you . . . lovers . . . ' He
kindly ignored my embarrassing cogitations and we started
at the beginning.

The police were very excellent in every way but of course
didn't fully understand the urgent loss of a book. Well, it is
indeed hard to describe. And as I cried – all night – really, I
couldn't stop, it felt like grief, I wondered whether I was
overreacting. I still had my health, I still had a roof over my
head, I still had the memories of my grandmother, if not her
necklace. Why was I quite so upset and angry? Stephen Fry
had kindly texted me to share his condolences as he could
imagine the horror of losing a creative baby. I felt reassured
my grief wasn't misplaced. He reminded me I wasn't the only
writer to have lost a book. Jilly Cooper left *Riders* on a
London bus (the fact it took fourteen years for her to rewrite
it must have been indicative of the pain of the loss). Dylan
Thomas lost *Under Milk Wood* three times ('to lose one

manuscript may be regarded as a misfortune, to lose three
. . . well, what a tit'). And Ernest Hemingway of course lost,
well, all his early works, and said in *A Moveable Feast* he
had never seen anyone cry as much as his wife trying to tell
him the manuscripts had been stolen. In a letter to Ezra
Pound a month after the loss he said, 'All that remains of
my complete works are three pencil drafts of a bum poem
. . . some correspondence . . . and some journalistic carbons.
You, naturally, would say, "Good", etc. But don't say it to
me. I ain't yet reached that mood.'

I was in good company. Although obviously nothing
compares to a generation losing a pet memoir by a comedy
actress. I think we all can see that would be a *far* greater loss
than Hemingway's early works or Dylan Thomas's master-
piece. *Under Milk Wood* versus *Peggy and Me*. No contest.

As dawn broke after nil sleep, I also experienced something
of a personal dawn. The reason for my grief, I realized, was
because they stole, not a great manuscript the world couldn't
be without (I am afraid, lest you didn't recognize my sarcasm
above, this is no *Oliver Twist* or *Tale of Two Cities*, or
anything by Hemingway or even, let's be frank, Jilly Cooper,
so please put it down immediately if you consider it might
be), but they stole my time. Not only the valuable weeks I
had carved out to work on it specifically, but all the weekends
I said no to because I had to get the book done that year;
the evenings I had spent pushing on with it; the few hours
working on the plane instead of relaxing watching a movie;
the couple of mornings on a cherished holiday. All gone.
They had stolen that most treasured commodity: my time. I
was grieving missed moments I could have had with friends
and family; swims or walks in beautiful scenery; or simply
a drink in a pub or watching a fun film. All the things I claim

to want to spend any spare cash on instead of the valuables the police would have understood in a burglary. All the things that are so important to me, I had sacrificed for work. Perhaps there is an interesting lesson to be learnt here. Perhaps this was a God-like intervention, and in future I needed to stand firmer than I thought I already was, in planning things on my timescale in a way that would get the best out of me creatively and give me time to, well, have a bit of a life. It is surely nonsense to have a moment of success then find yourself unable to enjoy it because, through fear of not being popular in a few months, or whatever it may be, you are run into the ground through overwork. I have lots more on that, and our cultural state of busy-ness, but I'll save it for another time and, perhaps, tome.

I never got the laptop back. I had no time left to rewrite it in 2013; 2014 was already planned with a stand-up tour, a film, and the writing and doing of the *Miranda Finale*; and 2015 was needed to recover and reclaim some of that stolen time with friends and family. So here we are. And although I still feel frankly very cross about it, I am going to consider rewriting it because well, for starters, I don't want those burglars to have won. Plus what I do remember about the book was that it included some simple life lessons I had learnt through a small dog's behaviour. I am not talking about how to wash my bum with my tongue or take a pie packet out of a bin and lick it (although I might have done that at university one morning after a late one – the latter, not the bum-licking, just to be VERY clear). The lessons were more, spiritual, for want of a better word. And perhaps the person who buys this book would find them useful. (And hello again to you, have you decided where we are dining? As you are paying, how about the Oxo Tower in Central London or somewhere in

New York – you can get relatively cheap flights . . .) I also remember it being, if I may be so bold, vaguely amusing. For I have got myself into a few scrapes over the last nine years of owning my dear pet – you can't be a little clumsy and silly in life and come out unscathed from a vet's or a dog groomer's. So perhaps my reader friend also needs a bit of light relief. (Or we could go and get sushi in Japan . . . ?)

Golly, I hope I can remember it all. If I can't, what else could I learn from the experience of losing an entire book, my hard work and time? Patience, I suppose. That things often don't go according to plan. And indeed, you will be constantly disappointed if you assume you are entitled to a perfect planned life. But because life is messy, you can really love and savour and be seriously joy-filled in the times it isn't. And attempt to be more accepting when it is. I must try and deeply relish the present moment, which is often less messy than we all make it. Perhaps the exercise of repeating an activity that was stolen will force me to be present in a way I never was before, making better choices with what to do with my newfound appreciation and understanding of time. Goodness me, I am sounding SO WISE. Move over Dalai Lama, there's not room for the both of us. *strolls to bedroom, changes into Gandhi loincloth (bath towel) and Mother Teresa headgear (tea towel), returns, resumes writing* 'Blessing in disguise' can feel like a phrase bandied about rather tritely. But surely 'tis true, 'tis true. So I am going to start again and feel hopeful for the lessons I have learnt, my personal blessings in disguise.

At this point I don't know how far I will get. I don't know whether I will finish it. I don't know whether, if I do finish it, it will be as good as it was, or whether I can remember enough and get it to an even vaguely acceptable standard.

None of this is an excuse – if it offends you, please write to my publisher, not to me! But I am starting to rewrite it because, if nothing else, I do find the subject matter amusing. And my muse for the, I hope, amusing musings, is my dear dog Peggy. Who gratefully this isn't posthumously about when it could easily have been had I not taken her with me that fateful day. Losing a laptop, all personal and creative documents, all photos and all music was hard, but it would be nothing compared with losing a best canine friend. Oh golly goodness no. She's priceless. So, as she looks up at me from her self-made bed on my discarded jumper by my desk, I'd better start writing about her.

Oh and yes, for the record, I now know exactly what iCloud is. I used to think 'backing up' was someone politely describing constipation, but now I am going to back up my introduction (three different ways) and crack on with this book. Again.

CHAPTER 1

Animal Lover

So here we are, Chapter 1, Take 2. And I think we should begin with an official welcome. So welcome, welcome to you, to my jolly old book. If all goes according to plan, we shall have a whole book to romp through together, and may I say how absolutely delighted I am that you've chosen to romp with me. In the literary sense only, I hasten to add. I do like the word romp but let's not euphemistically misconstrue, particularly if you are reading this before noon on a weekday.

So, MDRC, which for the uninitiated is short for My Dear Reader Chum. I don't know where you were for my first literary outing, *Is It Just Me?* (available in all good retailers). Perhaps a large picture of me on the front of that book was off-putting but now there is a DOG on the cover, you will consider my musings. Rude. (And for those of you saying there are two dogs on the cover of this book. Ruder. But funny.) So yes, MDRC, might I ask what in particular made you choose this book? Rather than, say, a slick psychological thriller; or a beautifully bound collection of medieval maps of the Peak District; or one of those peculiarly popular 'clean-eating' books of cake recipes without dairy, wheat, sugar or indeed anything vaguely edible you would want in a cake. Perhaps you settled upon this book purely by accident. Perhaps you were playing a game with a friend called 'Blindfold Book-Shopper', in which you tie a scarf, or sock, over your eyes and charge into a bookshop at full tilt and have to buy the first book you grab or, more likely, knock over. (Actually, I think I have come up with something there, do give me a shout next time you're playing and I'll jog along and join – well, walk along, I am over forty with large breasticles so jogging is not good for me.) Or perhaps you had a few too many wines of an evening, stabbed at some keys on your laptop and woke to find your bank account ten pounds lighter and me on your doormat, beaming up at you, begging to be read. In which case, I can't apologize enough, but let's try and make the best of it and you might like to think about switching to lime and soda on a weeknight in future. Not that I am judging. I too have been known to partake in an 'online tipsy-shop'. One recent morn I woke to a delivery of gluten-free muesli, a life-size cut-out of Prince William and an adult Disney Princess dress. I can only imagine the gluten-free muesli was an attempt to slim down to fit into the dress for the imaginary 'Wills to Miranda' Royal Wedding. Moving on. Perhaps you bought this book in haste, glimpsing only at the title, mistakenly believing that it was a biography of the late, great Dame Peggy Ashcroft. In which case, I'm so sorry and I hope that you find what you're looking for elsewhere, what a dear and wonderful actress she was. Or perhaps, and I'm keeping my fingers crossed here, you bought this book because you saw the hopeful, furry little face on the cover (talking about the dog, thank you very much) and you were seduced. Perhaps you guessed, correctly, that this was to be a book in celebration of all things doggish, all things pet-fancying, and all things concerning the ins and outs of my life with my wonderful hound, Peggy. If so, hoorah! MDRC, you are very much in the right place.

Let us begin our romp with a brief look at how I ended up like this. A dog-biscuit-clutching loon of a woman, with such a deep and mad love for her pet she feels it's worthy of a whole book, worried half to death that she won't manage to fully convey to the world just how marvellous dear Peggy is, the yapping, fluffy light of her dreary old life.

Well, I've always been a bit of an animal lover. When I say 'a bit', I mean obsessive. Obsessively drawn towards our four-legged friends. Initially as a young child it was all about persuading my parents to take me to any and every small-animal care centre/farm so I could get my hands on cute and fluffy creatures, although so obsessed was I that even a wiry piglet would be heavenly. In my early teens, however, my interest in animals became largely political. In the mid-1980s the RSPCA began their, 'A dog is for life, not just for Christmas' campaign and I'd recently become aware of the existence of the World Wildlife Fund. Consequently, I had a sticker book full of pictures of endangered species, coupled with my own worried musings on how the animals were all going to hell in a handcart and just what I could do to stop it. Sample musings:

15

July 1984. **PANDAS.** Really worried about the pandas. They seem in a bad way. But I don't quite understand the problem. Is it that maybe they don't have enough bamboo to eat? Because Mum and Dad have got a bamboo chair and I'd be really happy to send them that. Would they want the cushion as well, because weirdly it has a picture of a panda on it? But I don't know if animals know what they look like because they don't have mirrors and they might attack it. I read somewhere that some pandas in one zoo weren't making babies and that was the problem. When Flora Huntington's mum and dad couldn't make any more babies it was because Mr Huntington was going off for something called 'dirty weekends', so perhaps we should talk to the zookeepers about whether something similar could be the problem with them? Might be worth me writing a letter. I HAVE to do something.

March 1985. **DODOS.** Apparently these are already 'extinct', which means that there aren't any of them left, which I think is just SO sad. I am going to hold a funeral for the dodos on the main school playing field at 3 p.m. on Saturday, which I hope will raise awareness of how sad it is that there aren't any more dodos. I mean imagine if there were no more cats or rabbits. Dodos first, what will be next? I will follow the funeral with a vegetarian tea (apart from ham sandwiches, because you can't have sandwiches without ham, and people are bored of sandwich spread or else just eat it from the jar with a spoon).

My political streak – fun as it was for everyone, I'm sure – gradually faded away as I moved into adulthood and began to see, among other things, the comic potential of animals. Goodness me, they can be hilarious. As a comedy profes- sional, I find this humbling. I can sweat for hours over a joke, a scene, a vignette, yet a cat can reduce a crowd of *millions* of YouTube viewers to helpless, near-dangerous levels of mirth, simply by fumbling about a bit whilst trying to drag a stick through a cat flap. (Mind you, I have attempted a similar type of gag holding a large broom and exiting a door, but it was no way as funny.) And the stick-cat-flap fun is before we get on to those magical one-in-a-million clips, the freakishly wonderful ones. The husky dog that howls 'I love you.' The seal that plays a tambourine. The bear befriending a piglet (insert any other unusual animal friendship): always brilliant. Or the ducklings being blown over by a mischievous gust of wind. (MDRC, I know it sounds cruel but please get thee to YouTube immediately and check it out for 'tis very entertaining.)

Yes, I've spent many afternoons idly at my computer typing 'cat dog duck video singing falling over funny' and sitting back to enjoy what pops up. And I don't count this as wasted time, or something to be ashamed of, for it is life-affirming, heart-warming stuff and can make me guffaw like nothing else. Plus it's the perfect way for writers to recover from the post-lunch slump. As an aside, somebody said to me the other day: 'If you want to avoid the post-lunch slump then . . . ' I was breathless with anticipation, eagerly hoping for a solution to this tricky, often debilitating moment in one's day and the answer was, wait for it: 'Just avoid lunch.' Sorry? AVOID LUNCH?! I don't think I have ever looked so startled, confused and horrified in all my life. Had to share. Not my lunch, the anecdote. I don't share food. Right, back to the matter in hand.

Joy-filled animal merriment. Wonderful stuff. But, more importantly, if you bought this book as a fellow animal lover (and not because of too much white wine), you might also share an appreciation of animals' power to inspire, educate and move. Call me a sentimental old fool, but I'm a sucker for an inspirational story of Man And Animal United Against A Cruel Fate, Animal Rescuing Man From A Cruel Fate, Man Rescuing Animal From A Cruel Fate, or Man And Animal Losing Their Lives Together, Victims Of A Cruel Fate. *Born Free*, *Lassie*, *Beethoven*, *Black Beauty*, *March of the Penguins*, *Homeward Bound* – you name it, I've howled helplessly through it, to the embarrassment of my companions.

Once I got teary with joy and some sort of pride and concern, as if it was my own, when a goose ran across the stage during a theatre production; so you can but imagine how much I cried for the horses during *War Horse*. I thought I might have to be stretchered out and given a sports drink to replace the lost fluids. Again, I am talking about the theatre production. Not the film. An important distinction because let's not forget the horses in the theatre were PUPPETS. I do admit I spent the first ten to fifteen minutes watching only the puppeteers. Slightly bemused by their job, and their attempt to wear clothes that might blend in to the scenery when, sorry, WE CAN ALL SEE YOU. I was giggling as they began to take on the movements of the horse, to run or trot, or turn dramatically, when their body shape wasn't really made for any kind of sudden movement nay exercise full stop (I don't want to be mean, it's just puppeteers are not necessarily athletes). Then, as the story developed, I stopped watching the puppeteer completely and those puppets, well, they became magically real. Forgive me puppeteers for my initial patronizing sniggles, nothing but respect coming your way. And the ending – well, no spoilers here – it was just too much. There is something about the horses' duty and innocence in their suffering. I was crying enough to enter the nose dribble zone. Never an enjoyable zone when in public. The production ended, the lights came up, and it seems I was the only one quite so moved (despite a number of school parties in that day). And cue: 'Excuse me, sorry, I have terrible hay fever . . . yes I know it's December . . . I get it from a particular . . . it's . . . I'm allergic to . . . scarves.' Exit, exit. Exit stage left, wishing I was being pursued by a nice cuddly bear.

And then there are those astonishing stories, the ones where you can never quite figure out if they're true or not. Dog drags owner from a burning building. Dog brings child lollipop during hypoglycaemic episode, saves child's life. Cat spots breast cancer missed by the finest doctor in the land. Llama successfully pilots crashing plane to a safe and happy landing (I might have made one of those up). I always wanted to believe these tales, to believe there was some magical connection, some profound, unshakeable bond between people and their pets. Otherwise intelligent, emotionally balanced friends who had dogs would leave parties at 8 p.m. to 'get back to Treacle; she gets lonely if I leave her for the whole evening'. People would return from holiday two days early because 'the cat feeder called, Rufus didn't finish his Whiskas pouch and I'm worried he's pining'. A woman I know converted her laundry room into a 'soft play area' for cats, complete with real, climbable trees and catnip-stuffed kitty-beds (which of course the little idiots never went in, opting instead to hole up in the airing cupboard and scratch the best towels to bits). Even Booker Prize- and Nobel Prize-winning author V. S. Naipaul (who interestingly also lost some of his works in the 1970s) said the following after the death of his apparently beloved cat, Augustus: 'I feel a deep, deep grief . . . he was the sum of my experiences. He had taken on my outlook, my way of living.'

Presumably at this point one of Naipaul's mates, perhaps some sort of jolly, ruddy-faced chap from whichever golf club Nobel/Booker Prize champions like to hang out in, saw fit to say something like, 'Buck up, V. S.! Needn't be so awful. Why not take a turn round Battersea Dogs & Cats Home, see if they've got a kitten or two in need of a warm place to sleep? Or even a guinea pig, could be jolly.'

But no, our feline-loving brainbox friend had no such plan. He merely said: 'The terrible part of this is that people suggest to me that I get a new cat, that I invite this new cat into the home I shared with Augustus. As if this one should just be replaced so soon. It shows a lack of understanding.'

Golly. V. S. Naipaul. I mean, really, really not someone you'd expect to be going goggle-eyed over a furry friend. But I certainly understand. It always strikes me how peculiar and fascinating these smaller passions of our hearts are that make us all unique. Because, personally, I don't know about V. S., I didn't *choose* to be so goofy around animals. I didn't *choose* to feel such compassion for any beady-eyed four-legged animal that could reduce me to tears of laughter or empathy. I didn't *choose* to be the type of person who would rather spend a weekend on my own with a raft of small fluffy mammals than pretty much any other human. I didn't wake up one morning and say, 'Right, I know what I must do to make my life more complete: I must become weirdly obsessive about animals.' It's just how I am wired.

In many ways it would have saved me a lot of bother had I not entered the world with the animal-goof gene. No one turned up to the Dodo funeral on the playing field that day, despite the whole school getting written invitations. I got into a lot of trouble when I carried a goose from a nearby lake to our back garden, because I was convinced it wanted to spend some time with me. (I was ten, this wasn't recently.) And I wouldn't have been bitten on the nose by that lovely sheepdog who then had to be put down (too awful), had I not been quite so desperate to stroke and befriend it.

At least these were simple misguidances of youth. But the animal-goof gene hasn't eased in the slightest as I have grown into the deeply mature, intelligent and wise adult I am now (say nothing). Anytime I go travelling I will head straight to the nearest zoo. Which is all very well, but when you are in your thirties and forties with no children and you don't mind sporting one or ideally all of the following: Crocs, a cagoule and a bum bag, you look what I call, suspicious. Then there was the time I was caught chatting to a seagull in Australia. No, MDRC, no need to read that sentence again, you read right – I was chatting to a seagull. I thought I was alone on the beach and Sid (the seagull, for he had to be named) was following me as I walked, a couple of feet behind. It was very sweet. 'So Sid, what are you up to today? Catching some fish later? Can I just say, Sid, I think you have the whitest shiniest feathers of any sea . . . ' I turned around to see a lifeguard staring at me. ' . . . gull.' Amusingly Sid continued pottering along behind me as I ran away, which made me look weirdly Doolittle. But also made my heart skip for some reason. I didn't choose it but I get a ridiculous amount of joy from communing with animals. Even a blooming seagull.

In times when I was unemployed as an actress (for 'times'

read 'years'), I volunteered as a 'pet visitor' at Battersea Dogs Home. It involves sitting in the cages chatting to the dogs, playing with them, getting them used to sharing their space with a human. Socializing them. It was fine, and lovely, apart from the awkwardness of being in the cage when people came around to look at the dogs they might want to rehome. I couldn't help but feel self-conscious as they stared at the dog and talked about its lovely eyes and playful nature. 'Are you talking about me? Ha ha!' Blank faces, silence. 'Pick me!' Nothing. 'I am joking . . . it's just I am in the cage so you could be trying to rehome me . . . to be honest I wouldn't be averse to a bit of rehoming myself, if you were interested . . . they've gone . . . ' I quit, before I was the first person *ever* to be sacked from a volunteer scheme.

Then there was the time I went to Thailand and spent a week in Chiang Mai. The hotel I was staying in suggested a trip whereby you could spend the day at an elephant sanctuary. Well, I was all over that, like Nutella on Rafa Nadal. The sanctuary was utterly beautiful, set in the middle of flat dry savannah grassland, itself surrounded by luscious jungle, a muddy river running through it and a wooden building in the centre where the staff and volunteers lived. Fabulous long tables for communal living, a place to encourage the swapping of travelling stories and no doubt answers to solve every world problem there is, particularly of the animal variety. Those coming for the day were shown around and given the chance to feed and bathe the elephants. You can imagine how happy I was. I was in a childlike state of thrill and awe.

These elephants were once wild but had been captured, used and abused for money-making schemes like being ridden (yes, sorry, I know you might have thought the elephants liked it), or shuffling around the towns and cities at night handing out bananas and bags of nuts. The 'owners' making a pretty packet whilst this wild elephant pranced about in a state of terrified submission. But this sanctuary was recapturing them, allowing them to live with their own again, start to mate, live in the wild once more. Having been tamed they allowed you to feed them, and wash them – I will never forget having to dash out of the way as the elephant I was scrubbing with a long-handled broom decided to flop on to its side in the river. Luckily these beautiful creatures are so lumbering this manoeuvre takes long enough for you to have time to get out of the way. (Much like me heaving out of a bath after a high-calorie day – there's an image.) That said, I was so happy scrubbing down the elephant that I honestly wouldn't have minded dying because of it. Can't think of a better way to go, to be honest. Collapsed upon by a noble beast. I imagine that if I had died like that, all the beasts of the wild would have attended my funeral, out of respect. A lion would have read a poem, zebras looked on weeping as my coffin was carried by low-flying eagles. That sort of thing. Even minus the zoo funeral, I would surely have been deeply praised by my human peers for my heroism. 'She gave her very life in order to provide a soft crash-landing for a tired elephant.' 'So self-sacrificing! What an extraordinary woman she was.' Invariably, as the years go on, the story would suffer from dinner party anecdote exaggeration, and the next thing you knew I would have died throwing myself into the path of a herd of charging elephants in order to protect a not-so-elephant-proof primary school. Or perhaps I wouldn't have died at all. Perhaps it would have been more a case of: 'Well, I heard she got elephantiasis and emigrated to Papua New Guinea where she makes money in a freak show.

Towards the end of the day the sanctuary headmistress appeared – actually, what is the term for a sanctuary leader? Sanctuary Commander? Sanctuary Abbess? Whatever her title, she was someone impossible not to develop some kind of boarding school hero-worship crush on, with her tanned, leathery skin, super-sporty live-off-the-land slimness, perfect pins peeping out of khaki shorts, broad-brimmed canvas hat, deep voice fit to boom across the valleys. In short, she conformed to every stereotype of the 'animal sanctuary runner' and I would have been disappointed with anything less. The Sanctuary Team Captain-Abbess-Leader-General gave us some tea and took us into a room to show us a video of how the elephants were initially captured and why the sanctuary was so passionate about reclaiming them whenever they could. She said that some people might find the imagery harrowing. And she wasn't wrong. By the end of the video only two of the twenty people were still in the room. Yours truly included. I was crying. Buckets. We had gone way past the nose dribble zone.

But actually I would defy anyone, even those without the animal-goof gene, not to be upset. These elephants, for weeks and weeks, were kept in a tight wooden cage totally unable to move. Shackled by metal chains. Every time they attempted to bolt or cry for help they would be stabbed with knives on the end of wooden poles by their captors. Finally, bleeding, sore, exhausted, they would realize the only thing to do was to be quiet and be still. Their very nature, their very soul, their very essence beaten out of them. They were in complete submission. After this gruelling process they were taught various tricks. Surprisingly, worst of all would be if they were picked to be an elephant us tourists could ride. Their wild instinct would revive as their captors attempted to put seats and straps on top of them – and cue severe lashings with metal chains until they stopped.

At the end of the video they showed you how the elephant was and should be in the wild up against the lumbering, listless, beaten-down image of them now, wandering the city as a tourist attraction. Apparently they are permanently exhausted because every noise and movement and person is a shock of fear, but they can't bolt for terror of their owner. They are in a loop of fear. Sorry, talk about bringing the mood down. Here's hoping you weren't reading this book out loud to your beloved over a candlelit anniversary dinner. Though if you were, why were you? There are thousands of volumes of love poetry out there, and you chose to read from *Peggy and Me* to set up a sexy mood? Weird!

I was a wreck having seen the footage, dismayed at just

how cruel we humans can be towards animals, but I was also buoyed up. Really buoyed. Because I had made a decision. A rash decision sure, but I was certain: this was to be my life now; this was my calling. Saving elephants. That was it, I was going to stay put at the sanctuary. Yes, I had spent fifteen years trying to get into acting and was meant to be going home to write the second series of my sitcom, but that would all have to change. I imagined writing the email: 'Dear Friends and Family. This is a tiny bit random but I have decided to move to Thailand and save the elephants in the Chiang Mai area. They need me more than you do. Don't worry, I will be looked after by a brilliant woman with leathery legs and cool khakis. Please send Marmite and my DVD of *Born Free*. This might seem weird to you but don't try to understand me, man! Just love me. Yeah? Take care. Miranda.'

Joking apart, laughter aside, MDRC, I genuinely did consider staying out for a few weeks. It totally spoke to me that place. But I realized I didn't have the choice. I must go back to the job I had at the time. Plus, you would have to sleep in dorms and the toilet is a wooden shack. No, but come on.

Despite the fact that a normal flushing toilet got between me and the Thai elephant sanctuary, I think we can officially say: I am an animal nut. Which of course meant when younger all I wanted was a pet. Forget Scalextric, forget even *Annie the Musical* LP, I wanted to feel that deep connection and bond with an animal. In an attempt to get as close as I could to being my heroine Joy Adamson of *Born Free* fame, I wanted that pet to be a lion cub. But after giving it a bit of thought, even I was forced to concede that there was a teeny tiny chance that a lion cub could potentially grow up into, well, a lion. And a lion might not go down so well in suburban Hampshire. Think garden centre, village fete, and 'ooops he's broken into the butcher's again'. It would never have worked. So I quickly gave up on the lion front, and instead lobbied hard for the next best thing: A golden retriever (to my mind the lion of the dog world).

A campaign of determined proportions began. Christmas lists over the years went something like this:

Dear Father Christmas
    Please could I have 1. A dog 2. A dog bowl 3. A lead 4. A dog bed. 5. Some dog food.
    I have been very good. From Miranda Aged 7

Dear Dear Lovely and Handsome Father Christmas
    I know I have asked for the last two years, but I am going to have to ask again. I really really really really want a dog. Ideally a golden retriever. If you think that would be too big then I would probably be happy with a spaniel. Love, Miranda Aged 9.

Dear Mummy and Daddy
    I have forgiven you for lying about Father Christmas so I really do think you could get me a dog in return. Thank you, Miranda Aged 12

Dearest Darling Mummy and Daddy
    You really are the most amazing parents ever and I don't think I tell you that enough. I am genuinely so grateful for all that you have done for me in my life. My Christmas list this year is really simple.

A Dog.

And I will forgo all other presents.

Your loving daughter who loves you so so much,
Miranda Aged 14

Mum and Dad

This is a total joke now. I want a dog, all right.
What's the big deal. M Aged 15

P.S. The hamster's shit and not a dog substitute.

The dog was never forthcoming. Mum was a gardener and
it wouldn't do for a dog to be tearing up her plants, and Dad
was in the Navy and away at sea a lot so Mum would be left
to deal with it on her own . . . Yeah, yeah, blah, blah, blah.
(I'm totally over it.)

Right, well, what about a cat? The parental petition began,
because, I thought, cats are surely the convenient gateway
drug to dogs, and a notch up from a hamster, plus cats are
cool. Cats don't ask much of you. They'll come and go as
they please, in their own sweet way. You can leave a cat alone
for three days with just Radio Four and the automatic cat
feeder for company and they'll be sort of fine with it. I
sometimes get the sense that cats enjoy their alone time. They
use it to formulate a few thoughts, chill out, meditate, ponder
whether or not to write their memoirs then think, nah, won't
bother, I'm too cool for that. I'll just lie here listening to
Woman's Hour and lick my bits. There's none of the neediness that you seem to get from dogs, none of that 'oh-my-
GOODNESS-please-don't-leave-me-I-LOVE-YOU-what's-that-
what-oh-you're-going-on-holiday-take-me-please-take me-
take me-please-TAKE-ME-WITH-YOU-OR-I-MIGHT-DIE-

OF-GRIEF-I'm just-going-to-have-to-dig-up-that-shrub-you-just-planted-eat-your-new-shoes-and-HOOOOOWL-through-the-night!' No, cats are more convenient, cheaper, quieter, easier to skin and make lovely fur hats out of. (I assure you that was a joke, MDRC. I have never knowingly made a hat out of a cat; in fact the closest I've ever come was treading on a guinea pig so that it turned into a sort of fur bootee, but I promise you that was a mistake.)

On deciding a pussy was for me, if you very much pardon, I found myself a few weeks later communing with six little kittens. I was doing work experience as a runner on a TV show. A Ruth Rendell mystery set in a Hampshire village, and one scene was filmed in a pet shop. The film unit had secured a number of small animals for the set including some rabbits (or rabbi, as someone had put on the daily filming call sheet, causing much confusion as to what kind of pet shop this actually was), tortoises, but also – much more interestingly to me – six balls of fluff otherwise known as kittens. Beyond sweet. At the end of the day the assistant director shouted to all cast and crew, 'Does anyone want these kittens? Anyone?' No response. 'Right, I am going to throw them in the river . . . ' And cue six women, clearly single and slightly on the edge, in Fruit of the Loom sweat-shirts (I can disparage as I was obviously at the front of this screaming pack of desperate ladies) rushing to the box o' kittens sucked in by this deliberate ploy from the assistant director. I arrived first and a black and white kitten jumped up out of the box straight into my arms. This was clearly to be my pet. I took her home and named her Ruth in honour of the TV role, then had to rename her when I found out she was a boy. I do wish the vet could have been slightly less patronizing about it. 'And why are you calling this male Ruth?'

I laughed. Nothing from the vet. No smirk. I felt rather stupid. But come on, how many non-vet people know how to sex a cat (that sounds wrong)?

So Ruth became Casper. And I was fine with just Casper. More than fine. He was an amazing companion. One of those cats that followed you around. Always on my lap whenever and wherever I sat down, doing his manic 'kneading' before settling. He would even sometimes sit by the gate if I walked to the shop and miaow desperately until I returned. He was an eccentric dog-like cat. I was very happy and the dog obsession waned. And indeed the absolute nail in the coffin as regards possible dog ownership came when I noticed in my twenties I truly feared becoming a dog person. In my (then very limited, somewhat snooty) view, dog owners were eccentric, far more so than cat owners (even taking into account the more extreme 'mad cat people', the mad wandering cat-urine-scented ladies, a squalling ginger Tom in each of their fifteen carrier bags and one on their head for good measure, referring to them as her 'disciples' and buying them all hats at Christmas). No, dog owners seemed to me to be a breed apart (pun intended, MDRC. Please assume throughout this book all puns are very much intended). There are five key things about a dog owner that I believed at the time made them unique and, shall we say, societally marginal:

1. **Constantly bringing the conversation round to the subject of dogs, in particular, their dog.** Nothing subtle about this. You'll say, 'Absolutely fascinating this welfare reform business, isn't it?' And they'll respond, 'Mmm, yes, funny you should mention welfare because my Billy's been a bit peaky lately. He did a runny poo in the flowerbed which isn't

really like him and he's been shedding hair like crazy. Have you met Billy? No? Oh, I must have told you the story of the time we took him to the vicar's as a puppy and he thought the antique ottoman was his mother and . . . ' One can very easily be trapped like this for hours, unable to move as dog anecdote after dog anecdote is blasted into your face by a relative stranger.

2. **A light coating of dog hair on all clothes and exposed body parts.** It seems that dog ownership also removes one's ability to use a clothes brush. Either that or the onslaught of hair is so relentless that one has only just finished de-furring oneself when yet more hair appears, akin to painting the Forth Bridge.

3. **Odd items in pockets.** I can't even begin to tell you the number of times I've seen a dog owner reach into their pocket for a tissue and pull out a large rubber bone, several small freeze-dried meat pellets, a lead, a spare lead, and a fistful of depress-ing-looking small plastic bags which you just *know* they're going to use to pick up unimaginably disgusting things. Which brings me on to . . .

4. **Unusually high level of comfort around excrement.** Honestly, I have met dog owners who have picked up poo with one (plastic-bagged) hand, while eating a cream cake with the other and making a phone call. As if it were the most normal thing in the world. Well, it's not.

31

5. **Unusually high level of *joie de vivre*, sense of responsibility, sense of purpose, and a merry twinkle in the eye.** This was the one that gave me pause for thought. Which made me wonder, from time to time, whether there really was something in this whole dog ownership business.

But no, I thought. Absolutely and totally not. Dog ownership was not for me. Even when dearest darling Casper passed into cat heaven, I didn't want to switch teams and turn into a crazy, hair-covered, meat-smelling, poo-grabbing lunatic. No way, siree. I'll stick to being happily pet obsessed-free, thanks, merely stroking the odd cat when the fancy takes me and placating my animal goof gene from time to time with *The Planet's Funniest Animals*, YouTube videos and the odd zoo trip.

And then, My Dear Reader Chum, along came Peggy . . .

CHAPTER 2

Hello Peggy

So, how did Peggy come to be? Not literally. I am not
starting a chapter with the disgustingness of a dog and
its multiple births. That would involve words like 'canal' and
'sac', which to my mind should only ever be used in the
context of boating and postmen. Anything else would not
be appropriate for this kind of highbrow manuscript. So let
me gently tell you that I was introduced to Peggy in 2007,
on the set of a sitcom I was acting in at the time, Lee Mack's
Not Going Out. She, her mother and her siblings belonged
to the lady who made the costumes for the show and, my
goodness, you can't even begin to imagine the cuteness. It
was off the scale. It's a well-known and pretty jolly obvious
fact that puppies can veer slightly towards the adorable end
of things but these . . . these were something else. These
puppies were a shih-tzu/bichon-frise cross. I call them a Shitty
Frise (pleasing) but I believe the technical term is, 'OH MY

33

GOSH, THEY'RE SO SMALL AND FLUFFY LOOK LOOK JUST LOOK AT ITS LITTLE SNUFFLY-WUFFLY-NESS, TINY PADDY PAWS-EES, TEENY KISSY-FACEY FLUFFY-WUFFY SNUGGLE-Y WITH ITSY-BITSY SHINY LITTLE NOSE-Y NOO.' I know I am not the only one who can become so overwhelmed by the cuteness of a small animal that such utterances burst forth. I have a friend who I won't name (Sarah Hadland), and I have often heard her say, as she tightly clasps Peggy's head in her hands, and I quote, 'Peggy, you are so cute, I want to snap your head off, put it in a pie, cook it and just eat you all up.' Please don't call the RSPCA. If anything, call a psychiatric nurse. No really, don't worry; she too just has the animal goof gene.

Now, it's quite hard to distract me when I'm on the set of a show, in particular, a studio sitcom. I take enormous pleasure in the process of making a television programme; watching the ideas and jokes move from read-through to rehearsal room to studio to screen still feels completely magical to me, a veritable *Willy Wonka's Chocolate Factory* of excitements, and I never wish to skive. Even when I'm not in a particular scene, I want to linger and watch rehearsals. I hated going to sit in a stuffy dressing room on my own, and not just because they aren't exactly what you'd imagine. Sorry for any disillusionment here, but there's no chaise longue, no scented candles, no butler. Instead there's a tiny two-seater sofa that makes me feel like a giant as I attempt to get comfortable on it. I know most performers are smaller in real life but, come on, we're not Oompa-Loompas. There will be a bottle of warm Diet Coke (already opened), a mouldy tangerine, a Wham bar and a vague but relentless smell of body odour, not helped by the fact that the radiator is stuck on high and it's July. So the room itself was no incitement to linger. But even if it had been the palace of my dreams, I wouldn't have stuck around, principally because it would have meant missing the magic, the banter, the energy, the creativity, the excitement, the life, the escapism and the laughs my job brought me. And with Lee Mack and Tim Vine on set you were always going to get laughs – two of the funniest and quickest people I know.

I would often sit amongst the bank of empty audience chairs and soak up the atmosphere of the expectant studio. Waiting for bums on those seats to entertain was both terrifying and thrilling in equal measure. I wanted so desperately to hear the reason I was in the business to hear: laughter. It was never guaranteed, never assumed, but if it came, it was magic. And even more so in this particular studio in Teddington. Tommy Cooper had been in this room, for heaven's sake. Morecambe and Wise recorded their last series here. Everywhere you went there were photos and blue plaques honouring the greats who had graced the studios. I felt an impostor, but an impostor who was going to make the most of it and soak it all up. I was writing the pilot of my own sitcom at the time, so I had added reason to be a studious studio sponge. All these feelings I share as a testament to just how cute the little doggy puffballs must have been because I found myself curiously drawn towards the costume department, every spare second I had. A department that – if I am honest – isn't my favourite under any other circumstance.

I know a lot of actresses who love the whole dressing up side of the business, but when you get cast as 'characters', slash misfits (god bless them), costumes aren't going to be glam. And when it came to Barbara in *Not Going Out* it was a question of a sweatshirt, tracksuit bottoms, a tabard, socks and Crocs. An outfit I was glad of since we are currently in

2007, hailed for the birth of Peggy and, I confess, very much the peak of my 'fat years' during which I was regularly mistaken for someone about to give birth. (Women and girls, you need to be at least 350 per cent sure it's pregnancy before offering any congratulations, and men, just *don't*.) I always used to say with a stern look, 'Yes, I am pregnant, with the love child of Ben and Jerry', causing much confusion and/or embarrassment. Bring on the tabard. And the distractions of a gorgeous puppy.

Peggy was originally called Eunice. A true abomination of a dog name if ever there was one. No offence intended to any Eunices, or Euni?, out there. I'm sure that for the right person – perhaps an imperious octogenarian piano teacher in a starched governess dress, wielding an ivory-topped cane – Eunice is a most becoming name. But not on a hopeful, yapping little baby dog. No, absolutely not. There was a very good reason, however. Peggy's mother was Doris, and her siblings were Gladys, Mavis, Boris and Elvis. Do you see? Someone was going to get lumbered with Eunice. To be honest, they could have done a lot worse, name-wise. MDRC, I boggle at the world of dog naming. Absolutely boggle. It's a proper minefield, and nothing causes me greater pleasure these days than to sit back with my own now-beautifully-named hound, and ruthlessly observe the foibles of the dog-Christening world.

First up, the upper-middle classes, with the adorable tendency to name their dogs as if they are members of their family line (Saskia, Henry, Tamara) or their favourite foodstuff (Pesto, Parma, Pellegrino). Next, the frankly completely mad people of all social classes who favour traditional, straightforward names (Bonzo, Treacle, Scout) but who compensate for this by dressing their dogs in sailor suits/Father Christmas outfits/adorable little Colombo costumes. Then there's the more emotional types who call their pets Fluffy and Cutie, and post endless photographs of them on social networking sites with captions like 'Fluffy's doing the big sad eyes again, must be overdue for her cuddly time!' And let's please not ignore the Pedigree Crufts dogs with their regal multi-barrelled ancestral names: Bram Valley Conquistador the Third, Royal Oxford Castle Mr Muggles, The Intolerable Genghis Khan (this one will inevitably be a miniature poodle). I've thought about it and Peggy's would be: Miss Peggy Sue Chef Hart The First (thank you).

There seem to be a few completely arbitrary rules when it comes to naming pets (oh yes, MDRC, we are absolutely going to the nub of this issue). Human names work best on animals if they end in 'ie' or 'y', for example, Peggy, Jonny, Flossie, Betty, Polly. I don't know quite why this is, but imagine a guinea pig called Keith. Absurd. Keiths are geography or maths teachers. Keiths love maps and marry women who collect teaspoons (I do love a stereotype). Keith is not a guinea pig, or indeed any small, fluffy animal. Ditto Derek. If someone were shouting 'Derek, Derek!' in a park, you would assume they had lost a middle-aged rail enthusiast not a cocker spaniel. But weirdly, Dave works. Someone who calls their dog Dave is kind of cool, confident in bucking the dog-naming trend in a way that is inexplicably acceptable. Why this person can shout Dave and look cool and the woman standing next to him shouting Derek looks like a prize fool – nay lunatic – is a mystery.

Then we move on to animals named after other types of

animal. A dog called Tiger, a cat called Mackerel, a guinea pig called Kestrel are always sort of brilliant. And finally and most importantly, two absolute no-no's as regards dog naming. Firstly, never succumb to allowing your young children to name your new puppy. You might think it an amusing game at home hearing their suggestions but you will end up with a dog called Ketchup or Felt Tip or Poo Hole. Small children, you are charming and lively and this world's great hope, but you are not to be trusted to pick names for pets which won't make your parents want to curl up and die when they shout them in the park. Secondly, and this is even more crucial, never ever name an animal after a current pop culture phenomenon. The creature is bound to outlive the trend. I predict that fifteen years from now there will be upwards of fifty thousand elderly dogs called 'Gangnam', whose thirty-something owners will be rendered near-suicidal by having to explain their pet's name to every new person that they meet. 'No really, it was a song. Lots of people liked it. There was a dance . . . ' *starts moving like a drunk horse, dying of shame* Just don't do it.

I have just done a big old fat digression. I can only apologize to you, MDRC, for I was in the midst of sharing my initial experiences with Peggy. Our first meetings. Our courtship, if you will. You were on the edge of your seat, revving up for drama, and I wandered off into an enormous ramble about dressing rooms and poodles called Conquistador. So, yes. I was quite enamoured with the lovely little Eunice, and I found myself spending more and more time with her. Even with all the excitement of a television programme being made in the next room, I could most often be found crouched over her basket, watching her play, or watching her sleep, captivated. Her tiny sides going up and down as she let out little marshmallow snores, her skin flimsy as a petal, her little wet nose a juicy nub of loveliness, her hair like angel-fuzz . . . getting a bit carried away. But my goodness, if you only could have seen her! She used to curl up in my shoe. A hopeful ball of animated fluff, sitting comfortably in my trainer, peeping up at me. I should add she was very small – I don't have size twelve feet or sport clown shoes to work. And she made me laugh. Which I know small creatures do, but Peggy seemed unusually adept at this. I was particularly grateful for the laughter because, despite my perfect job, life had recently dealt me a bad hand. But more anon: let's return to the wonderful doggy distraction that is Peggy.

I put her gift of comedy down to her show-business heritage. Oh yes, this little pup is a descendant of show-biz royalty. Peggy née Eunice had a mother, Doris, whose owner was the aforementioned costume lady. And Peggy's father (the shih-tzu) was owned by none other than all-singing, all-dancing, all-beer pulling in the Queen Vic-ing, Samantha Janus. I know, fun fact. But you just wait until you hear who her grandfather was owned by – only the comic legend

Michael Barrymore. I know! What a thrill. Well, it was to me because I loved him and he inspired me greatly. Younger reader chums, you may have to look him up on YouTube because in the late 1990s things, very sadly, went a little awry in his life. Let's just leave it at that. I don't like to gossip.

I felt safe laughing at 'show-business Princess Peggy', getting to know her, playing with her, allowing myself to become fond, because she was already spoken for. Eunice and her siblings, unsurprisingly enough, had had owners lined up and waiting for them since birth. Which meant that I could frolic to my heart's content, in the knowledge that there was no risk whatsoever of my ending up 'with dog', as it were. UNDER NO CIRCUMSTANCES was I even going to consider thinking about entertaining the possibility of a dog. I was still an animal nut, of course, always to be so, but very much in the cat camp when it came to cat versus dog as a pet option, favouring the astute, independent, nonchalant vibe over the relentless neediness and excitability of a dog. And in any case I was just beginning to get regular work as an actor, and dog ownership is, to say the least, wildly incompatible with the acting lifestyle. Unlike cats, dogs need routine, stability, company; as smooth and predictable a life as possible. Actors have to be able to drop everything at a moment's notice so they can vanish off to stand in a wet field in Surrey in an enormous bonnet saying things like, 'But forsooth, Mr Bradshaw, it's a way to go by horse if you plan to be in Lower Loxfield by sundown.' Actors need to be able to say yes to a supporting role in a musical running for five months at the Dundee Grand, the first week of which may well be spent sleeping in the boot of a Volvo to save on costs. Actors have to leave at dawn, rehearse all day in a damp church hall on the wrong side of town, and come back home at midnight, tipsy, to a solitary, disorganized dinner of petrol-station pasties and Prosecco. I knew you couldn't do any of this easily if you had a little creature who was depending on you for food, comfort, exercise, and a place to call home, or at the very least enough of a disposable income that you could pay someone else to provide these things on your behalf.

What's more, I had almost no experience of looking after anything. Not successfully, at any rate. I've never kept a pot plant alive for longer than a week. I tend to run shrieking from the room when friends ask me to water their gardens for them. And what I haven't admitted to you, MDRC, is that I have a certain amount of what the criminal justice system might call 'previous' as regards animal care. My only real dog-handling experience was a couple of truly disastrous days spent looking after a dog called Charlie. Charlie belonged to some friends of my parents, and he was a merry little Scotty with a big bushy beard and a cheeky glint in his eye. A marvellous little companion, notable for his love of balls (stop it).

One sunny Sunday, I was taking Charlie for a stroll across Hyde Park, when we happened upon a football game. A proper football game – none of your five-a-side shirts-versus-skins kickabouts here – this was serious stuff. Twenty-two grim-faced, burly men, settling a score. I found myself slowing down a little to have a look. For purely pervy reasons, I hope you understand, simply trying to catch a closer look at some men in shorts. Alas, as I slowed, eyes firmly on the well-muscled thighs, all Charlie saw was the ball. The bouncing, glistening ball, completely irresistible to a keen little Scotty

41

such as himself. He charged into the middle of the field and grabbed his prey, puncturing it, and galloped off with its leather carcass dangling from his mouth, chased by twenty-two now-furious men. I steamed across the pitch after him, deeply embarrassed and screaming his name. Thank goodness for his sensible dog name, and I didn't have to run at twenty-two men shouting 'Poo Hole'. Although, unfortunately, as it transpired, it was the same name as two of the men playing, which caused all sorts of confusion. 'Charlie! Charlie!' 'Yes.' 'No, not you, the other Charlie.' 'Me?' 'No, the other one.' 'Who, me? I thought you said it wasn't me?' 'NO NO, FOR GOODNESS' SAKE, THE DOG CHARLIE!!!' 'Are you calling me a dog?' 'No, no, THE DOG IS CALLED CHARLIE, WHY IS EVERYONE CALLED CHARLIE!' I took one look at the furious footballers, panicked, and for some reason thought it best to shout, 'He's not my dog! Not mine!' as I picked him up and prised the ball from his teeth. Which made me look like a bellowing lunatic dog thief of the highest order.

Not my finest hour. Not my worst, either, as it happens. No, my dog-owning nadir came when I took Charlie to a student party where some of the guests were in the living room, fashioning a, what I call, 'funny cigarette'. They'd left some of their 'special grass' on the coffee table and Charlie, thinking it was some sort of marvellous plant-y dog treat, jumped right in and snaffled the lot. And then became ridiculously stoned, wandering around the party bashing into walls and hoovering up great big giant bowls of crisps until I got terribly worried and took him to the vet, who laughed and laughed and laughed, and called in her boss who laughed and laughed and laughed, and said that Charlie would be fine but that I ought to take his car keys off him, not let him make any important phone calls until the morning, and that on the way home he might want to stop off for some munchies, have a good cry and get a bit huggy.

Childhood experiences of caring for pets were hardly more successful. At the age of twelve (just prior to the Save the Dodo campaign), I briefly had a hamster called Nellie. Note the word 'briefly'. Also please note my aptly named pet with an 'ie' ending. Well, Nellie, bless her, scampered merrily off when I let her out of her cage for a potter around the living room. I know I shouldn't have let her out but I thought they must get so bored in their cages. I don't think a hamster wheel can be in any way fun; it's a cry for help, it looks desperate. It's the hamster equivalent of a London commuter finally losing it and walking in little circles on the concourse at Euston Station shouting, 'All is lost! All is lost!' And I was not going to embarrass Nellie and put her in one of those spherical transparent balls that force hamsters to pedal around bumping into furniture whilst towering humans laugh and point. So I let her run around. Roam free, across the living room. I don't quite know what happened or where exactly she went but, at the time of writing, Nellie is probably still decomposing pungently somewhere underneath my parents' floorboards.

Some years later we risked getting a budgie, who I named Ernie (I need recognition for my consistency in pet naming). But Ernie also met with a sticky end when I let him out of his cage for some exercise. I think I may have watched *Born Free* a few too many times by this stage of my life. I thought I had shut the door to the living room, but it hadn't clicked shut and the next thing I knew (and please don't laugh at this and those of you who do are WRONG IN THE HEAD), Casper had snuck in and Ernie flew straight into the slavering jaws of my beloved cat. An incident which led to a hilarious-in-retrospect-but-at-the-time-truly-horrible Benny Hill-esque scene involving my parents chasing me chasing the budgie-wielding cat round and round the house knocking into furniture and each other as we screamed, 'Get the cat', 'He's killing my budgie', 'Call the fire brigade!', 'Why the fire brigade?', 'DON'T QUESTION ME, MOTHER, THIS IS ALL VERY TRAGIC.'

Yes, you could fairly say that my confidence in myself as a caretaker was not especially high. I did tend to, well, kill things. Not in a murder-y way, you understand – just stuff happens (which ironically sounds exactly the kind of thing a murderer would say). The list of my victims now reads something like: 1 x budgie, 1 x hamster, 15 x pot plants, 1 x rhododendron bush (no, I don't know quite how I managed that one either), 1 x oak tree (drove into it in a miniature digger, long story), and 1 x Tamagotchi (yes, it's just a computer, but it's still really sad when they die). I was reluctant in the extreme to add '1 x adorable small dog' to the list.

However, one morning at work the costume lady informed me that the owner who was lined up for 'Eunice' was no longer going to be able to take her on, due to having had a fall and needing a hip replacement. It was suddenly a possibility that the puppy who I'd thought of as mine, but who I comfortably knew could never become mine, was now available to become, well, mine. I had a stern word with myself, told myself it just wasn't possible. I was not going to get a dog. Eunice seemed to feel differently. I know it sounds completely mad, but it seemed that her behaviour towards me changed when there was suddenly a possibility of her becoming mine. She became needy, beguilingly so, clambering over her siblings to reach me when I came to visit. Jumping up and yapping at me when she so much as saw me pass the door of the costume room, and gazing up at me with her adoring little orphan-like eyes as if to say 'adopt me, lovely lady, adopt me, take me away and make me your own', in what I imagined would be a squeaky Cockney sort of little Tiny Tim-type voice. 'Don't abandon me to the workhouse, Nice Miranda lady, where I'll be shouted at by the mean orphan-master. Take me home, and tuck me up nice and cosy by the fire. That'll be luvverly, nice kind lady, won't it? *Please* don't abandon me, please!'

I had my little heart in my little mouth, I really did. I kept running and running around in very very fast tight little circles. And yes, it's Peggy here. HELLO! I am very very excited to meet you. Oh dear, I have started spinning again. Something I am not so keen on doing because it is extremely dizzy-making and detracts from my dignity as a dog, and as a great thinker of our time, but for some reason when I am excited I simply must do it. *spins in the other direction to balance out the dizziness, sits panting*

Before I say anything more I must make it perfectly clear I sound nothing like a Dickensian Cockney. My voice is clear as a bell and very smart. I have modelled it on Penelope Keith (we listen to a lot of things with her in and I think she is marvellous; such a warm, rich, refined voice, it suits me well). I just had to butt in, seeing as Miranda's jolly well writing a whole book about me. I've always said she's a woman of exceptional taste. Tee hee hee. And if she's going to have her say, then I would really like to have mine. Without me, there'd be no book.

I'd go further. Without me, she's nothing. I just say it how I see it.

I see she is telling you about me when I was a puppy. Oh they were happy happy happy days on the set of Not Going Out. *Me and my brothers and sisters got lots of attention (rightly so – we were ADORABLE) and cuddles (ditto) and I got to watch all the crazy television people messing around being silly. They say it's a job but it isn't, I mean it really isn't. They spend all their time taking costumes off and putting other costumes on, and when they're not doing that they just sit around talking about food. I mean, literally, their whole day is filled with eating meals, snacking, between-snack snacking, and attempts to make new, exciting snacks out of unlikely food combinations. Miranda's latest one being a Nairn's oatcake atop a Dorito atop a slice of ham draped in a slice of cheese with a thin film of peanut butter on the top. Disgusterama. I wouldn't touch it. And I am a dog.*

But that said, I really liked Miranda, she seemed kind. Although her trainers stank. And I am a dog. And I must concede that she's reasonably entertaining (though I wouldn't go further than that).

Oooh, there's a leaf, oooh, sorry, leaf, hang on. *rushes off to catch a leaf blowing in the wind, leaps to get it, it blows in another direction, leaps in the other direction, it blows back in the original direction, stops and sits on floor, intellectually confounded by what has just happened. Licks paw* They are naughty leaves, you think you have it, then whoosh, gone. It's really really funny. Here it comes. Nope, can't get it. TOO funny.

Where was I? Yes Miranda. Gladys, Boris, Mavis and Elvis all teased me for liking her. They called her the *'bizarre-o-mega-tall apron lady with the oatcakes who sometimes gets mistaken for a man'. But when my original owner pulled out I was really really scared I might be left with no one. It's really really scary when people come and choose you because you see they might NOT choose you. So I went all out on the charm front. I wouldn't want you thinking that I'm some kind of manipulative flirt, but it is hard to have looks like mine and not want to use them to your advantage. I just say it how I see it. So I pulled out all the stops for the 'bizarre-o-mega-tall apron lady with the oatcakes who sometimes gets mistaken for a man'. I gave her the Orphan-Eyes, the Cuddle-Me-Tail-Wag, the I-Like-You-the-Best scramble over my siblings and it absolutely worked. I'd heard her talking about how she didn't have time to take care of me, but surely I thought . . . I mean, just look at me. *cocks head to one side, lets out a cute yap* Oh yeah, I can work it, baby.*

But no, absolutely not. Out of the question. I am not ready for the commitment. I mean, I am barely an adult. Nine times out of ten I forget to pierce the film on microwave meals before microwaving, and consider anyone who remembers to do so to be 'quite the chef'. As we know I am in no fit state to look after another living creature. And due to life's recent knocks I was protective of my space and solitude. As I was staring over the bundle of puppies, stroking little Eunice who was having what seemed like a frightening dream, the costume lady suddenly asked me outright, 'So, would you like to take her?' I paused, confident in my response. 'I'm sorry but . . . Yes. Yes I will.' WHAT?! What just happened? She immediately started excitedly talking logistics. 'No, wait, stop, hang on . . . Did I just say . . . '

I went into the tightest of running circles a young pup has ever been in. It was the best moment in my life. I had a new owner. The 'bizarre-o-mega-tall apron lady with the oatcakes who sometimes gets mistaken for a man' had picked me. I was hers. I remember Boris saying 'good luck', which I didn't understand until a few weeks later. That moment was just beyond exciting. *darts into a small circle remembering it*

What had I done?

How very rude. *washes bottom*

I promised myself I would never join the dog-owning brigade. But there I was. I suddenly had my very own dog, a dog of my very own. Both a wonderful gift from the universe and, frankly, the absolute last thing I needed at the time. MDRC, as I've hinted, all was not well with me around the time that Peggy appeared in my life. I'd just ended a long-term relationship and the Hart heart (serious circumstances call for merry wordplay, I find) was not in the best shape. Coupled with that, almost as soon as my new pet crossed the threshold of my home, I succumbed to a miserable stretch of glandular fever. I was hit emotionally and physically pretty hard and I was feeling very lonely, very isolated, very depressed, and frankly, very uncertain whether I could ever love or be loved again.

Which brings us on to what this book's going to be about: my journey with Peggy, from this moment forth. If you were hoping for some sort of ever-so-clever philosophical treatise on the wider ramifications of pet ownership in our increasingly individualistic society, you're going to be disappointed. You should know by now that I like to get right into the nuance-y nub of things, the awkward little moments, the daft happenings of life which, if left undiscussed, have a tendency to eat away until you're shrieking in the mirror with the sheer blinding horror of it all. In this case, that means the things you won't see covered in the pamphlets you pick up at the vet's. We'll be delving into the pet-ownership equivalent of breaking wind on the massage table or having a job interview over a coffee and answering a serious question with a 'frothy coffee moustache', or greeting someone with a second kiss when the other person was only ever committing to the one. And we'll begin where we are: the pair of us back at my flat for the first time, sad and worried, uncertain whether or not life was ever going to be all right again.

Desperate for a bit of fun in my life, I rechristened Eunice 'Peggy', because it reminded me of the word 'Piggy', as in 'Miss Piggy', the thought of which made me feel vaguely positive and strengthened. Plus Peggy was my heroine in *Swallows and Amazons*, and reminiscing about youthful freedom with not a care was at the time deeply appealing. Then, in a flash, my present reality overwhelmed me. It was as though the exhaustion and the sadness of being alone punched me in the stomach. I crumpled on to the kitchen floor in a heap and burst out crying. I couldn't stop. Deep guttural sobs. I can still remember, vividly, Peggy lying there patiently in my arms as my tears trickled down her fur. I was grateful to have something to cuddle. And I thought then, perhaps this dog's going to turn it all around. Perhaps that's why I found myself saying yes. Perhaps I'll learn to love again via a perfect dog-woman relationship? Perhaps this will be the start of something beautiful . . .

CHAPTER 3

Reality Check

THERE IS POO ALL OVER MY FLAT . . . !!! I repeat – there is POO ALL OVER MY FLAT. How is this helping? This is not beautiful. This is the opposite of beautiful. This is brutalist architecture meets a burnt omelette meets sweaty back hair meets a politician in *Celebrity Big Brother*. By which I mean, THIS IS DISGUSTING. How could something so sweet and fluffy and small, during one relatively short night, create what can only be described as a landfill of poo? A mountain range of poo. A post-apocalyptic world where, after the blast, all that remains is poo. MDRC, forgive the indelicacy, but don't say I didn't warn you. I promised that we were going to dive, unafraid and unashamed, into the nuts and bolts of pet ownership. And it just so happens that at this stage of proceedings, all those nuts and bolts happen to be made of . . . faecal matter. Oh no, that sounds worse, let's stick with 'poo'.

It was extraordinary; if there'd been perhaps one tiny, apologetic pile on the doormat, and a worried little puppy curled up beside it begging for mercy, I could have understood. But this, this poo apocalypse or poocalypse – thank you, I am very pleased with that – was something else altogether. This looked as if Peggy had waited until I'd gone to sleep, then jumped out of her basket, and said, 'This evening I fancy myself as a cutting-edge conceptual artist, and tonight my medium is poo!'

I stood at the top of the stairs, surveyed the situation, and despaired. Please remember that at the time, even before the poocalypse (still pleasing), I was hovering around the doldrum area, to say the least. I was in fact clinging on to the edge of a black pit of misery, desperately trying not to spiral to the bottom. And I don't think any medical textbook or search engine would respond to the question 'What's the best way to cheer up my depressed friend?' with the words, 'Great idea and relatively simple this one. Fill her living room with as much dog poo as you can find.'

Matters were made worse by the fact that on the morning of witnessing this devastation, I was a tad sleep-deprived. For, in addition to her delightful pooing habit, it appeared Peggy had a bit of a taste for whining in the night. And what whining it was. Not a thoughtful song, not a pensive moan, not even a short, sharp imperative expressing an urgent need for attention; more a Chinese-water-drip-torture of intermittent piercing shrieks. Unpredictable, too, irregular in volume, duration and pitch, so that just when I thought it was over, and I began drifting off to sleep, I'd be ripped from my slumber by a wild volley of canine misery-noises. Like most of us in this modern age, I am obsessed with how much sleep I get. 'Right, I have to set the alarm at 6.30 tomorrow so let's work back', and cue crazed backwards counting on my fingers to see where eight hours takes us – because we've got to get our eight hours' sleep, right? 'So that's 10.30 and I need half an hour to get to sleep, so bed at 10 p.m. please, Miranda.' These sleep mathematics begin at around 8 p.m. so the next two hours become a frenzied and frantic quest for a state of calm. It gets to 10.15. 'Help, I am not in bed yet, quick, quick, got to get my eight hours.' I might get into bed at 10.45 with wet hair (no time to dry it, got to get my eight hours), a towel on my pillow and the washing up only soaking (can't do it now, got to get my eight hours), but soaking is sort of washing up – it's self-cleaning, isn't it. Quick, lights out, sleep. Sleep now. Get to sleep. I have only got seven hours and forty minutes now. GET TO SLEEP! Where did this pressure come from? Suddenly a generation is wandering around with what feels like a government warning above our heads: WE MUST ALL GET EIGHT HOURS' SLEEP OTHERWISE OUR LIVES WILL FALL APART AND WE WILL GET STROKES AND DIABETES AND BECOME OBESE AND GET A BUNION AND NEVER HOLD DOWN A RELATIONSHIP AND WILL SLOWLY GO MAD AND END UP DRIVING A RIDE-ON MOWER THROUGH A GARDEN CENTRE WINDOW WHILE SCREAMING, AND NAKED. The fear of not getting the allotted eight hours has now put so much emphasis on sleep we can't sleep. Our evenings are spent panicking about when to have our last drink so we don't wee all night; when we must stop the caffeine (and is that just coffee or is tea really as bad?); whether watching TV in bed will mean our brain is melting . . . and so it goes on. Gone are the days when we would have a couple of glasses of wine, sod the consequences, and slumber peacefully.

So, I'm lying in bed in a wired state of fear, my eight-hour window reducing by the minute. I reset the alarm to 6.45 so that psychologically getting into bed at 10.45 hasn't caused damage and I slowly calm down, eventually dropping off. About an hour later, I am woken with the first Peggy whine. In my confused state I briefly forget I have a puppy. 'There's a coyote in my kitchen,' I shriek. No, let's think this through, we are not on an Appalachian ranch. Bear in mind, MDRC, that I am in the very worst half-asleep state here. Not the kind where you're all toasty and floaty and snuggled up like a litter of kittens. More the kind of reluctant, twisty-turny semi-sleeplessness where you end up having a good long think about life, and decide that you have no hope and no talents and all your friends hate you and as soon as it's getting-up time you're going to look into pursuing a career as a submariner. Just me? Another whine from Peggy. I jolt miserably an inch further towards wakefulness. 'Racoon? Possum? BEAR?! Again, Miranda. Not on a ranch. Or in a cartoon. Must be an urban fox, snuck in through the cat flap. No, wait, I don't have a cat flap. It's torn up the front door, mutilated itself on the way in . . . THERE'S A HORROR MOVIE-STYLE MUTILATED ZOMBIE FOX IN MY LIVING ROOM!'

I bravely venture downstairs, switch on a kitchen light, see little Peggy the pup and am reminded of my new reality. The minute she sees me she abandons all signs of distress, wags her tail, tilts her head to one side and tries to leap out of her crate. 'Urh, no, no, little doggy, it's now something called night-time, and we must all get eight hours' of sleep during it or, according to government guidelines, we are likely to die the next day, so settle down please.' I switch the light off and retreat quietly up the stairs. It's 11.35 at this point, so we are now into hour six which feels most unstable. Reckless, even. But I fall asleep. Then . . . I am woken up with a start – the whining is more extreme. Oh please let it be just before my alarm is going to go off and I have randomly had a really solid length of sleep. I look at the clock. IT'S 2.30! Nooooo! I shout at Peggy, 'Night, night, puppy, sleepy sleep time.' The noise doesn't stop. I go downstairs. Immediately the wagging and jumping starts. Oh, it's too sad, she just wants to be with me. I explain to her I have a job on television that means I need to remember lines and that is only possible on EIGHT HOURS' sleep. Surely a dog with her show-biz heritage would understand an early call time?

I run upstairs like a . . . well, frankly, like a sleep-deprived actress who's far too exhausted and panicky to come up with a decent analogy. Just before I clamber back into the delicious-ness that is my still-warm bed a high-pitched yelp emanates. 'Right, that's it.' I switch on my lamp and start desperately scanning Cesar Millan's puppy training book. He says that to avoid issues around separation anxiety the key is to leave the puppy in its crate, move to another room for thirty seconds, then return without giving the dog attention. Then leave it for one minute. And repeat regularly until it eventually gets to thirty minutes. The puppy will then not fear being alone and should settle quickly in the first few nights. To which I start shouting: 'Cesar, Cesar Millan, it is 3.15 IN THE MORNING, not in the afternoon when it is acceptable to be awake at 3.15 but 3.15 IN THE MORNING, when it is only acceptable to be awake if you are under twenty-five and in a nightclub, and under no circumstances am I going to spend my night walking to and from various rooms at timed intervals; oh and also, your name, well IT SOUNDS LIKE A SALAD!'

I am quite pleased with that insult and victoriously switch

off my lamp and pull the duvet over my head. And cue whining. I try and shove in earplugs but all I imagine is Peggy's little face and I feel brief guilt and sadness. I know Cesar Salad Millan (with salami not chicken I suppose) says under no circumstances allow the puppy into your bed because they then think they are top dog and blah blah blah. Well, bum holes to that. Thank you for your service, Cesar, you big salad-named dog-fancier, but I say BUM HOLES to your advice because some of us can't lie around all day being named after salads, some of us have to go and be vaguely amusing in tabards at the crack of dawn and NEED SOME SLEEP, AND IDEALLY EIGHT HOURS OF IT.

So, defeated, I go downstairs and pick up the happiest puppy there ever was and put her on my bed. I nip to the loo for the last what I call 'insurance wee', and on return find she is curled up in the tightest ball in the middle of my warm bed, already fast asleep. Tempted as I am to wake her with a revenge whine and then do the same again at twenty-minute intervals, I creep in next to her and finally fall asleep. For TWO hours. And thus ended my first night as a highly skilled, disciplinarian dog owner.

During those two hours Peggy must have come and gone from the bedroom to the sitting room to deposit her 'art' and in my morning daze I whacked a clothes peg on my nose, put on some gardening gloves, and began the hideous business of de-pooing my flat. This, I thought (arguably a tad melo-dramatically), is what it must be like to have a new baby. In fact, I thought, and please remember, I hadn't had a great deal of sleep, this was *worse* than having a baby. This new Peggy-and-me situation seemed to have all the most disrup-tive, miserable elements of baby-having – poo, sleep depri-vation, mushy food, a being that cries/whines that you are supposed to love but just want to shout, 'Why can't you tell me what you WANT?' and the general sensation of a bomb having gone off in one's life. But without any of the positives. At least a baby's probably going to grow up and go to university and get a nice job in financial services and one day pay for me to end my days in a mink-lined old people's home in Whitstable. A puppy's just going to turn into, well, a dog. Which will grow up and become an old dog, and then we will be back at further poocalypses but add in dank breath emitting with every yawn, and a sense there is one long continuous fart occurring (actually not dissimilar to some of my past relationships).

At least a baby eats and drinks slightly endearing, Cath Kidston-esque things like breast milk and sugar-free pureed apple served in an upcycled biodegradable pouch. Dogs eat things like Munch-A-Lot Jellied Hearts In Liver (Haddock Flavour) which look like hell and smell how I imagine the First World War trenches would have smelt if all the major battles had been settled using stink bombs. And here's the nub of the thing, MDRC, at least with a baby you get *sympathy*. People saying things like, 'You are doing so well'; 'You are going to be a great mother'; 'Lack of sleep is so awful, try and top up with lunchtime naps, got to get your eight hours'; 'Don't worry, I've got sick on my cardigan too.' Whereas with a puppy you are simply meant to be full of the joys. When people ask, 'Why are you shuffling outside Starbucks in stained tracksuit bottoms trying to remember if you are going in or coming out? You've got a what? A *dog*? Oh. Right. Anyway, let me tell you what my baby did last night . . . why are you crying?' I did in a dark moment consider buying a pram to take to the shops to justify my crazed tearful appearance.

New mothers are able to connect their friends to their new arrival by showing photograph after photograph. If you were to do this at length with a puppy, within an hour someone would be discreetly dialling the number of a mental health professional. (Although once you are through the initial stages and look vaguely sane, there is absolutely a time for pet-photo show-and-tell – more on that later.) Mothers can take their babies into shops, whereas we new dog owners have to leave our charges outside, searching for a heavy object to tie them to (nothing worse than the dog following you in dragging a chair or shop sign). We are essentially leaving them at the mercy of kidnappers who want to pinch our hounds and use them as bait in terrifying illegal dog-fights in multi-storey car parks in the rougher boroughs of Britain's inner cities. It's entirely possible that I've been reading too many tabloid newspapers. I bought them to cover the floor of my flat, thinking that as I had a creature doing dirty protests, it would be rather satisfying to see it being done on – insert unnamed offensive celebrity or politician; I can't name them for I'd be stooping to tabloid level. Taking a stand.

Also, I thought, as I sanitized my hands for the billionth time that morning and crouched down low over a glistening puddle of dog wee, that at least with babies you can put them in a nappy. With dogs you have to let them out to wee or face the consequences. Although I did wonder and found myself googling 'Dog Nappies'. Sure enough, thanks to good old America, of course, there was such a thing. I jest you not. Please google Dog Nappies and look at the images and enjoy – well, don't enjoy, just wonder what next. Cat bibs? Protective headgear for squirrels? Fish bonnets? I won't lie to you, on that first, bleak, poo-sodden morning, I wondered whether I'd completely ruined my life by bringing this dog into it. On top of that, I felt incredibly guilty. Shouldn't I be surfing on a golden wave of love? Shouldn't I be ecstatically grateful to have the adorable little creature in my care; this hopeful bundle of fluff, this sweetly dependent little thing who'll be mine for ever, if I choose to keep her? And she *was* cute. Even through my heartbroken, depressive poo-goggles (poggles – again, thank you), I could see that she was pretty damned adorable. Like an alive teddy bear. And sometimes, when she skittered across the floor towards me and looked me straight in the eye, I felt a surge of . . . something. Not love, not even kinship, but a sense that one day, one far-off day in the future, this might be all right. I knew that the only way out was through. It was time to tackle the problem head-on, by plunging into what I call dog-min. Which is short for dog-ministration, which is short for The Myriad Small Acts Of Administration Required In The Successful Ownership Of A Dog.

Um, excuse me, hello, hello, *jumps up at the table legs* can I please get a word in, while Miranda's carried away with her pompous 'what-I-call-dog-min' overenthusiastic speechification business. For I, Peggy Hart, need to defend myself, Your Honour, before I am taken down. (We watch a lot of crime drama.) For it seems to me, Peggy's Dear Reader Chum (oh wow, I do really really love that), that all this poo talk is a bit of a smear tactic. Yes, I do realize what I just said. It is not funny actually. This is all really really upsetting indeed.

You see, me lud, the reason *suddenly scratches an awkward itch*, apologies, Your Honour . . . the reason I thought it was acceptable to poo on the carpet was simply this, the carpet was already the colour of poo. Miranda has

59

a few gifts. I think. So far I have only seen that she is quite good at balancing a cupcake on her head to take from the kitchen to the sitting room as she announces herself as Lady Cup of Cakeshire. Which I do admit I find a bit funny. But an interior designer she is not. I mean, when I first came in here I thought, it is lucky I am dog, albeit a dog with exceptional taste and a very good eye, because even a student would come in here and say 'oh dear, no thanks'. I just say it how I see it.

What I did on her carpet IMPROVED it. Also, ladies and gentlemen of the jury, it had quite simply not been made clear to me at the outset where I was and was not supposed to defecate. I was certainly not going to sit over that shining white lake within a bowl thing, which empties itself with a horrendous WHOOSH the second somebody presses down on a lever. Terrifying and unhygienic. Who else has sat down on that bowl before you? I like to feel the wind around my haunches as I go, thank you very much. I am a classy lady. *wipes arse along the floor*

And as for the whining, me lud; I must confess that well, actually, if you really really must know, I was feeling really really frightened. You see, this lovely tall lady who I really do think I sort of love, takes me on as her own, and then at night-time wanders off and curls up in her own basket BEHIND A CLOSED DOOR without so much as singing me to sleep. This I did not expect. I have been used to sleeping with my siblings. Aaah, I really miss them. We used to huddle up in a row to keep warm and take turns to be the one on the end. I REALLY REALLY miss Boris and Elvis and Gladys and Mavis. I hope they are all right in their new homes. I wonder if I will ever see them again. *wells up*

*So yes, frankly, I believe Miranda deserved everything she got whine-wise. And why she fears not getting eight hours when she naps more than me I don't know. Oh, and, final point to the court . . . sharing a bed with her when I was finally allowed in was NOT easy. I may have whined but she . . . Well, I don't like to be a snitch but . . . well . . . Teeth grinding, dribbling, farting, snoring, farting, sleep-talking, thrashing, constant trips to the white bowl, farting, grinding . . . Case closed, Your Honour. *sits down triumphant* *sneezes**

The first and most urgent piece of dog-min seemed to me to be the not-so-small matter of, well, puppy training. Specifically in the toilet department. Sit, fetch, beg, dance, roll over – all of these could wait, my living-room carpet could only take so much punishment. The training, according to Cesar SALAD Milan, whose book I'd retrieved from the skip, seemed to consist of taking the little beast outside once every two hours, standing up tall and, in my best Crufts-competitor voice (in case you're curious, it's a cross between Princess Anne and an angry drunk at closing time), instruct Peggy to do her business. Initially, I chose the straightforward command 'WEE!', but found it excruciatingly embarrassing wandering the streets of London bellowing it, to the point that every time someone heard me I felt forced to hide the offending word by burying it in a sentence, 'WEE! . . . were just going for a trot round the park, might you care to join us, good sir?' Or 'WEE! . . . are looking lovely in that hat today, aren't we, madam?' I made a few new friends that way, but it wasn't a sustainable strategy.

I experimented with some entirely random words (Lifeboat! Sandwich! Condiment! Counterpane! Vogue!), which were fun to shout, but ineffective. I knew that I had to steer well clear of any word which I use regularly in everyday life, lest my shouting a cheery 'hello!' to the postman be misconstrued by my canine chum as a command to urinate on his shoes. It's a minefield, I tell you, a minefield. And another something new mothers don't have to contend with. I ended up plumping for 'wee-wees'. Which I am now entirely at peace with, but when first used caused something of a kerfuffle. I stepped out of my door before putting Peggy on the lead; she wandered off and I shouted 'wee-wees' after her whilst smacking directly into my approaching neighbour. 'What did you say?' he said, assuming I was addressing him. 'I said . . . ummm . . . *oui, oui*, because . . . I was just agreeing with my French flatmate upstairs.' 'I didn't know you had a flat-mate.' '*Oui, oui* . . . ooh, there I am again.' 'I'm going to need their name and details for the buildings insurance then, please.' 'Oh right, yes, well *oui oui*, of course . . . their name, ummm . . . Gerard . . . Depardieu.' He stared sharply. Understandably.

At the time I didn't have the reassurance that this kind of interchange was great fodder for my future sitcom character. I was just mortified. This dog ownership lark was not going well. I wouldn't have had this problem with a cat. I should have got a cat, I thought. I was not in a fit state to deal with anything more than a cat. Clearly. I just tried to tell my neighbour I was living with Gerard Depardieu. Plus, that morning, I had been to the doctor, who told me the glandular fever had segued into chronic fatigue. Fabulous. Life was beginning to feel physically and emotionally like wading through treacle.

However, against many odds, things progressed reasonably well. Filming had finished and being between jobs gave me the time for intensive dog-min. I took Peggy out once every two hours, as suggested, and pretty soon we seemed to be communicating better, and the carpet took a bit less nightly punishment. After a week or so, I felt brave enough to face another key part of dog-min: The Park. Up to this point I'd just thought of the park as, well, The Park. A pleasant enough place to wander through on my way to somewhere else, but never an event. So when, as a new dog owner, I first had the notion 'perhaps I should take Peggy down to the park and see how she likes it', I was initially daunted by the concept of park culture. The park was a communal room really, key to all parents and dog owners (and joggers, but let's ignore them). An entirely new world to me. Then, there was a sudden rush of unexpected excitement. I'd remembered, you see, the one piece of information I have about my local park, which is that it has a reputation for being a place where people run into their future partners. A quite freakishly high proportion of single people have wandered into the park with a lurcher on a lead and wandered out twenty minutes later, arm in arm with the love of their life. I exaggerate not. One friend of mine got chatting to a gentleman caller walking his retriever at dusk, and so engrossed did they become that they didn't realize the park had closed. He then had to gallantly find a way to escape from their inadvertent prison. Every woman deep down wants a good rescuing (if you pardon) and any man loves to portray a knight. It was the perfect courtship. They are now happily married with a merry brood. Fact. So, like a debutante off to a dance, I slapped on my second-cleanest tracksuit bottoms (still pretty depressed, remember) and dragged a yapping Peggy off down the road.

The Park

I arrived at the park to find myself confronted with what would be best described as a 'wall of dogs'. Or perhaps a sea of dogs. A glut of dogs. A . . . lot of dogs. Each dog, of course, attached to an owner, and each owner representing what seems to me to be a very specific 'type'. Before my first, mind-boggling hour in this modest West London park was up, I felt that I'd encountered and made polite conversation with every possible variation of dog owner in the Western world. Many of them seemingly so crazy that the entertainment value more than made up for my not yet having met my prince charming. It would give me no greater pleasure, MDRC, than to walk you through these said types. Please follow me.

First up, we have **People Who Talk Through Their Dogs**. A surprisingly common one this. They'll bound up to you with their red setter, ignore your polite, human greeting, look your dog straight in the eye and say, in an oddly intense way, 'Ginger would like to know your name.' Confused about whether they mean you or the dog, you'll say, 'Uh, Miranda. No, Peggy. I'm Miranda, she's Peggy.' They'll then – still avoiding your gaze – say, perhaps in a weird out-of-the-corner-of-their-mouth, dog-voiced sort of way, 'Well, a hearty WOOF WOOF to you, Peggy! My name's Ginger, because I am a red setter! RrrrrRRRRRWOOOF!' At which point you'll jump back in shock because, well, a middle-aged man in a Puffa jacket is barking at you. At which point the Person Who Talks Through His Dog may well become passive-aggressive, and say something like, 'What's that, Ginger?' *cocks ear towards silent dog* 'You don't think that lady wants to be friends with us? Well, she doesn't know what she's missing out on, does she?' And man and dog will turn on their heel and stalk off, and you'll be left wondering whether or not you just accidentally had an argument with a red setter.

Still, this man's nothing compared with number two on my list. For next on our perambulation we have: the **Brisk Posh People Who Ask Lots Of Questions**. Now, these people can generally be spotted by their outfits, which will comprise of padded gilets over a long-sleeved cashmere jumper, corduroy trousers (often red), and a thick-sock-and-walking-boot combination more suited to a hike in the Andes than to a Wednesday morning stroll in an urban park. They'll generally be about fifty and will have, regardless of gender, a giant bouffant of a hairdo which extends out further than the average cycling helmet. There is no question that their dog will be a Labrador. These people are always impeccably polite and friendly, but waste no time in diving in with their posh brisk questions, and have a habit of speaking louder than is necessary. 'So, what's her breeding?' Before you can even attempt to answer the next question comes hurtling at you: 'Will you be showing her?' I start panicking: 'Urh . . . showing her what? Do I have to show her things? I was sort of hoping she would work things out for herself.' 'No, showing her, you know, competitions? Which kennel is she from?' (Er, the costume department.) 'Will she be a working dog?' (Um . . . perhaps the odd advert, if she's pretty enough?) By this point I've become so hysterical that I can't even remember what breed of dog Peggy is and, indeed, whether or not she actually is a dog at all, and I want to shout, 'I don't know! I think she's a dog. A little dog! I'm teaching her to do wee-wees! Stop shouting at me, your hair is scaring us, is there another dog underneath it?!' before running off into the bushes.

Then there's the younger crowd, which almost always includes our third dog-owner type: **Sweet Teenage Girl With A Puppy**. Often a completely adorable type of puppy, a Jack Russell or a beagle. The combination of hopeful, youthful, slightly cool teenager and prancing pup generally sends me into a tailspin of eager-to-please-ness and I decided irrationally and uncontrollably that I simply *must* become friends with this person. I think I wanted to know I could commune with this age group, proving I am bang on trend and by no means middle-aged. These days I am full of the joys of middle-age, so much so that I oft want to skip out of my forties straight into my sixties, where eating dinner at 5 p.m., spending forty-five minutes deciding what to order from a menu, and growing a light moustache are even more acceptable. But in my post-relationship breakdown state of being, friendship with this teenager was the order of the day. I just wish I hadn't sidled up to her, doing what I've come to call my 'special Rude Boi swagger', a slouchy, rolling gait meant to signify youthful insouciance, which might be better described as 'the creepy drunken-sailor lollop', and said, wait for it, 'So . . . any discos this weekend?' WHAT?! DISCOS?! I had all things puppy to compare and chat about and I ask her if she is going to a DISCO? All any actual self-respecting fifteen-year-old wants to do is sit on the brick wall outside the Post Office swigging vodka Red Bull from a shampoo bottle, before engaging in a little light shoplifting and spending the night in a skip. Or, more likely, they're all now busy with their million-pound start-up companies and ten million YouTube channel subscribers. A DISCO! For goodness' sake, Hart.

Let's shuffle immediately on to our next type, the teenage

girl's male counterpart: **Scary Youth With A Staffie**. I should
be clear, I say 'scary', but the scariness is, I freely admit,
all in my own head. I don't know why I am proper well
fearful of the male yoot and his Staffie (not a euphemism).
I have never been attacked, bullied, victimized or made to
feel in any way unsafe by either a youth or a Staffordshire
bull terrier. Nevertheless, my initial reaction upon seeing
an under-twenty-one in gym gear with a square-faced dog
straining at the leash is almost always, 'Run! Run! He's
going to try and sell you marijuana which is actually just
grass cuttings, then stab you in the face for not wanting
it!'

Next we have, and please welcome and feel free to stand
and applaud: the **Person With A Problem Dog**. The Person
With A Problem Dog can generally be found hovering on
the fringes of a group of jolly middle-class dog owners, who
by rights ought to be his friends. They're all standing together
fifteen feet away from him discussing things he'd really love
to be in on – Tuscan retreats, kale recipes, bathroom tiles,
granola – but he can only join in by straining to hear what
they're saying, then bellowing his contributions over his
shoulder while his dog (which could be any dog, but is
probably something slightly too large for him to handle like
a Doberman cross or a Dalmatian) moves in tight circles
around him, barking wildly and wrapping the lead around
his ankles. He can't move any closer to the group as he is
well aware that if he does his dog will immediately take a
chunk out of nice Mrs Kerrins's poodle before chewing
through its lead and making off across the park, galloping
through beautifully manicured topiary, scattering children
and the elderly, before charging on to the nearest main road
causing a cartoon-style pile-up, which will most likely involve

a lorry full of ball bearings and a treacle-tanker. This dog has been to every single dog-training school in the Greater London area, thousands of pounds and generations of dog-training expertise have been spent on trying to get it to obey rudimentary commands, but every single attempt has led merely to a shrug of the shoulders and the words, 'Some dogs just aren't trainable.' Not even Mr Cesar Salad Millan would have a go on this animal. Pride prevents the owner having the dog rehomed with somebody more suitable (perhaps a small but savage militia in need of an attack dog), so the owner grimly pops a fistful of Valium before braving the park, telling himself that 'He'll learn. One day, he'll learn.' (He won't.)

The Problem Dog will also, if female, be on heat at least 90 per cent of the time. 'Being on heat', for those delicate souls unfamiliar with the condition, refers to the couple of days when your dog effectively becomes the female-dog equivalent of Jessica Rabbit. She will stand, innocent, while male dogs lose control of themselves, flock towards her like an army of Russell Brands, and start humping wildly. This will result in you having to deal with two equally horrible tasks of a) having to peel a sexually aroused dog off the rear end of your own dog, and b) having to engage in awkward banter with the owner of the offending dog, usually involving mutual pretence that what the dog is doing is in no way sexual. 'Gosh, sorry, he's just giving her a little hug – ever so friendly, aren't they! Ha! Ha! Isn't the weather glorious?' (It's pouring with rain.) Mind you, a dog upon your dog, as it were, is a notch down embarrassment-wise than a dog that suddenly attacks one's own leg and begins a, shall we say, 'vibrant humping'. Always awkward.

The fear you feel when a randy mutt approaches yours, or your leg, however, is nothing compared to that which takes hold when confronted by that great park figure, the next on our list. Follow me, you at the back please keep up, for we are now to meet: **The Professional Dog Walker.** A professional dog walker, for those who have yet to encounter one, appears to the untrained eye to be a small, vulnerable human being towed along by up to a hundred dogs of varying sizes. Well, usually six to eight dogs, but still it's deeply unnerving. It looks like the human is being taken for a walk. That somehow a gang of dogs on a day out have taken pity on this defenceless diminutive person and have grabbed her to be part of their pack, to show her their favourite haunts. Which is to say, it gives me the willies. But massive kudos to anyone who even attempts it.

Last but by no means least on our park potter, we have my very favourite breed (pun, as ever, very much intended) of dog owner: **The Husband Who's Been Made To Take His Wife's Dog For A Walk**. These poor unfortunate men are identifiable by the fact that they'll be walking a dog of quite striking effeminacy – Afghan hound, miniature poodle, Pekingese, Pomeranian – which will generally be professionally groomed to within an inch of its life. The hound will know precisely how beautiful it looks (very, very beautiful) and will be prancing accordingly, stepping out with a fine, high stride, sniffing the air and cocking its head flirtatiously at passers-by. The man, on the other hand, will look as ashamed as it's possible for a man to look outside of the penal system, staring at the gravel three feet in front of him and shuffling along as if heading to the electric chair. Occasionally somebody – generally a female somebody – will stop this man and say 'Oh my goodness, what a beautiful dog', to which he'll respond, in a mumble, ''S-not-mine it's-my-wife's-just-taking-it-for-a-walk' before trundling off. You see this man is consistently mistaken for gay and has never been confident enough in his male-ness to shrug that off as the nothing it is. Walking a small, fluffy dog with a pink, fluffy lead is really the last straw for this put-upon husband. His nemesis is of course the **Jogging Alpha-Male That His Spaniel Can Barely Keep Up With**. If our lovely man walking his wife's effeminate hound sees this alpha male in his rugby gear (not that he has played since school but 'I can still get into the same gear, what what?! Not like fatso Hugo and big Biffy ha ha!!') running with his equally alpha, muddy, to heel, spaniel, it will be enough to force him to join the guy on the park bench with a Special Brew. God Bless Him. So there we are. A pretty definitive list. Thank you, I hear you say. Oh stop it and indeed, thank *you* for promenading with me, MDRC, for you make a fine companion to promenade with.

Of course it was all a bit of fun assessing all the dog people but I realized that some of these people would have to become my acquaintances, and possibly friends. At twice-daily intervals we were all going to be walking our dogs. In some way, they were going to become part of my life now. My tribe. Oh dear, did I have anything in common with them? Was anyone feeling as desperate, lonely and confused by life and their hound as I? What sort of dog owner was I? If I'd had to categorize myself at this point I would have said, **Reluctant Dog Owner Wishing Their High-Maintenance Dog Were A Low-Maintenance Cat.** Was anyone else feeling utterly overwhelmed by all things dog-min? At this point the only thing I knew I had in common with them was the need to poop-a-scoop. Which is a ridiculous word for it, isn't it? Because there isn't really any scooping involved these days? Yet the word 'scoop' has become so entwined with the word 'poop' that you can't hear one without thinking of the other. Which is a travesty, quite frankly, and if I were the leader of the Ice Cream Scoopers' Union I'd be wasting no time in starting a riot over how inextricably linked with dog shit my once fine and noble profession had become. That is as political as I get. Stand Up For The Scoopers. Reclaim The Scoop From The Poop. This is my manifesto. Forgive the digress, but really it has lessened the enjoyment of my very favourite treat – the scoop (nay four) of ice cream. Most upsetting.

That first day in the park observing my new peers, I marvelled at how confident and non-disgusted the other dog owners seemed, picking up piles of excrement as if they were simply grabbing a dropped sock. I, on the other hand, found the procedure reduced me to an emotional wreck. Not only did I feel that gathering up Peggy's warm droppings warranted Marigolds, alcoholic hand gel and a bit of lavender spray for afterwards, I found myself crippled by an irrational fear of accidentally picking up another dog's poo. Whilst Peggy's droppings were, let's be frank, 90 per cent disgusting, the faeces of a random hound were at least two million per cent disgusting, and to be avoided at all costs. In those early days it wasn't at all rare to see me tapping a stranger on the shoulder, pointing to a pile of dog poo and saying, 'Excuse me, sir? Is that yours or mine?' (And I wonder why I haven't yet met the love of my life in the park.)

As I assessed hopefully what common ground we may all have, I was struck by a worrying difference. It was plain to see that all the other dog types at the park seemed to have, well, *relationships* with their dogs. An ease, a comfort, a familiarity. Which made me wonder whether or not I'd ever find the same with Peggy. I felt as if the pair of us were still essentially strangers, reluctant flatmates out on a walk (albeit slightly peculiar flatmates where one has to scoop up the other's poop). Still, I persisted. And next on the dog-min agenda . . .

Puppy Classes

The first thing to say about them, however useful they may be – they are WEIRD. WEIRD I tell you. Puppy Classes are basically Monkey Music for dogs, where anxious new young dog-parents congregate to show off their offspring and, crucially, compare themselves unfavourably to other new-dog owners, to the detriment of their mental health. The classes took place in a West London church hall, and reintroduced me to the various different type of dog owner from the park, this time in embryonic form. The People Who Talk Through Their Dogs were only just starting to discover the joy of whispering passive-aggressive cutesy nonsense in little tiny puppy voices; the Brisk Posh People Who Ask Lots Of Questions were just beginning to find their weirdly loud voices (I think these types assume everyone else is mildly deaf, I don't get their volume). And the Person With A Problem Dog was there, as you'd imagine, blissfully oblivious to the fact that the mad, yapping creature at his feet is never going to turn into the serene Lassie-esque creature of his dreams. I felt more at home in the Puppy Classes than in the park. It was reassuring to spend time with others who seemed as tentative around their dogs as I was. We compared anxieties and neuroses and all knew that each of us behind the banter was thinking, 'Please don't let my puppy be the first to wee on the floor.'

As the weeks went on, whatever the cause, it became clear quickly that Peggy wasn't terribly well suited to all of this. She just about mastered 'sit' and 'stay', along with everyone else (except, of course, for the Problem Dog, who repeatedly misheard 'sit' as 'climb the curtains'), but when it came to Pass the Puppy – just as it sounds, a handling exercise to accustom puppies to human contact – Peggy revealed herself as a terrible squirmer, wriggling hysterically away from all who grasped her, as if she were a high-net-worth princess and they were a burly band of balaclava'd kidnappers. This prompted much concerned whispering: 'bit needy', 'thinks she's top dog', 'probably sleeps on the bed'.

I felt judged. I was clearly reeking of newly-single-lady-so-desperate-for-intimacy-she-is-sacrificing-her-dog's-training-for-cuddles. The Bridget Jones of the Puppy Class. The sort of woman who only got a puppy because someone told her it was a good way to meet men and all the salsa-dancing classes were booked up. Someone not only terrible at owning a dog, but clearly a bit dodgy at life as well. And this despite the fact that I'd tried to cram in a sneaky bit of advance preparation for the classes. Still feeling low and trying in vain to write my sitcom pilot, I spent a number of long, lonely afternoons teaching Peggy tricks. Quite advanced, circus-ish tricks too: walking on her hind legs (entirely unsuccessful), jumping on command (only worked if I dangled a treat above her head and suddenly jerked it skywards) and barking the alphabet (she *definitely* made a noise which sounded like 'f' at one point, but let's not book the Wigmore Hall just yet). My poor, addled brain had thought something like, 'Well, if this sitcom isn't any good, then at least Peggy can become a superstar advert dog and we can earn a living that way.'

I started spiralling in negative thought. I definitely should have stuck with a cat if I was that desperate for a pet. A Casper replacement. There would have been very little cat-min and instead of a needy dog asking me to teach them how life works, a cat in all its self-sufficiency would more likely have sat at my keyboard, nudged me out of the way and purred arrogantly in my ear, 'Let me write your sitcom, you have no idea what you are doing, I'll just do a few scenes and then make you dinner.' There was, however, a brief pause in the negative spiral with a marvellous discovery. It turns out that the number one most useful tool for dog training is . . . wait for it . . . frankfurters! Yes, the humble frank. Peggy would do almost anything for a tinned frankfurter. And so, it seemed, would I. As Peggy proved enthusiastic about the franks, willingly performing all manner of tricks in her search for a smoky meaty treat, I started to become rather partial to them myself. I began shamelessly bribing myself as I wrote 'One more joke, and you can have another frankfurter.' 'One decent scene, and you can have two.' I wondered if having a dog was starting to turn me into a dog. Well, at least hear me out. Between the writing, the ongoing emotional wobble and having to stay in with the dog, I seemed to be living a life of meaty snacks, napping and the occasional walk. It felt as if the only real difference between Peggy and me was that she had slightly more fur. Is this what happens, I thought? Am I going to become progressively more and more canine, until I'm one day shot by a farmer for chasing sheep? I felt myself spiralling back down the misery pit as I realized that so far dog ownership was letting me down. And even, dare I say, post-Puppy Classes, my dog was letting me down.

Peggy wakes up and stares at Miranda wide-eyed and open mouthed Letting her down? LETTING HER DOWN? Oh I'm really, really upset she thinks that. Whilst Miranda stands at the fridge door staring into the light I must speak my piece. Why do humans stare at the fridge like that by the way? Open the fridge door and just stare, nibble, shut the door again, walk away, turn back, open it again, stare. What do they think is going to be in there that wasn't there five seconds ago? It's really weird.

PDRC (Peggy's Dear Reader Chum – I still really love that, it makes me very very happy *sits up smiling*), I am again having to defend myself. In this instance over my wriggling at the Puppy Classes. Or, as I called them, the terrifying-hippy-commune-touching-shouting-cult-meetings-OF-DOOM. Ladies and Gentlemen, how would YOU feel if you went off for a lovely evening out with your mistress perhaps hoping that you were going to be taken to the *opera, or at the very least the legitimate theatre, only to discover that you were going to some vile hall where enormous shouty women pick you up, squeeze you, and bellow, 'HELLO, MY DEAR LITTLE FLUFFY ONE!' in your face with their rich, porty, breath? I mean I am a classy, cultured lady with a show-biz heritage who should be on a chaise longue in a West End dressing room of an evening, not in a grotty local hall. Where would she take me next – Bingo? Go Ape? The roller rink?*

And the thing is, PDRC, I can tell you why I was wriggling as I was passed around the cult-commune . . . *shakes her coat and presents as if about to perform a Shakespeare monologue at The Globe* You see, I was really, really scared. I wanted to be with Miranda and stay in her arms. What I had learnt from her is that the world is a scary place and we don't need to be with other people. And I thought she might need me. For protection and cuddles. She often picks me up for cuddles as she wanders around the flat. It's really nice and I like seeing things when I am high up in her arms, especially when we look out of the sitting room on to the street. And I feel really safe with her. I think I might have been starting to really . . . love her. So really . . . there. Excuse me. *trots off to snuggle in her bed, sits pensive, trots back*

Me again. Oh I do love chatting to you. One more thing. On the subject of fidgeting and squirming, *scratches ear* I'm going to be a bit cheeky, PDRC, and tell you a thing or two about what my Miranda gets up to when she's 'writing'. Tee hee hee. Other than the breaks to try and teach me to bark the alphabet and the regular napping I have noted the following:

Eating Frankfurters: All right, we both like frankfurters.

*But Miranda works on a strict 'one for you, two for me'
policy.*

*Animal Frankfurters: Pretending to be an animal with
the use of a frankfurter, her most successful being
elephant, and her favourite as she shoves a frankfurter up
each nostril, the platypus.*

*Frankfurter Olympics: In which Miranda lays a number
of frankfurters out on her desk, and encourages them to
'race' one another and 'jump over' one another, awarding
gold, silver and bronze chocolate coins – to herself.*

*Frankfurter Winter Olympics: Moulding a little man out
of cheese which she stands on 'frankfurter skis' and
pushes down a mountain made of Pringle tubes into her
mouth.*

*Frankfurter Pop Star: Singing 'Nine to Five' by Dolly
Parton on the hour, every hour, whilst dancing using a
frankfurter as a microphone.*

*Frankfurter Boyfriend: Where Miranda acts out
romantic scenes with a frankfurter that she calls Gary.
There are also girl frankfurters with strawberry shoelace
hair that she calls Tilly and Stevie.*

*So. I think you will find that my wriggling is a very
minor crime, in the grand scheme of things. Tee hee hee,
naughty Peggy telling you all that. *rubs her eyes, slight
pause* Do you think she likes me? I really hope she likes
me. I wonder what Boris, Mavis, Elvis and Gladys are doing
. . . I really really really hope she likes me . . .*

Perhaps a nice way to finish this part of my story would be
with our improved visit to the park. Important to end on a
positive, or as near to a positive as I can summon up from
this slightly bleak, worrying period of my life with Peggy.

About a fortnight after our first trip, Peggy and I went to the park again. I still felt mired in dog-min (who knew a dog needs a blooming toothbrush), and far from happy. I wasn't looking forward to seeing all the extreme-dog-owner types again; I didn't really want to talk to anyone, if I'm honest. Particularly after a moment of courage when I tried to impress a potential dog-owner friend with my majestically wonderful poop-a-scooping motion, and ended up flinging a turd into an ornamental pond, very close to a woman's open handbag. Now THAT would have been funny. Don't judge me, MDRC, you know it would! But it didn't happen. There was nothing to laugh at and I bowed my head in shame, afraid I would be recognized as the single loon from the Puppy Classes, and shuffled on, Peggy and I still like reluctant flatmates.

As I circled the perimeter of the park, staring at the ground, unwilling to engage, people came over to me, said hello, recognized Peggy from our previous visit or were just struck by her puppyish fluffiness, and I was forced to share a few moments of grudging communion with others, albeit not necessarily the others I'd have chosen for myself. I could feel my fog of misery start to lift a little, and I felt grateful; momentarily, pathetically grateful to Peggy for lifting me out of myself, forcing me to engage with the world. Without her need for a walk, I certainly wouldn't be in the park. I would probably have the curtains closed and be escaping via some sort of degrading telly binge-a-thon. (*The O.C.* anyone?) But, surprisingly, my spirits rose – a bit. I knew as I walked, that sure, I was far away from the old spring in my step, and I was certainly far away from being one of these people at ease with their dog, and their place in the dog world. But I felt OK with that. I felt a bit better with my Peggy-and-me awkwardness, our odd not-quite-there-yet flatmate relationship. If I was meant to become a proper dog owner, then maybe that would happen in time. And if not, not. So be it. If it came to it, there would be no shortage of willing families to provide her with a loving home. But I had to admit that this little puppy had taught me a lesson here I would otherwise have never learned, or certainly taken a lot longer to. I would have balked at the idea of fresh air and small talk to aid a weary heart, but it turns out that being in beauty, and gaining a sense of community, really is health to the soul.

I could tangibly feel it affecting my body language, and it took me out of my self-pity for a moment. By communing with others I was forced to think outside of myself. I wasn't the only one on this planet and, more to the point, wouldn't be the only one in pain. I noted from Peggy that part of her joy of the park wasn't just the exercise, the freedom, the new surroundings, but she went the most giddy with excitement in communing with her doggy friends. You know – that mad running-in-circles thing dogs do. I slightly wished we could do that as humans. Just gambol up to each other and trot round and round, giving out unconditional, joyful friendship vibes without having to endure the excruciating self-inflicted torture that is small talk. All that trying to give out signals that you'd like to be friends with someone, without actually saying it out loud and making yourself vulnerable. Miserable, pointless, and the sort of thing that only humans could create. Much easier, surely, if we could give someone a sniff and, if interested, do some energetic bounding, perhaps a gentle skip or two and incite a little chase, see if it's reciprocated. If not, move on, nothing lost, and a bit of exercise too. No drinks parties, canapés or 'and what do you do?' Bliss.

Human sniffing and bounding silliness aside, I had learnt

my first spiritual lesson via dog ownership here. That is, we may want to isolate ourselves in tough times but what we actually need is comfort through community and thinking outwards. Just then Peggy gambolled back over to me, happy from her exercise and communing, looking for all the world as if I was the best owner she could possibly have. My heart lifted a little as I saw her and I felt not happy – but hopeful. A notch more hopeful than before.

*You know I DO think you're the best owner I could have. I was happy the minute you brought me to your flat (even though it had a poo-coloured carpet), but I am really worried you don't love me as much as I love you. Miranda? *remembers sitting at the bottom of Miranda's feet, a paw on her shoe and staring, neck straining upward* Miranda? I am doing my cutest face. Look . . .*

CHAPTER 4

My Family

Over the next month or so, despite remaining ambivalent about my new life as a dog owner, constantly worried I'd made a dreadful mistake, I can say things improved. Not dramatically; I was still pretty fatigued with the remnants of glandular fever in my system, which left less room and energy for the animal goof gene to rear its beautiful head. Perhaps my fragility was a blessing in disguise in this instance. The animal goof gene is such a powerful force it can lead a woman very quickly from 'oh hey, perhaps I'll get a dog' or 'maybe I'll do a season at an elephant sanctuary' to a life of semi-feral hermitry, never out of wellies, conversing merrily with chickens, sleeping eight-in-a-bed with a litter of piglets, and nervously calling up Santander to see about applying for a joint mortgage with a sheep. So my need to recuperate physically kept me, I think, grounded safely in normal human life.

Despite my fatigue, the sun began to peep gently out from behind the clouds, emotionally speaking, and life got a little brighter. Thanks to all the walking I began to lose a bit of weight (even with the frankfurter craze not wholly waning). This, combined with the fresh air in my lungs and the sense of satisfaction born of having negotiated the recent poocalypse and other dog-min, meant that I began to feel a bit better about myself and the world. I was now on nodding terms with the other dog owners in the park and had introduced Peggy to my nearest and dearest, even feeling moments of pride as they cooed over her. And we had got into a few quite sweet little routines. She now recognized basic commands. If there was a savoury snack in the offing she was pretty committed to sit, stay, come here, down and even play dead on a good day. It was pretty impressive but we weren't quite *Britain's Got Talent* contenders yet. I was always rather envious of her training regime and thought if an instructor dangled a Greg's sausage roll over some weights at the gym, I would more likely consider membership. Perhaps they should start a new gym class: 'Plus-Sized Aerobics: Jump for Canapés'.

She responded to my picking up her lead pre-park with an intensity of excitement more commonly seen in rank outsiders winning Olympic Gold in front of an audience of millions (whatever I was feeling I could not but smile). When I sat on the sofa, she'd come and sit at my feet and look intensely up at me, hoping against hope for the slightest crumb of approval. And indeed crumb of whatever it was I was most likely eating.

I now understood and made use of a thing called a Kong – oh yes, hard-core dog-min. For those of you without dog, it's a sort of rubber item betwixt a tube and a bowl in which you stuff dog food, apparently making it more entertaining for them to eat from as they have to imaginatively throw it and push it, or delve right down deep with their tongue to release the squished deliciousness. Doesn't sound entertaining to me. Imagine being presented with a roast, watch it being pulped and stuffed into a tight tube, given boxing gloves to wear so you can't get an easy purchase, and be forced to lick out your meal. NOT FUN! (Although there's probably a similar Hollywood diet regime endorsed by Jennifer Aniston et al. 'Pulp and lick your food – takes days to eat one meal.')

She would do her nightly wee-wees quickly and efficiently, then take her bedtime treat and bury it somewhere inappropriate – towels, pillows, sofa cushions. If I ever caught her burying I would quickly video it, such was my amusement at how movements like 'dig a hole' or 'cover up with earth' were so instinctual they would happen when there was no need, no earth, she was the only dog in the pack, on a sofa, and the only thing she could possibly consider a predator would be a John Lewis scatter cushion. But the digging and burying ritual always abounds. I became accustomed to falling asleep to a waft of dribbled-upon rawhide and was no longer woken by her plaintive whines as she'd become accustomed to her basket in the kitchen.

She thought she had successfully trained me to do so but, PDRC, between us, I CHOSE to stay in the kitchen. I really loved her squishy bed and sometimes crept up there in the day (there is still a patch of mud on her bedspread I once ruined, tee hee), but I could no longer handle the nights.

I cannot begin to explain the heady combination of a

six-foot-one-inch woman's thrashing, grinding and wind-breaking. Once she knocked me off the bed right on to the floor when her leg kicked from the surprise of being woken by a fart. NOT ACCEPTABLE.

We'd transitioned from reluctant flatmates – perhaps flatmates who found one another on Gumtree and signed a tenancy agreement without really thinking it through – to the sort of flatmates who share the occasional meal and ask the other if they want to add anything to their darks wash. (Something weirdly intimate for a Brit about our 'smalls' sharing a washing machine; and beyond blush-making to hang them up to dry. Way too much handling of a flatmate's private department.)

On which flat-sharing note, during this cautiously, newly fond phase of my life with Peggy, I moved house. In an attempt to make a fresh start post-breakup and post-illness, I moved to a new, considerably more swish rented place. MDRC, lest you become envious, I should say that 'swish' is all relative. In this instance it simply means one working toilet and the absence of a decade-old fried egg stuck to the skylight. (If you are wondering how it got there, well, via a game I like to call 'Can you stick a fried egg to the skylight?' Obviously.) I was still struggling to earn into double figures with my writing and acting, so high-end swish was a way off. But I had just secured a regular part in a new ITV comedy drama series called *Monday Monday* playing 'Tall Karen'. Yes, <u>Tall</u> Karen! I mean who else were they going to give the part to? It was me or *Dragons' Den*'s Peter Jones in drag. Thanks to Tall Karen I finally had enough funds to rent up a notch.

Without Peggy, I would have been a tad nervous. For the first time in my life, I was moving into the sort of place which people might actually want to come and visit. A proper, grown-up little house, with wooden floors, and things estate agents delight in calling 'period features'. The sort of place that cried out for little tea lights in little glass holders, and African art that you can say you got on a safari but was actually from the local market, and a vintage hat stand. Which will only ever be used for coats and scarves and possibly towels, because who on earth has enough hats these days to justify a stand? What kind of quasi-Victorian loon has the seven hats required to fully occupy a whole multi-pronged piece of furniture?

Oh, PDRC, I have to tell you I was SO relieved when we finally found the new house. Because it meant one totally brilliant brilliant thing. No more of those REALLY weird human things called estate agents. How strange are they, PDRC?! SERIOUSLY!

Have you seen how small the cars are that they drive? I don't think even I could barely fit in, yet a posh six-foot-five-inch boy called an estate agent somehow squishes in and drives off. It's really spooky.

I also don't like their voices; they speak really really loudly and it hurts my ears.

And I think they may have some quite serious spatial awareness issue because they say things like 'that metre-squared kitchenette will make for dinner parties of eight', or 'that elbow-sized dent in the wall made by a previous tenant with an anger issue is a walk-in wardrobe'. I think they should all see a doctor. And soon.

And they used to phone Miranda ALL THE TIME. I would be settling down for a nice nap, to be startled by a weird estate agent on speaker shouting, 'Just phoning about something interesting that's just come up. It's very nearly what you're looking for – a two-bed in West London was it? This one is actually a fifteen-bedroom equestrian property outside Inverness. But 'tis going to be snapped up and I'd never forgive myself if I didn't at least offer you a viewing.'

But we never wanted to live in Inverness and I am terrified of horses. WHAT'S WRONG WITH THEM?! Are they ill, PDRC? I know a dog behaviourist who might be able to help them. All I know is they defo need help.

There, I have said my piece on the matter. *rushes, proud of her speech, to make her toy dog squeak* Every time it squeaks I just LOVE IT. Every time. I dig my teeth in and squeak, squeak. SO FUNNY. On its own, no noise. My teeth and it squeaks. TOO GOOD.

Did this new house mean I suddenly had to become some kind of 'adult'? Someone who knows how to bleed a radiator and read an Ordnance Survey map? Somebody who can stand in front of an open fridge in the dark and not pretend they are in a spotlight on the Wembley stage as an international pop sensation? Someone who puts crisps in a bowl rather than have them straight from the packet/tuck them inside a pasty to add a bit of texture? Someone who *irons their clothes*? Is this who I was going to have to become, if I wanted to live in this house? Owning Peggy was really the only thing which qualified me as any sort of adult human; without her, despite being a year or two into my thirties, I felt little more than an overgrown sixth-former to whom someone had randomly and inadvisably given a job.

With these thoughts whirring around in my head and my nerves a-jangle, I did all I could to settle into my new home.

I polished the wood floors, put down some lovely rugs, settled Peggy into her basket in the living room, lit a scented candle, then thought better of it (nothing's more likely to alienate your neighbours than a yowling, on-fire dog sprinting through their garden, even if that dog does smell faintly of ylang-ylang and rosewood) and curled up in my brand-new bed, excited. I really felt that things were on the up. It was unlike me in my recent slump to dare to hope. But hope I did.

I came downstairs the next morning to find myself confronted by . . . well, you simply won't believe it, MDRC. I know what you're thinking, 'Miranda, not poo. No. Please. Not another poocalypse. Not in your new house. And, more to the point, do we have to read about poo yet again in this silly book of yours; I wish I was reading about Peggy Ashcroft now if I'm honest.' Well, I am sorry, but yes indeed, after daring to hope, and frankly I deserve full sympathy for this and if you laugh I will come and find you and gently smack you on the head with a spoon, for I came downstairs and there was POO ALL OVER MY HOUSE!

History, to my great dismay, had repeated itself. Worse, this time it wasn't just poo, brace yourselves and put that snack down, for it was poo and sick. Deal with it, MDRC, deal with it! And it was, shall we say, lavish. I was about to get furious with Peggy but then I saw her. In the middle of the battlefield lay my poor little doggy, on her side, breathing heavily and gazing up at me with the look of – well, someone with a serious stomach bug. She looked like nothing more than a pre-Dioralyte human dealing with gastro-intestinal carnage, but without the knowledge of what to do to help herself. She was so weak she couldn't move; just lay there listless, her eyes wide and frightened. It was the saddest thing I've ever seen, quite frankly – so much so that I couldn't even be cross about the fact that a) my brand-new, shiny, rented living room now resembled an instructional video on the perils of eating raw chicken, and b) I was supposed to be starting a new acting job that very day. Leaving in twenty-five minutes, in fact.

I didn't know what to do; I felt ripped in half. This blooming dog, who I still wasn't 100 per cent sure I wanted, had ruined my pad and placed me in an untenable professional situation. I wanted to get on with my new house, new job, new life, yet this foot-long fur-ball was seemingly determined to quite literally shit all over my hopes and dreams. This was the first read-through for my ITV debut, my comedy drama debut. Tall Karen needed me and I needed her. But then there was that poorly little furry face . . . oh, my goodness, you should have seen it. Such fragility. Such dependence. MDRC, I felt a rush of what I can only assume is maternal feeling – the sense, the knowledge in fact, that – come hell or high water – I had to protect this fluff-ball. Whatever she was suffering, I had to do everything within my power to fix it for her.

I called work to tell them . . . what? I didn't know what to say. 'My dog is sick' sounds perilously like a pulling-a-sickie type of excuse. Also, are you allowed to take time off for a sick pet? A child, yes, of course, take as long as you need and rightly so. But a dog? Really? It's a dog. And to someone who doesn't get the whole dog thing, a dog's little more than a hugely expensive, vast and weirdly clingy rat. It's an animal. It's . . . self-repairing, surely. Just prop it up in the corner with a bowl of water and a dead mouse and it'll be fine. This is the first thing my new colleagues were going to learn about me – she is staying at home because her dog is poorly.

It sounded utterly pathetic. I was already worried that people were wondering what sort of weird giantess was going to tip up to play Tall Karen (couldn't she just have been called Karen?!). The whole thing was paranoia-making enough, without a sick dog situation bundled on top of it. Tom Ellis, who I was keen to persuade to be in my sitcom pilot, was in the show, and Fay Ripley, an actress I had always loved but never met. I really wanted to impress on both counts. It was Job versus Dog. I, like Natalie Imbruglia before me, was torn. But a few more seconds spent looking into Peggy's sweet, dehydrated, dear-God-please-don't-let-me-die eyes convinced me that canine Calpol and abandonment wasn't a realistic option. I made the Call of Shame to work, bundled Peggy into a thickly newspaper-lined crate, and we were off for our very first visit together to The Vet.

The Vet

Fortunately, due to the gravity of Peggy's condition (or perhaps just because she was emitting terrible smells), we were rushed through pronto and were spared the horror of the vet's waiting room. Waiting rooms have always made me nervous. I am not so much scared of being ill than I am a doctor's waiting room. What are you going to catch on top of what you already have? Why is it so hot? Dare I touch the magazines? What does the person sitting next to me and invading my personal space have? Would it be rude to offer him some alcoholic hand gel? Why are there posters telling me that if I feel a little tired and a bit headachy I probably have a Type 1 this or a rare that. Hideous places. And a vet's waiting room I find equally discombobulating. There'll generally be something in the region of two dogs, one rabbit, a hamster, three cats including one with a bandage round its paw (always sinister) and at least one weird animal like a parrot or a tortoise or a creepy lizard on a string. A situation that feels to me as if it's merely moments away from some kind of jungle kingdom anarchy – the parrot nips a dog owner's hand, causing him to drop the lead, at which one cat will let out a terrible yowl and the dog will panic and attack the tortoise, and another cat will jump up (bandage on paw) and go for the parrot, and the whole thing will escalate until we all perish in a tornado of shrieking and feathers. It's a room of ominous expectancy, and if anyone is going to be chatted up by the peculiar older gent with the lizard on the string, it is me I tell you. And that does nothing for the self-esteem.

So, as the whimpering Peg and I reached the vet's consulting room, I was thinking, 'Right, let's get this sorted out as quickly as possible so I can get on with my life as a serious professional actor adult who doesn't want to be surrounded by one-eyed parrots and . . . woweee.' The last thing I was prepared for, MDRC, was a hunky vet. And he really was hunky. I mean he looked like a Viking. Like Asterix crossed with a slimline Oliver Reed, chiselled out of Nordic stone and adorned with the very finest shock of blond hair that nature could create. (I may be overstating this a little. He probably looked like a normal, quite tall blond vet. But please remember that I'd pretty much spent the last months alone indoors with a dog.) I gathered myself, but then, just to tip me over from 'a bit flustered' into 'jibbering and jabbering and dribbling like a bloodhound with a cavity', Dr Hunky-Viking-Vet (all names have been changed) took a look at Peggy, smiled, and said: 'Nice dog. My ex-wife used to have a shih-tzu.'

Ex-wife. *Ex*-wife. EX! Dr Hunky-Viking-Vet was only jolly well single. Well, this was it, I thought. This was why Peggy had been brought into my life. She was the device which would guide me towards my romantic comedy ending, my life spent with Dr Hunky-Viking-Vet, perhaps on a ranch in the Australian bush, surrounded by kangaroos and possums who loved us, but not nearly as much as we loved each other; or even a ranch in Colorado where we'd huddle together on a bearskin to keep safe from mountain lions, while some sort of delicious ranch-y cornbread bakes away behind us. Or, and hang on a minute, perhaps this is the chance I've been waiting for to open my Elephant Sanctuary. Perhaps I have now finally found my partner in elephant-ing! Suffice to say, my mind might have galloped ever-so-slightly off with me. But why had he made the point of saying his EX-wife used to have a shih-tzu? He needn't have said that. Unnecessary vet chitter-chatter there. He could have just said 'nice dog' and cracked on with his business. But no, he made the point of telling me of his EX-wife. His wife of NO MORE. There was only one very obvious answer, MDRC – he had taken one look at me and fallen. The man with the lizard on the string would have to keep on dreaming. Dr Hunky-Viking-Vet was my future.

I suddenly felt stiflingly hot, hotter even than the first flush of infatuation warranted, and it occurred to me that the heating was on full blast in the vet's consulting room. Perhaps he'd recently been treating a tropical bird which required rainforest temperatures, I don't know. To make matters worse, there were no windows and the walls started coming in on me. I felt claustrophobically hot. You know the kind of heat that makes you want to tear all your clothes off immediately and sit in a fridge. The kind of heat you feel in winter when outside temperatures warrant thick jumpers, a coat, hat and scarf, but when you enter a shop, within twenty seconds your wool prison creates such a searing rage you want to kill. Dr Hunky-Viking-Vet asked in a calm, caring voice, looking intently at me like he would actually listen to the answer (what a man):

'So do you want to tell me the problem?'

'Ah that's kind, I'm OK, just very very hot . . . not in that way . . . temperature-wise . . . although I can be hot in a hot-to-trot sexy way if, anyway . . . wow, I'm just sort of menopausal hot really . . . I could kill . . . not really, maybe just a punch . . . I should add I'm not actually menopausal . . . I just meant . . . '

'No, you look too young . . . '

'Stop it . . . ! People do say I have good skin . . . No, the problem is that I think mainly I have just been lonely and . . . '

'I meant the problem with the dog . . . '

'Ah yes, of course . . . *unnecessary laughing* . . . the dog, my dog . . . similar to your wife's dog, your wife that is no longer . . . hello, I'm your number two . . . what? . . . right . . . ' *more unnecessary laughing*

Oh my golly golly goodness golly me . . . *slowly removes paw from over eyes* Peggy's Dear Reader Chum, all I can say is this crazed display from my owner was WAY more nauseating than the condition I was actually suffering from and I was feeling really really sick. What Miranda didn't know was that the day before I had found a very old KFC bucket from the bottom of a bin and scoffed the lot. Please don't say. She usually stops me when I go near bins, but she was chatting to one of her doggy friends and me and a schnauzer went off scavaging. Hee hee.

The vet man was very calming and nice, but nothing to warrant Miranda's kind of attention. She looked sort of unstable. I just say it how I see it.

And, actually, excuse me, I was the one who needed attention. Because can I just say it's bad enough when you have to go to the vet because you are probably not very well and actually, even if you aren't ill, you get a person with plastic gloves shoving their massive hands in your mouth to look at your teeth, which is just disgusting and really terrifying, but I need to let you know how really really terrifying the enormously HIGH vets' tables are.

Not to you, to you they're hip height, or to Miranda, calf height. Tee hee hee. But for the likes of me and my animalian brothers and sisters, they are, basically, sixty feet in the air. Imagine you are feeling unwell and a bit dizzy and when you get to the doctors they make you receive treatment on top of Tower Bridge. That is how the table feels to us. So just have a little think about THAT. *sneezes triumphantly*

'And what sort of food do we like?' Dr Hunky-Viking-Vet said whilst examining Peggy.

'Oh, well I would never say no to Thai . . . '

'I meant the dog . . . '

'Again, yes, I see . . . sorry.' I really had to gather now. It was gather or go. But I couldn't leave Peggy and I felt I could claw it back (claw – PUN). There were beads of sweat forming on my upper lip and I was concerned I might tip over into full sweat-moustache but, as if reading my mind, Dr Hunky-Viking-Vet leaned behind me and popped on a fan. Well, now, I was thrilled. And I shall tell you for why. A youth spent watching 80s and 90s music videos has convinced me, rightly or wrongly . . .

Wrongly . . .

. . . that I look my absolute best when positioned in front of any kind of wind machine. If you move the air around me – even a fraction – I turn into Olivia Newton-John, vogueing madly as my hair fans out behind me like a halo. In wind (of the meteorological variety), I become regal, sensual, the sort of woman who can writhe standing up. Magnificent.

If by magnificent you mean like a crazed fisherman navigating his boat through a squall . . .

I gently vogued before the fan, mentally picking out my wedding dress as the vet prodded away at Peggy. I felt that nothing could possibly go wrong. I was redeeming myself, I was only inches away from the arms of the love of my life, until he uttered the immortal words:

'Has it mostly been brown vomit, or greeny-tinged?'

Now, I can't remember specifically what it is he says to her in *Casablanca* in order to seal the deal, but I'm fairly sure it wasn't 'Has it mostly been brown vomit, or greeny-tinged?' Still, I thought, nil desperandum! Perhaps our story's going to be a bit more of a gross-out knockabout romantic comedy, a *There's Something About Mary* sort of set-up, where the path to love is paved with hilarious misunderstandings over which mug's got tea in it and which one's got the sample to be sent off to the lab. I continued gently vogueing, and replied:

'Goodness . . . . it's hard to say. Perhaps greeny-tinged with gentle, rustic brownish hues? Like a . . . beautiful Canaletto painting of the mud on the bank of the Venetian canals . . . Have you ever been to Venice? Gorgeous, isn't it?'

Nice work, Hart. Way to keep it sexy. Steer the conversation back to romantic matters. Steer it with the determination of a tugboat pulling a tanker into dock. But we were very much in the days I got stuck in a verbal diarrhoea and once I had begun it somehow seemed easier to keep going than to stop. An odd social tick.

'Do you think Peggy is going to be OK? She looks a little deathly – like a dying opera hero . . . Opera in Venice anyone? Wow that would be . . . People love or hate opera, don't they? I find it very sensual . . . oh sorry, don't know why I said sensual . . . horrible word . . . nothing sensual about sensual . . . oh dear, still saying sensual . . . '

WHAT IS HAPPENING? Is this flirting? Why can't she just stop talking? Honestly, what is it with you humans and your 'flirting' and 'dating' rituals? What is wrong with sniffing a bottom? That way you know instantly whether there is any future. SO much easier. Nobody has to buy a push-up bra or do strange wiggly supermodel walking or get stuck eating a three-course dinner with somebody they don't much like. It's madness. Why ON EARTH would you want to eat dinner with someone anyway? How do you know they're not going to steal your food? Though I do know that is one thing Miranda never does. She never ever ever shares food. And I have great respect for her on that front. But this, this vogueing and constant repeating of the word 'sensual', is utter madness.

I had let myself down a little . . .

A LITTLE . . . !!!

. . . and was suddenly acutely aware again of the heat. I had to take some clothes off NOW. I felt like I was in a sauna in a duffel coat eating a curry. But hang on, this was my opportunity, my chance to seductively take off my jacket, then remove my jumper in one fluid movement to make the shift from asexual scruffy dog owner to Bond-esque girl siren, a viable option – nay serious catch – for Dr Hunky-Viking-Vet. I attempted to calmly make the sex-siren shift, and, well, buckle in, MDRC – you see, my jumper was a polo-neck and there was no fluid movement for the polo-neck got stuck on my head. I panicked and started shouting desperately, 'Pull me off, pull me off, vet . . . '

This is the end, it can't get worse. I cannot take the shame. Someone, rescue me. I am a rescue dog. RESCUE ME!

He yanked my polo-neck off my head as if I was an oversized child. Why did it have to be a polo-neck? And WHY do polo-necks DO that? Adhere themselves to you like a second skin, or a plastic bag blown at you by a gale, or a stalker? Because, and tighten that seat belt even more, I hadn't realized that said polo-neck had also removed the T-shirt underneath. I was now standing in front of him, IN MY BRA.

Oh no, my bad, it can get worse. HELP ME. There is now six feet of sweaty, out-of-control, semi-naked flesh. She looks like a giraffe who's just been given an injection.

The only plus was that I had a joke for my on-screen character, but it wouldn't be until much later I could see that positive side. Dr Hunky-Viking-Vet dealt with the situation with aplomb, didn't mention it, and as I put my T-shirt back on cleared his throat and went ahead with his follow-up question to the vomit-colour extravaganza of disgustingness. Which was 'and what consistency are her faeces?' at which point I was just (but only just) thinking that it might still be worth asking him out in an amusing 'now you have seen my bra . . . '-type way. After all, even in her current state, Peggy was still pretty damn cute. That had to cancel out some of the revoltingness of the situation, surely?

Well, most certainly. I am cute enough to cancel out most revoltingness. Have you seen me? I mean, you've seen pictures, so you've probably got a fair idea. Basically, like a little silver cloud breathed by angels. But you can't REALLY understand the marvellousness until you meet me in the flesh and fur. It's heart-melting. Seriously.

As I drew breath to deliver my best chat-up line ever and rescue myself, he came out with (sorry, but time to put down your snacks again):

'Hmm, yes. The thing about these breeds is that they often get blocked anal glands. What you need to do regularly with these dogs is puncture the glands and release the fluid.'

Just ignore that please. Still beautiful.

At which point my focus quite firmly shifted from 'continue to flirt with vet, despite polo-neck-bra-reveal-incident and mild ongoing disgustingness of situation' to 'try to exit the room as quickly as possible without throwing up on the floor'. Anal glands, MDRC, for the love of James Herriot: what vet would inflict the words ANAL GLANDS on an unsuspecting woman obviously new to the world of dog ownership? And how had I never been warned about this? Why had no one taken me aside and said, 'Oh, you're getting a dog, how wonderful and adorable, I hope somebody's told you that every few months you have to puncture their anal glands in order to release fluid.' *Born Free* and my other childhood animal research had never mentioned such things and I felt briefly duped.

The vet explained to me exactly what the process would involve. I'll spare you the gory details. Suffice to say that as he spoke the colour drained from my face and my belief in any kind of benevolent, ordered universe abruptly left me. Dr Hunky-Viking-Vet (who I think we'll now rechristen Dr Bum-Gland-Disgusting-Man) had officially ruined everything. This was the end of the affair. I stepped away from the fan (didn't want it to render me alluring against my will) . . .

AS IF!

. . . and responded to Dr Bum-Gland-Disgusting-Man's next question ('would you like me to teach you how to deal with the glands so you can do it yourself at home?') by drawing myself up to my full height and declaiming:

'Good sir. I would sooner eat your tray of surgical instruments than have anything at all to do with that particular area of my dog. I have no intention of EVER getting anywhere near something that calls itself an anal gland, let alone one that needs fluid removed from it. The word anal is bad enough, the word gland is truly hideous. You have put the two together and suggest I become intimate with such a thing. No, no and thrice no. This is precisely why people like you become vets so people like me are able to throw good money willingly at you to address such VILE things. Good day to you.'

I turned on my heel and stormed out of the office, before turning on my other heel and storming back in in order to reclaim my – by now pretty confused – little hound-let.

So. Our first trip to the vet was one of thwarted romantic ambition, extreme heat, polo-necks and unimaginable disgustingness. Not the smoothest entrance to the veterinary world, but it did at least reveal that Peggy was in no way seriously ill, merely suffering from some kind of dog bug, or food poisoning. Walking home, a partially cured Peggy bleating at me from her crate (she probably could have walked, but I felt I ought to allow her the luxury of being a bit 'regal', given the indignities she'd just suffered), I felt an eclectic bunch of emotions. I felt sad again knowing that I was going back to an empty house with no one to share my day of shame. But, as Peggy looked up at me, I felt – perhaps – a connection. I wasn't alone. I had to look after another living being. Peggy and I were somehow grafted to one another. She was mine, and I hers. 'We belong together,' I thought.

I was heartened by this new sense of a familial bond between Peggy and Me. I began to think having a dog is really a miniature, less-socially-acceptable version of having a child. But as I thought of motherhood, I began to worry, then to fret, then to outright panic. I am not dealing well with temporary custody of a house with period features and one small dog, how would I ever be able to consider a child if and when that opportunity came? What would I be like with actual living, breathing human children? As the cursing of self began again, I wondered: am I somehow responsible for the ways in which this pup is going to develop or not, personality-wise? I don't think a firm conclusion was ever reached on the old 'nature versus nurture' debate, was it? Which of my appalling personality traits might I be at risk of passing on to my poor innocent hound and turning her into a sociopath . . . ?

Oh dear. I feel guilty now. I don't want her to worry about what she could pass on. Because, actually, I think she's doing a really really good job. She is very lovable. I just wish <u>she</u> realized she was. I don't think the end of her relationship did her any good, self-esteem-wise. Generally in her life it seems she has been scarred by arguments and mean things being said about her that just aren't true. And I don't know if she realizes that I, well, I love her. She is all I have. She's definitely my family. And here are the qualities that I believe my mistress Miranda has, so far, passed on to me. *pauses briefly* No, no, hang on, there are some. *looks into the air, thinks* Ummm . . . Hang on . . . Yes. I know.

Number One: If in doubt, eat.

Number Two: Have lots and lots and lots of worries, because worries keep us safe.

Number Three: General air of kindness and jollity.

Number Four: Need for constant inflow of frankfurters and biscuits in order to maintain general air of kindness and jollity.

Number Five: If in doubt, eat. No, I have said that one.

OK, but I am on the spot here. The point is she is lovely. And I could really be a lot worse off.

I had ruined my cosy feeling of a sense of family by going down a rabbit hole of worry. (It took a good few years to learn how to stop those unnecessary negative thoughts ruining an otherwise pleasant day.) Once again I had that nagging feeling I had made a mistake with this doggy. I felt trapped by the responsibility, a responsibility that Casper never brought me.

The third afternoon after our eventful veterinary trip and attempting to push away any sense of regret, Peggy rolled in some mud on a walk (*serious* mud, the sort of thing you wouldn't be surprised to find a hippo rootling about in). I tried to shampoo her in my bath and it led to some serious matting. I could ignore it no longer, I had to face my next dog-min challenge. And I knew this was going to be make or break in the whole dog-ownership connection. Peg and I had to make our first visit to . . . the dog groomers'.

I suspect you might be thinking: 'Who do you think you are, Marie Antoinette? Can't even take a brush to your own dog? Wimp.' Well, MDRC, bit harsh but I see where you're coming from. But you must understand that when dealing with a dog of Peggy's level of fluffiness, it really is jolly hard to deal with it yourself. My attempt at bathing had turned her soft flowing locks into the texture of an oven scourer. I nearly considered putting her at the end of a mop to do some hardcore cleaning. I am not saying I was going to get her groomed like some people do their large poodles, you know, like topiary. Topiary Dogs I call them. It was just for a wash and brush. And, it turns out, Peggy really needs professional help on the fur front.

Speak for yourself.

The Groomers'

It's a crazy, crazy world at the groomers', I'll tell you that for nothing (or, if not nothing exactly, then the arguably very modest price that you've paid for this book). Before I went, I imagined, slightly madly I concede, that it would be just like a doggier version of a normal human hairdressers'. Dogs sitting under tiny little dryers, dipping dog biscuits in teacups of water and flicking through *Horse & Hound* magazine. Dogs sitting in those strange gowns which are like silky versions of backless hospital gowns, gossiping. ('And sweetheart, her *breath*!') Actually, the dog groomers' looks a bit more like the sort of place a Bond villain would keep his victims immediately before taking them through to the inner sanctum of his lair and disposing of them in a bath of gold. The dogs sit in cages, waiting their turn, and when the time comes for them to be groomed they're taken out and strapped to what appears to be an executioner's table. I should stress that the dogs are treated humanely – wonderfully, even – at my local dog groomers', and any resemblance the place bears to a torture chamber/Bond-villain lair/Guantanamo Bay is purely an aesthetic accident. Still, I'm ever so grateful that I, as a human, don't have to go through such an earthy, public process in order to look vaguely presentable. I decided the human equivalent of what Peggy goes through at the groomers' would be having one's bikini line off in a shopping centre outside Poundland whilst strapped akimbo to a board surrounded by some whimpering men in cages awaiting a public back, sack and crack.

As we arrived, Peggy started visibly shaking. I hadn't seen this before. It was both impossibly cute and deeply concerning. The grooming lady explained dogs often shake because they sense their owner is nervous. I was back to thinking, 'Help, you *can* pass traits on to dogs.' But she also informed me that they can shake deliberately to get out of a situation, knowing a human may take pity on the vulnerability of the shiver. Either way, I found myself terribly confused and worried. If there was a profound connection between owner and dog this was my first experience of it. I suppose this was the motherhood equivalent of the first day at nursery. I handed her over, gave her a little kiss, and rushed off before I got too emotional, convinced the shaking was genuine terror.

Of course I was terrified. But not for any reason you may suspect. I don't mind being preened in public. When you have supermodel-quality looks, you feel it's something you owe the public. I court a coo. It's in my genes. And it's what I deserve. The reason I was terrified was because there was this dog at the groomers' that I quite fancied who looks like Michael Ball. Do you know about Michael Ball? He is very gorgeous. Although, however much of a fan I am of musical theatre, I have to listen to the Lloyd Webber collection on a loop, A LOT. It wouldn't be too bad but Miranda drowns out any female voices in the duet parts singing them herself. She is silly. I do love 'All I Ask Of You', though – that's when she stands me up on my hind legs and duets with me. So I was hoping that the Michael Ball dog would be impressed by what they were going to do to me. So no, I wasn't shaking because I didn't want to be separated. I mean really . . . no . . . well, maybe a little bit. It's just I didn't want her to go off and do her acting stuff, and be around that Tom Ellis man and Fay Ripley woman and forget all about little perfect wonderful me.

I was meant to be writing the final draft of my sitcom pilot the day Peggy was at the groomers' but I found I couldn't remotely concentrate. I was pacing, waiting eagerly for the call that she was ready to be picked up. It was akin to waiting for a family member to come around after a tricky operation. I kept wondering if she was ok, if she was playing nicely with the other dogs, if she perhaps . . . missed me. Was this normal dog-owner behaviour or was I going sentimental and weird? Certainly my reaction to getting the call she was ready to be picked up was at a surprising level of excitement. Anyone would have thought I had just won a competition to become the fourth member of Take That. But, may I say, my excitement was very much warranted.

She was like a new dog. A half-shaved, pouffed and sculpted movie-star dog. Like a snowflake made out of cotton wool. Like the inside of a Milky Way bar crossed with a cloud. As she was handed to me, my heart leapt. She started clambering to get into my arms, licking me all over (well, not all over, but you know what I mean), and I allowed it. It had been our first experience of lengthy separation from each other and I was so so so happy to have her back. I had missed her. I thought just how far we'd come together. It was all still new, still tentative, but Peggy really felt like family now. The groomers' had thankfully been *make* not *break* and I was learning my next lesson from my dear dog. In that instance, what my acting colleagues or the Nordic vet beauty thought of me didn't matter. I had a little being that adored me, indeed, who I think might just love me – approval from anyone else wasn't necessary. If you have a loving family unit, any stings from others can wash over you. And, more to the point, I found myself realizing that it's better to be single than in a relationship that doesn't give a kind, loving and trusting approval. And in that moment, something in me had changed. I felt my heartbreak begin to recede. I drove home teary. I had a being that loved me. And, right then, it didn't matter to me that it was just a dog.

*Finally, she's getting it. I DO love her. I DO, I really really really do. And I am happy to skate over the 'JUST a dog' bit. I mean REALLY. *jumps from Miranda's arms, and prances off down the street* Just a dog. Duh. Have you seen me? Hello, hello everyone. I am so beautiful! Look at* *me all groomed, like a super-duper movie star! Or a beautiful vase of flowers! The Sistine Chapel! Oh, isn't the world lucky to be able to gaze upon one so stunning as myself. What a treat I am. Get a load of this, Michael Ball dog. Have a sniff on this . . . *adds in a dainty high hip wiggle to the prance**

This genuine bonded feeling was cemented a few weeks later when Peggy went to the vet (to a new practice – I thought it best that Dr Hunky-Viking-Vet wasn't subjected further) to 'be done'. The removal of all lady bits and bobs. I felt sad that no Peggy puppies would ever be possible, but was advised that unless you knew for sure you wanted to breed your bitch, it was kinder and meant less chance of disease in the 'downstairs departments'. When I picked her up from the operation, still a little groggy, so relieved to be 'with Mummy', and me desperate to get her home, I knew our family unit was fully fused. I admit I was still mired in dog-min, house-min, work-min and general working-it-all-out-alone-min but I felt this might be the beginning of what the younger me writing all those letters to Santa wanted from her mythical golden retriever. And I no longer needed a golden retriever. Actually Peggy, the Shitty Frise, was my perfect dog. Although not quite perfect at the time as she was sporting the delight that is the post-op animal 'cone'. Too tragic, but rather funny.

FUNNY? They are NOT funny. How would YOU like to be seen with an office bin around your neck?

It was as we were trotting around the park the day she'd been to the groomers', and pre-Peggy's op, that I first truly marvelled at how perfect she looked. So so beautiful. Fresh, fluffy, fragrant, and fabulous. Only slightly marred by the fact that her new 'do' made her – how can I put this? – 'poo hole' look a tiny bit more pronounced than usual.

How very rude. *immediately rolls in fox poo*

Noooooo! Family eh?

CHAPTER 5

True Love

So, MDRC, what did I say at the beginning of the last chapter? For those who can't remember, frankly I'm disappointed; surely it should be etched in your memory, such is the utter thrill of this book. Well, in as much as a book about a dog can be a thrill, I'm not Dan Brown. If you were expecting a roller-coaster ride of a story, I am afraid you have got the once-around-a-merry-go-round kind instead. No adrenaline junkies here. And I make no apology for that. I'm the kind of woman that gets enough of an adrenaline kick walking to the Post Office without a bra. Let's not dwell on that image. I shall remind you what I said. At the beginning of the last chapter I uttered the immortal words 'I'd made a dreadful mistake' as regards my bringing Peggy home that fateful day. I briefly painted a picture of myself in love with Peggy. We weren't Romeo and Juliet, or Eric and Ernie, or Jedward, we were more something halfway between The Odd

Couple and Bill and Ben the Flowerpot Men. Only border-line-happy bedfellows, at best.

Well, My Dear Dear Dearest Most Beautiful Reader Chum (the slightly more extravagant and generous tone of my writing reflects the happy and glorious subject matter of this chapter) – it finally happened. I finally Got It. Got It to the extent that I feel compelled to use capital letters where no capital letters are strictly called for. I Got why people buy little cowboy/Santa/Sherlock costumes for their dogs, and sit them up at the dinner table in front of a monogrammed bowl. I Got why people try to phone their dogs at the kennels when they're away on holiday; sit up at night with them when they're ill; talk incessantly about them to strangers in the park; enter them in huge, mad dog shows where they're made to trot out in front of fifteen other dogs in a green baize ring while ruddy-cheeked ladies jot down notes about their gait. On which note, for me, when watching Crufts, my eye is always unavoidably drawn not to the dogs, but to the dogs' handlers, specifically the dogs' handlers when they are forced to jog around the perimeter of the ring next to their animals. So much funnier and more interesting than the dogs themselves, not least because the handlers tend to be people wildly unsuited to jogging. Most likely due to a combination of oversized bosom/unsupportive bra/lavish man-boob/hefty tweed. And yet they jog gamely along, despite these significant limitations. Often with a slight hint of panic, as if a chip-pan fire had just broken out in the village hall and they're staggering to safety. And some of them can't run at ALL, and so adopt a sort of nervous waddling emergency-run-like-walk similar to penguins scooting down a glacier. It's wonderful. I love them. You must look.

I actually have more on this. That is, the moving spectacle

of the un-athletic being forced into an activity which transcends their skill level (see Puppeteers in Chapter 1). It fascinates me (it should be my *Mastermind* specialist subject), but I fear this is not the place. Where was I? Oh yes, I was Getting It. If you pardon. I mean, of course, as regards the understanding of a true love for a dog. Yes, I Got It, I Got It all and, lucky for you, My Dear Reader Chum, I Got this – I Got why people write books about their dogs. And I feel it's only right I tell you the story behind this moment. It's a bit of a yarn, but bear with and, I hope, enjoy. This would be a good time to refill your mug o' tea or chosen beverage. Except you on the sherry, I see you, we're not quite halfway through our romp together; pace yourself please.

Love Trip

A few months into our life together, Peggy and I went on our first trip away with a particularly doggy friend of mine, Katie. She invited us to come and stay with her in Devon. This involved a very long car journey and my first experience of proper travel with Peggy. I was a little nervous. It seemed odd to me to travel at speed in a motor vehicle accompanied by what is only a few smidges of domestication away from a wild animal. What if she went feral, grabbed the wheel, and the last anyone saw of us was me screaming in a car on speed-camera footage being driven by a crazed shih-tzu/bichon-frise cross? And what if, oh I can't believe we're talking about this again, but here we go, what if there was some sort of horrendous in-car poo incident? If it was bad in a two-bedroom house, then goodness only knows what a poocalypse would be like in a fast-moving, sealed, glass-windowed container on a hot sunny day.

111

With this in mind, I stopped at pretty much every available service station in order to allow Peggy ample opportunity to do her business, which meant that by the end of our journey I felt I was the Michael Palin of petrol stations. They are of course basically completely horrible places, but there's something about the remoteness, the this-is-your-only-snack-op-tion-for-fifty-miles-now-make-the-best-of-it-bitch-ness which makes them indescribably addictive and alluring. TV bosses, if you ever want to make a series charting the history of the dog-owning woman's relationship to petrol stations, then I am the girl for you. I'm talking about the small service areas, the lesser known; you know the sort – one small shop, four pumps, a Little Chef if you're lucky and a disgusting lavatory into which someone has inexplicably dumped a pasty wrapper. AND – I can't let this pass without comment – to which you must gain access by asking the man in the shop for a TINY key on a MASSIVE wooden ring. Why? Why? Why does this disgusting loo deserve to be guarded like the crown jewels, or the players' dressing room at Wimbledon? Are they worried I will un-plumb and steal the basin? What is it about this substandard lav that could possibly warrant this degrading level of security, which compels the poor toilet-needer to publicly collect and return the Enormous Wooden Key Of Shame, which might as well be a huge sandwich board reading 'HELLO. MY BLADDER IS FULL, SOON I AM GOING TO TAKE DOWN MY TROUSERS AND EMPTY IT. IMAGINE THAT.'

Pre-Peggy, I would avoid these kinds of stops and forge on in the hope the next would be the Holy Grail of the service station: an M&S Simply Food. And cue the 'Hallelujah Chorus'. Well, come on, they have mini-millionaire short-bread in a tub for the love of Jane Asher. Thank goodness for the relatively new service-station signs that inform us what key facilities are available and within how many miles. There was nothing worse in the olden days than pulling in for a not urgent 'insurance wee', to be confronted by an off-brand stationer – not even a WHSmith's, for pity's sake – and a greasy spoon which looked like the setting for a low-budget zombie film, to later realize you were only seventeen miles away from an M&S. A bitter blow for any motorway traveller. They were tough times – those of you under twenty can but imagine such a thing. It was akin to going for a walk without texting. Actually looking up. Imagine, young people, just imagine.

But Post-Peggy, although I had control of my own bladder (though I won't attempt an unprepared bounce), I didn't have control over my puppy's, so was forced to stop at the lesser-known stations (no South Mimms or Clacket Lane for me – I told you I knew my stuff), which I previously only had a standard layman's relationship with. My pattern was as follows: out of the car, fill her up, brief moment of worry about blowing the place sky-high if my mobile rang (is this REALLY a threat?), pay for petrol, go for a wee in the loo with the key, then back in the car and off we go. With a dog, the petrol-station visit now had to include dragging Peggy over to the nearest bit of dog-friendly scrubland (one of those imposing, greyish roadside banks which look like a row of snipers might start firing over the top of at any minute). Where, suddenly, I was faced with a whole new petrol-station subculture. In addition to the dog owners, there were smokers, old people having a breather, a couple having an argument, and families who'd chosen The World's Least Scenic Picnic Spot. Have these strange gaggle of travellers always been here, I thought? It was all rather nerve-wracking. For some

113

reason, I'd expected roadside solitude, yet here I was presented with what felt like a muted, depressive park culture.

I didn't know how to interact with these 'verge people'. Did they have their own language, a strange sequence of winks which acted as an instruction to 'meet me by Pump Number Three for super-fun good times and the illegal exchange of recreational drugs'? I wanted the courage to approach the picnickers and ask why they had chosen their spot. I mean, do they have a condition where their blood sugar drops so dramatically they have to pull over immediately to inhale an egg sandwich rather than spend a few more minutes finding an attractive picnic spot? Or do they like eating a packet of crisps as lorries shudder their car and they get sprayed with mud. Is that somehow relaxing to them . . . these picknickers baffle me, MDRC.

I also wanted to ask the woman crying on her partner's shoulder whether it was because she had found herself inexplicably drawn to the imposing service-station public-weighing machine. Why do they have them? Who feels at their lithest and most health-conscious right after four hours on the M6? Yet for some reason we part with 50p in order to weigh ourselves fully clothed, immediately after having eaten a Full English Breakfast, in front of an audience of truck drivers and bored children, who will all witness us being classified as morbidly obese (which seems to be the case whoever you are). When I have made this mistake I'll then go outside, so depressed that it'll seem like a really fabulous idea to buy some new motor insurance from the man standing by the main entrance. 'I am the heaviest creature on this earth,' I'll think. 'I am so laden down with heft that I am surely likely to unbalance the mechanisms of any car simply by sitting in it. It would therefore serve me well to possess some incredibly expensive, comprehensive motor insurance. Yes. I must buy it now.' Perhaps the weighing-machine people are in cahoots with the insurance people. I don't know. And yes, it is possible I have started to overthink the whole service-station culture.

Making a connection with the 'vergers' turned out to be easy between dog owners. 'Ah cute, how old?' 'This is Rose, she's four months, Rose meet Peggy, ha ha.' 'Oops sorry, got our leads tangled . . . ' Always a tricky moment for the dog-walking brigade. When your leads mesh and you're suddenly breath-smellingly close to a stranger, tilted over sideways and slightly unsteady on your feet, as if you're in the early stages of a joyless, coercive game of Twister which also features up to three dogs who have absolutely no sense of personal boundaries. Not fun!

Let us now pull gently out of the service-station forecourt of this digression and back on to the motorway of our story, which coincidentally is where you'll find Peggy and me, zooming towards Devon en route to our first ever time away. My car, post-stop, was covered in crisps, a fact which wasn't lost on Peggy as she snortled her way round, hoovering them up like a pig digging for truffles. This aside, she was remarkably well behaved for the first part of the journey, curling up in the back seat and dozing. I thought that perhaps all my worries had been in vain; perhaps Peggy was going to be a model car dog, the envy of all who witnessed her Zen-like serenity in the face of five hours in a hot vehicle. However, sometime around hour three, the sun came out, the light hit her, and she leapt forward from her hidey-hole in the back seat, jumped on to my lap and shoved her head in my armpit, desperate to be back in the dark. It was quite sweet, but potentially very dangerous. Not in a position to pull into a layby, I shrugged in a doomed attempt to catapult her into the back seat where I could chuck some sort of rug or towel over her, but I succeeded only in nudging her down into the footwell, where she hovered terrifyingly between the accelerator and the clutch, very nearly disabling both. After a high-pitched negotiation (I do hope there is no CCTV footage), we eventually reached a compromise whereby I could maintain control over the pedals so long as she could sit on my lap while I drove, like a co-pilot, occasionally licking me under my chin by way of encouragement.

I felt a tad self-conscious about this. I imagined it looked rather strange to those around us when we pulled up at traffic lights. Though, frankly, given what some people get up to at traffic lights, a little canine face-licking is a mere trifle of an eccentricity. I'd say that it was one notch weirder than white van men who eat Ginsters pasties whilst smoking with the windows SHUT, but several notches less weird than people who continue their boisterous, audible-through-glass radio sing-along. I rather envy those people, actually, entirely comfortable continuing to bellow their way through 'Careless Whisper' as traffic either side points and laughs. I only dare go 'Full Beyoncé' in fast-moving traffic on A-roads. Their freedom is inspiring. It reminds me of a friend who sees a red light as an opportunity to turn to whoever's in the car next to them, stare intently at the side of their head until they're forced to look at her, and then to mouth 'I LOVE YOU' and wait for the red-faced confused consequences. Brilliant. Try it, MDRC – you're welcome. And on the dog front, I've seen people with an Alsatian sitting in the front passenger seat. An Alsatian is basically the size of a small person. It should be wearing not only a seat belt but a baseball hat and a gilet, reading a map and wondering how long it is till he can next get out of the car for a fag (unless it's in a white van, then of course just crack on, with the windows SHUT).

So. Yes. My minor Peggy-on-lap situation was, comparatively, small fry for traffic-light scenarios. Which didn't mean that I wasn't embarrassed enough to stop a mile away from my destination to pop her in the back seat so that my excellent friend and hostess Katie wouldn't think me irresponsible slash weird. I was a bit nervous about the visit generally, and the fact that Katie was a lifelong 'dog person' only made it worse. What if she took one look at Peggy and told me that I'd been horribly malnourishing her or (more likely) over-feeding her, or accidentally spoiling her or neglecting her, or grooming her wrong or that I'd chosen a command to wee which was widely considered enormously offensive within the dog community? I was going to have to lie, I thought, when Peggy did her usual, badly behaved routine of begging for food, or leaping up on to every piece of furniture before deciding where to settle. I was going to have to say, 'Oh my goodness, she's never done that before, how weird, Peggy get OFF that sofa,' and feel like a big fat fraud as I said it.

117

What's more, as I approached Katie's house, it occurred to me that Peggy and I had, in the relatively short time we'd been together, got into some pretty weird habits. Habits which might cause an outsider to raise their eyebrows in consternation/run screaming from the room to alert the nearest psychiatric hospital pronto. For example, whenever I got home from a few hours out, Peggy tended to run up and down the room in deep excitement at my homecoming. Which would be fine – bit annoying, quite sweet, well within the normal spectrum – were it not for the fact that I'd taken to running up and down with her and turning it into a marvellous Miranda-and-Peggy game. To us, this was completely normal. To an outsider, we would have looked as if we were being silently electrocuted; woman and dog being shoved from one end of the living room to the other by an invisible captor with a cattle prod. Were an onlooker to see a woman performing crazed, enthusiastic laps of her sitting room laughing hysterically to herself, they would likely class her eccentric.

It amuses me to think of all the possible dog-owner habits up and down the country of varying degrees of peculiarity. At this point in my Peggy relationship I only had a few: I'd recently tasted and become partial to an oat-and-honey dog biscuit (dip one in tea and you'd be hard-pressed to tell the difference between it and a digestive, I promise you).

How many times, they're MY biscuits. They're bone-shaped, for goodness' sake.

Then there was the 'Peggy as a hat selfie', where I would simply lie down next to a curled-up sleeping Peg and find the right angle to make her look like a Russian winter hat.

Fun. This would sometimes segue into me gently placing my head on her – when in a tight ball she is perfect pillow size – and singing her the following ditty: 'You're my little Russian Hat, I'm glad you're not a cat, sorry I don't always give you treats, I refuse to make you fat'.

Dreadful.

Thank you. That's kind of you to clap.

I doubt any of you are clapping but if you are please stop immediately.

And finally there was the 'night night nose lick'. As it sounds. When I went upstairs I would say 'night night' and permit one, only one, little nose lick. From Peggy to me, I hasten to add. Licking your dog's fur probably crosses a line. That said, I don't doubt we all do deeply unhygienic things with and to our pets when nobody's looking (as it very much were). I have a friend who leans in to sniff her cat's breath when he yawns, as she thinks it smells 'reassuringly savoury'. Her cat is called Prozac so that probably tells us everything. Though I think that rather brilliant. For those with the animal goof gene a pet is probably a better prescription than most anti-depressants.

It turned out I needn't have worried about my habits. Compared to Katie and her dogs, Peggy and I were normal. Dreary, even. Grey, dull and everyday. The John Major of relationships. Katie, it turned out, was properly dog mad, in a way I'd not yet seen close up. I'd suspected butterfly-net-standard dog lunacy in some of the park people, but I had no way of knowing for sure what went on behind closed doors. In Katie's case, I saw every last bit of it. She had two spaniels, and let both of them sleep in her bed – *in*, you'll note, not *on* – and she was completely comfortable with the pair of them licking her on the mouth, a proper tongue-kissing affair, which I think is most definitely crossing the line. Peggy is quite a licky dog, with a tendency to go for my lower legs just after I've got out of the shower; bit weird, but short of rudely kicking her away I'm not entirely sure what I can do about it. But mouth licking – no, no, I draw the line. Yes, they are our beloved pets, but also, and this is my simple argument: THEY LICK THEIR OWN BOTTOMS. Case closed. Say no more. There is no comeback to that. And if you really think there is, I just say this to you: THEY LICK *OTHER* DOGS' BOTTOMS. Thank you and good day to that argument. What's more, Katie cooked for her dogs. Delicious chicken meals, better than the human food we ate, lovingly slaved over for hours and hours, sautéed and seasoned and spooned reverently into the dog bowl (no Kong for her animals). I was astonished. It certainly made me feel better about me and Peggy's dirty frankfurter-sharing secret.

Katie could be classified in a league of her own – properly dog bananas – and, far from it seeming odd, I found it rather inspiring. To be so unashamedly, face-lickingly devoted to your pet suddenly looked like something to aspire to, rather than a peculiar condition to be avoided at all costs. I don't know if it was the fresh Devon air, the holiday atmosphere, or the unique experience of looking forward to dining on a dog's leftovers, but any residual doubts I had about owning Peggy were slipping away. I gamely compared doggy nick-names with Katie. Her two spaniels had no fewer than seventy-two between them, so I fessed up that I had at various points referred to Peggy as Peg, Peggles, The Pegster, Pegaroo,

Pegaloo, Mrs Pegglychops, PeggaPoppaLicious, Miss Peggy, Peggo, Le Peg and My Little Russian Hat.

I really do object to being called after a bit of headgear. I mean, REALLY. She also sometimes calls me her fluffy little bin. Yes, really. To compare me to A BIN. A bin. Me. Me a bin. I mean REALLY.

My friend told me that I was nothing more than a rank beginner and soon I'd be referring to her publicly and without a second thought as Queen Pegspialidocious, and The First Mistress of Pegmania.

Much better.

I went to bed fully reassured and looking forward to Katie's suggestion of a trip to the beach the next day.

The Beach

Peggy had never been to a beach before, and she went completely bonkers with excitement. She was running in circles, barking at seagulls, astonished by her own pawprints in the sand. I'd never seen anyone or anything take such a simple, uninhibited delight in their surroundings. I felt tremendously lucky to be witnessing it, and humbled by what a thrill I'd been able to give this creature, simply by taking her to a new place. It was a uniquely wonderful moment with my dog. Her sniffing at some seaweed, then sneezing twenty times in a row, provided me much more mirth than I would ever have expected. I couldn't keep my eyes off her as she rushed up to the edge of the sea and back again, spraying sand behind her, so fast was her joy-filled running-hopping combo. And her joy was infectious. I laughed at her wobbly walk as she negotiated a pile of stones and hoped there wasn't a sharp shell she could hurt herself on. I began feeling protective of her beach experience. More maternal than ever before.

And then, MDDDWMDDRC (my dear dear dearest wonderful majestic darling dear reader chum), it happened. At one point Peggy was trotting along at the water's edge, when an unexpectedly big wave came in and crashed down on to the sand. She flinched and ran away from the wave towards me, barking furiously, excited and scared, and as she approached I felt an overwhelming, transcendent, almost physical sensation of love. It was the same affectionate lift I'd felt when I'd picked her up from the dog groomers', times one million. Peggy jumped up into my arms – as she's done

many, many times since (she has quite a spring in her little legs) – and I caught her, held her close and whispered, 'It's you and me against the world.'

Over the last nine years the love I felt on the beach that day has unexpectedly deepened. Each and every time she rushes towards me I break into the widest of smiles that connects with my heart alive with love. My instinct at this point is to pull back a bit, to make gentle fun of myself, to apologize for a moment of soppiness, to defend myself to those who don't feel that way towards their dogs, but I can't do that, not right now. All I can say is that in that moment on the beach, I felt truly blessed. Peggy's joy, innocence and trust as she ran to me to protect her from that wave finally unlocked the Hart heart. I knew then that I would be able to love again, really love; animals and people and life itself. What a gift. And all from a little doggy.

Peggy bounds in, barking urgently; so excited that she is wriggling-while-walking in that extraordinary way that only a very excited little dog can Hello? Hello? Excuse me! While Miranda's gone all misty-eyed and staring-at-the-horizon-y, can I have a word? Thank you.

Well. SHE may be perfectly comfortable with blah-ing on about how blessed she is and making you think she's basically St Francis of Assisi just because she had a nice day at the beach, but may I make it perfectly plain that whilst it might have taken Miranda aaaaages to fall in love with me and to know that, dog-wise, I am very much The One, I've actually known since I first curled up in her massive trainer that SHE was The One for me (if she heard that she would be singing the Robbie Williams song 'She's The One' – we are big Robbie fans).

She was so late to the love party, if I'm honest.

But much much more to the point, have you ever actually been to the beach? It is THE BEST PLACE EVER. The Disneyland of smells! Things I smelled the first time I went to the beach included:

1. Other dogs' bottoms. LOTS of them.

2. Chips.

3. Sweat. A lot of which came from Miranda who has never exercised as far as I'm aware.

4. Seven different types of wind some of which DEFINITELY came from France.

5. Salt, which I could also taste and which tasted properly yum.

6. Posh ladies down from London for the weekend who were wearing expensive perfume which was majorly yuck.

7. A rotting seagull carcass, completely YUM, and which I rolled in on the way home – amazeballs, but which Miranda probably won't tell you about as she's trying to be all romantic and soppy and things.

Ooh, actually, can I tell you a thing about seagulls? YOU CAN'T CATCH THEM! It looks as if you can, but then you can't. Sort of like squirrels, only worse. They're soooo sneaky, they swoop down in your face and they're all 'ooh, look at me with my big flappy wings which look so tasty', and then just as you run at them they go up in the air, and if you try to jump up and catch them you usually fall on your back, and Miranda and her friend who makes the yummy chicken for her dogs (I only ever get stuff in packets) will point and laugh at you. And more to the point your fur gets lathered in sand. Which isn't too much of a shame on other dogs, but it is when you have fur so soft and, well, perfect as mine – no one likes a show-off but I just say it as I see it. Miranda's always saying she hates sand in her cracks. I don't quite know what she means but it sounds horrible.

Two other very very important things about the beach. One, if you see a small child eating what looks like a cloud atop a horn of gold, that is something called an 'ice cream', and it's crucial that you don't knock this out of their hand as children like ice creams very very much. And two, those squares of coloured cloth that people leave lying around are called 'towels' and it's REALLY REALLY FUNNY if you pick the towels up and run into the ocean with them; the people get so cross and they hop about all wet and shout at you. Tee hee hee. There ends Miss Peggy Hart's Guide to The Beach. *rests head elegantly on front paws*

So there we were, Peggy and me, on the expansive dramatic Devon beach, shocked by joy. Well, certainly I was shocked by joy. A light was suddenly shining through the greyness of the previous year or two, dominated by viruses, a breakup and a general physical and mental fatigue that had pushed joy firmly to the recesses of my soul, feeling as though it was irretrievable, frankly. Peggy seemed to bring it back when she ran from that wave. As we drove back to Katie's house, I reflected on how much it felt as if pet ownership had chosen me, rather than my choosing it. I imagine that the pet lovers amongst you will understand this; the rest of you (those of you who haven't yet cast aside this tome in favour of something more suitable, perhaps a book about *Vintage Diesel Engines*, or *The History of Grit*) probably won't. I was reminded of my animal goof gene. You've got to remember your animal goof gene when you're idling along a beach and find yourself near to tears because you've seen a dinghy covered in barnacles, and are suddenly worrying about whether the barnacles all had or still do have happy lives. It is both a blessing and a sickness. All in all, I think that it was my destiny to end up in charge of Peggy. She was my Joy Adamson lion cub. Any initial resistance I had to owning her was probably just a fear of doing the thing I was always supposed to do.

This led me to think about passions in general, and how important it is to follow your bliss. Or if not bliss, precisely – bliss can be pretty hard to come by, I find – then at the least the thing which makes you wake up in the morning thinking, 'Oh, brilliant, I'm going to do that today'; the thing which makes you feel a bit lighter, a bit more positive about the world. Or perhaps the thing you dreamed of doing as a child, told everybody you were definitely going to do, then somehow never did.

When I was eight, I wanted to be a vet. Over the years, I shoved that passion into the background but, much later, when I'd turned thirty and comedy and acting still wasn't really happening for me, I called upon my childhood enthusiasm and, wait for it, for I've never told anyone this before I don't think, I took a correspondence course in small-animal care. Don't mock, MDRC, it felt a sensible thing to do at the time. It was a bit of a halfway house; I couldn't face the thought of giving up comedy entirely and spending goodness knows how many years learning the anatomy and functioning of five thousand different mammals (I mean, for goodness' sake, they may treat a lizard one day, the next a llama). So I tried a miniature version of the veterinary life, specializing in small, adorable, fluffy things. It was a bit eccentric; one of the tasks involved stencilling a picture of a rabbit, which brought about an 'oh dear, help, what has my life become, I thought I would be married with children, whilst juggling a glamorous acting lifestyle and worthy charitable commitments by now?' moment – but I enjoyed it. I unearthed a surprising talent for guinea pigs, actually. I said DON'T MOCK! However, Operation Small Animal Care, or OSAC (which is a jolly acronym as it sounds as if I am singing an Elizabethan ballad to a sack: 'O, Sack!'), ground to a halt when I went to do a day of work experience at the vet and actually had to handle the small animals.

It wasn't a question of 'please keep these six perfect Labrador puppies and ten gorgeous tabby kittens company' which, let's face it, I was really hoping and expecting it would be; it was in fact holding and dealing with mice and rats, overweight gerbils (sinister), pus-riddled rabbits and one-eyed chinchillas. The coalface of fluffy animals. I got completely freaked out by their tiny beating mammal hearts, all hot and fragile and creepy near my hands. Even the guinea pigs – my specialist area. Also, there's something a tiny bit crazy about a grown woman with a love of the guinea pig. Hamsters and guinea pigs cease to be acceptable pets when one reaches the age of sixteen, I fear (although, according to Miranda's Completely Arbitrary Rules Of Pet Ownership, budgerigars and cockatiels become *more* acceptable as one enters one's early sixties and seventies).

So, no life of professional animal care for me. Probably for the best, really. I doubt that my comedic instincts would have been especially welcome in the operating theatre (scalpel moustache, anyone? No? Pin the Tail On An Actual Live Donkey?). But let's skip forward a few months from that day on the Devonshire beach. I'm not a small-animal care professional, but I do have one dog I love dearly just for being who she is. I was also learning my next dog-ownership lesson as I realized that whilst you can't always live your childhood dream life: perhaps circumstances prevent you from doing so; or perhaps it's not appropriate for you as an adult (not everyone can be an astronaut or a train driver or a ringmaster, and those city workers who are currently going into phone boxes pretending to be Superman should probably give it a rest), you can however incorporate elements of that dream into your current life, hopefully making it a happier and more rounded one.

My animal goof gene has come to the fore in a sensible and practical way for my life, softening other things around it like ambition and the need to achieve. Being, just hanging and playing with my dog, is now as essential and rewarding as doing. I still find some of the dog-min annoying: having to take Peggy for walks at ten o'clock at night to do her pre-bed wee-wee when I've just had a bath and I'm in my pyjamas, ready for bed. But I no longer perform it grudgingly; the whole business is carried forwards on a wave of affection and a sense of what a privilege it is to have the little creature so dependent on me. I even pick up poo like a demon (Peggy's only, thank you), generally managing to do it in one swift movement, albeit breath held. The dog-min now falls into the category of 'things you do for someone you love', and the day-to-day drudgery of it pales into insignificance next to the way it's opened up my heart. I wasn't ready for human love again – still too bashed-up by recent experiences – but a dog, I felt, was definitely the next best thing. Better, even. No talking back from a dog. Much less space taken up on the sofa. No compromises required over the TV remote, except during Crufts week when it's only kind to let Peggy have her way. I always get to choose our holiday destinations, simply because I Am Bigger Than Her. No sharing of food (apart from those delicious oaty biscuits). Always someone to blame farts on who won't answer back. The advantages are endless.

I wondered, as Peggy and I lay in a pile in front of *Strictly*, sharing a bag of Hula Hoops, whether I might love her a bit too much. It all seemed a bit sudden, this bliss. My sister's got a good test of whether or not a person loves their dog too much; it's the question, 'If you were travelling on a ferry with your dog, and it jumped off the back into the sea, would you jump in after it?' If it takes you longer than three seconds to reach the conclusion that no, of course you wouldn't, then you definitely love your dog too much and ought to consider some sort of aversion therapy. However much I love Peggy, I know the value of my life as a human is higher in this ferry hypothetical. Although I did scare myself once when Peggy ran, having been spooked by a large Doberman, out of the park entrance on to a busy road, and I sprinted after her without a care for what traffic might be hurtling towards me. I came very close to my end with a bus. But I knew when my sister posed the question that, no, I wouldn't jump off the ferry. I'm still just about within the normal spectrum, so much so that I turned down an invitation to a first birthday party for Peggy and her siblings, thrown by the woman who owns Peggy's mother, for fear that it would catapult me into full-on dog lunacy (my suspicions were confirmed when two weeks later I received a picture of the whole litter reunited, wearing little party hats and 'posing' next to a bone-shaped cake, presumably fresh from a hearty game of doggy Pass the Parcel and a fight over the last cheese-and-liver-in-jelly sandwich). I was still sane, still me, still normal. I just really, really loved my dog. Is that so wrong?

Absolutely not. What's not to love? I'll say it again, have you SEEN me?

An Interlude: Cats versus Dogs

What's that, MDRC? What are you complaining about now? You were all wrapped up in the wonderful story of Peggy and me, gagging to know what happened next, and here I am trying to fob you off with some sort of 'interlude'! Well, I understand your concern. It could be seen as remiss – nay, cruel of me – to divert you from our gripping yet reflective tale at this crucial juncture. But I feel we have important business to attend to before we proceed. Primarily, the gritty question of . . . feel free to do a personal drum-roll effect (particularly if you are reading in bed with a partner and wish to startle them for your amusement), the question of . . . **Cats versus Dogs**?! Not Cats versus Dogs in the 'I wondered who would win in a fight so I smeared a bull mastiff with tuna and put it in a cage with a cat' sort of way, more in the 'which is better, *really*?' sort of way. Let's jolly well get to the nub of this issue and put it to bed once and for all.

Because it does bear thinking about. Once I'd had the experience of falling rather wonderfully in love with a dog and understood this true dog-owner happiness for the first time, I became briefly worried. Does it mean that I was now a full-on 'dog person': barking at the enemy, flying the bone-shaped flag for Team Dog and hurling tins of Winalot over the battlements at the first sign of a feline interloper? Or was Peggy a one-off, a dog-shaped blip? My present might well be with Peggy, but my past, as you know, is intertwined with feline chums. So I felt that a formal pause for thought was called for before we go any further. Or, Paws for Thought, oh thank you, thank you very much indeed, you are too kind . . . OK, you can sit down now and stop cheering, it's embarrassing.

So, am I a Cat Person or a Dog Person? Do you *have* to be either one or the other? And does it really matter? And the conclusion that I've come to, is that yes, I do have to be one or the other, yes, it most definitely does matter and, most importantly, *yes*, I am now, quite decidedly, a Dog Person. It turns out that I was a Dog Person all along; there's no sense of treachery or turncoat here. My cat phase was just that – a phase. Cats were indeed the convenient gateway drug to dogs, or the boyfriend you think is The One before you finally meet the *actual* one. That's a weird thing, isn't it? Why do we spend months, years, with people who are patently so wrong for us? People who are literally an Identikit picture of Everything We Do Not Want In A Partner. And yet, we stay. Long after we've cruised through the honeymoon period and accepted it's never going to work out, we just . . . continue. Well, whilst we're here I'd like to boldly say to you, STOP. GET OUT. YOU CAN DO BETTER. You deserve your right partner, the one who makes you feel as if you've come home, every time you see them. Hold out and settle for nothing less.

steps down from regal sermon-y stance at top of stairs, removes bishop's robes self-made from sheets

Back to the Cats versus Dogs debate. And where I come down on it is this: cats are absolutely fine and dandy, but I can now stand confidently before you and say this: *takes deep breath, puts bishop's robe-sheets back on, stands on makeshift podium (coffee table – note to self – shouldn't have chosen one with wheels), intones*, My Dear Reader Chum, I would like to assert:

DOGS ARE BETTER THAN CATS

There. I've said it. Those who are now leaving the room in horror, cat in hand, please come back, for I have plenty more to say on the subject. I wouldn't dream of making such a statement and then vanishing in a puff of smoke; I must back up my bold assertion, and I'd like to devote this, what I call, Interlude, to arguing my case with all the bounce and vim of a beagle who's just spied a joint of lamb. We shall now launch into **Miranda's Bold And Bouncy Argument As To Why Dogs Are Better Than Cats**. Such fun.

Let's kick off – perhaps a little unfairly – with a look at the **Nutty Cat Owners**. I would argue that the sheer number of mad-as-a-brush cat owners is all the evidence one needs of the essential superiority of dogs. Of course, I'm well aware that dog ownership can drive a person mildly crackers (please refer to my earlier musings on the cross-section of Extreme Dog Owners to be found in my local park), and I'm also aware that I myself am at risk of becoming a crazy dog owner, absolutely yes (I have written a WHOLE BOOK about my dear dog, for heaven's sake) – but I'd argue that Cat Nutters are approximately 1,473 per cent nuttier than your average Dog Nutter (all statistics in this book are 87.5 per cent made up). Reasons to follow. I think this calls for a list. Who doesn't love a little list?

1. **Anthropomorphizing and humanizing cats.** This is of course the prime manifestation of most animal-related nuttiness, but also the one that gives an enormous amount of joy to us owners. And it officially appears so, so much madder with a cat than a dog. For example . . . oh, hold on, I think there's going to be a list within a list. Well, this is TREMENDOUS.

   i. Costumes. If you put, say, a little Spiderman costume on a dog to protect it from the rain it looks rather natty. Dapper. Happy to be all togged up, and hoping it's off to a party. Put an identical costume on a cat and it looks like a rugby player who's passed out on a stag night and woken up to find his friends have dressed him in a French maid's outfit. The cat looks, in short, abused.

   ii. Handbags. If you put a dog in a handbag (by which I mean something like a Chihuahua in a Burberry shoulder bag, not trying to stuff an Alsatian in a ruck-sack), it looks fine. Rather impressive, even. Smart. Kardashian-esque. If you were to put a cat in a bag and bring it to work, you'd look like the very maddest of the mad. You might as well wear a wetsuit to a Zumba class. Or marry your photocopier.

   iii. The way you interact with your pet. If you were to look at your dog and say, 'Buttons the Dog looks sad. Would you like a cuddle, Buttons?' you'd be thought of as a caring pet owner. If you were to do exactly the same to a cat, you'd be thought of as a merry lunatic, most likely projecting your own emotions on to the poor blank animal in the absence of any meaningful human contact. And I think we must all be honest about the vast difference between looking into the eyes of a cat, and the eyes of a dog. If, and please allow me a moment of poetry here, if a dog's eyes are like a fast-moving film reel of feelings, all of them sincere, most of them extreme (Devastation! Love! Hope! JOY! Devastation! LOVE!), then staring into a cat's eyes is like staring into a still oily puddle which may or may not turn out to conceal a bottomless pit. Unfathomable. Mysterious. Blank. At very best, a cat's eyes are those of that girl in your class at school, the one who was so effortlessly beautiful and chic that she didn't ever have to bother being anything else. Life, to her, was just one big staring contest, and she always won. Well, that's cats for you.

iv. Leads. When you put a lead on a dog, it's normal. A dog is meant to be attached to a human via a lead. It is an entirely natural state of affairs. Put a lead on a cat, and you might as well whack on a T-shirt bearing the slogan 'I AM A RAMBLING ECCENTRIC, PLEASE GIVE ME A WIDE BERTH OR I WILL COME AT YOU WITH MY WEIRD CAT ON A STRING.'

v. Shows. Ever wonder why there isn't a Crufts for cats? Thought not. Because we all know that Crufts for cats would be completely knockout stone-cold mental. Fact. Imagine trying to train a cat to go up and down a seesaw and in and out of poles. It would stare at you as if saying, 'Piss off, I'm late for *Newsnight*.' Plus you'd be back at needing to put a cat on a lead.

Now, if we can interlude within the Interlude – I know, I don't want to confuse you, especially as I have just listed within a list, but try and keep up, MDRC, I can't help being a literary maverick – I need to nip those of you asking 'yes, but who puts a cat on a lead?' in the bud. For I have witnessed this event, twice. Once on a pavement in a busy shopping street in Chiswick, West London. A woman brazenly walking a cat on a colourful ribbon as if it were perfectly normal (please note, a ribbon – Chiswick is frightfully middle class, no pieces of string here). However confidently this woman walked her cat on a ribbon, she looked CERTIFIABLE. There are a few – and only a very few, I'm afraid – people who can get away with this sort of thing. I would imagine Helena Bonham Carter could get away with it. And also maybe Grayson Perry.

Generally Americans can get away with cats on leads far better, which brings me to my second cat-on-lead sighting: a beautiful lady out walking some kind of pedigree puss in New York's Central Park. She seemed to carry it – and her leopard-print leggings and matching jacket, hat, shoes, socks and velveteen scrunchie – off rather well. But I think we can chalk that up as one of the many things Americans can do which British people somehow can't, along with running up to strangers in the street and asking them where they get their hair cut, eating burgers the size of their own face as a between-meal snack, visiting shooting ranges for fun at the weekend (if I did that my friends would assume that I was planning some kind of violent revolution), and weeping openly at political rallies (just *imagine* somebody waving a flag and sobbing at a Lib Dem Party Conference).

I did once have the privilege of seeing a rabbit on a lead in a square in Pimlico. And a ferret on a lead on a train from Blackheath to Charing Cross. I know, I clearly have a gift for spotting unusual tethered animals, although the latter was via a photograph from my fellow animal-goofer friend Ms Sarah Hadland. Both events made their owners look so deeply dotty that I just thought . . . no. Not for me. I love having an animal with me wherever I go, tugging gently at my hand from the other end of a nylon lead, but I'm not prepared to be a nutter about it. There's a reason that dogs look fine in these positions, while other creatures don't. Dogs are made for it. Cats aren't. End of. And yet people do do all these things: they do dress their cats up as Spiderman and Buzz Lightyear and Father Christmas; they do put them on leads and walk them round the park; they do swaddle them like babies. (MDRC, if you find yourself with half an hour to kill, I suggest you type the words 'cat sling' into Google, and get ready for the ride of your life.) And they do talk to their cats as if they were not just children but emotionally artic- ulate and culturally engaged life partners. And they do look, and I really didn't want to be mean, quite frankly, unstable.

Before I started analysing the whole situation in the depth I am now (and you're welcome), I did consider getting a cat to join the Peggy-and-me household. I thought it might be a way to stay in touch with my catty roots, and provide a fun friend for Peggy. I've read *The Wind in the Willows* a few too many times, and had visions of Peggy and the cat chumming up with a toad for some rollicking inter-animal adventures. But I realized pretty quickly that Peggy would be having none of it. She's a possessive beast at the best of times. When I'm out with her I can't so much as sit on a park bench or pause for an alfresco sandwich without passers-by getting barked at with considerable savagery.

Which brings to mind number two on the Dogs Are Better Than Cats list.

2. **Dogs care.** Dogs will risk their lives defending your chicken-salad wrap against potentially threatening passers-by, even when a human can see that there's no sensible reason for them to do so. Cats keep themselves to themselves. You could be being murdered right in front of your cat and it'd sit there watching, thinking nothing more than, 'Oh. I hope that severed head doesn't land anywhere near my freshly manicured paws.' Dogs are transparent, open and enthusiastic; cats are reserved and sinister, their cool façade quite possibly concealing fathomless depths of evil (or, more likely, nothing, but that's a bit boring; let's go with the 'evil overlord' theory).

Dogs are, historically, useful working animals, programmed in some deep, almost human way to serve, to work alongside their owners. Whereas cats are, well, essentially useless. Throw a stick for a dog, and it'll bound away and do its darndest to retrieve it for you come hell or high water. It wants only to please. Throw a stick for a cat and it'll sit on the carpet staring up at you with the disdainful, haughty air of a billionaire oligarch's wife, before strolling off for a nap on whichever brand-new jumper you were hoping desperately to keep clean for an evening out. Cats do as they please, day after day, and if what they do happens to please you (for example, lying in a particularly adorable position on your lap), then marvellous. But you need to know that they are not doing it for your benefit. They do not care what you think. And you will never, ever know what motivated them to do it. Because cats are, above all else, WEIRD.

3. **Cats are weird.** We may worship them as deities, create whole internet subcultures based on them, lose entire afternoons to YouTube videos of them, and declare them to be our favourite thing in the whole wide world, but, at heart, they're all deeply inscrutable oddballs with no desire to relinquish their outsider status. Cats are the slightly smelly child in velour dungarees who'd sit alone at play-time eating four Club biscuits in one, and chatting to her tangerine. (I am not describing myself. I am.) I will back this up with another list within a list. Don't say I don't treat you right.

i. Spiked fur. When frightened or in any kind of heightened emotional state, they don't do what any sensible animals (such as a dog) would do and either retreat whimpering or go on the attack. Cats, when stressed, puff themselves up, spike their fur and do an inexplicable impression of a hedgehog. Weird.

ii. They spray terrible things from their bottoms when they want to mark their territory. Even in your sitting room, on your sofa. Your house smells of cat-bottom spray.

iii. They climb up trees and forget how to climb down. Not so clever now. Or, and have you ever considered this of your beloved moggy, they do it deliberately so you have to embarrass yourself with a fireman. Weird *and* mean.

iv. They sit by closed doors scrabbling and whining and yearning to be let through, then when you actually make a move to open the door for them, they just sit there staring up at you as if to say 'What on earth did you do that for? I was enjoying the frustration of the door NOT being open. Now you've gone and ruined it.'

v. They are sneaky. Super-sneaky. You can be working quietly away in what you thought was blissful solitude, then suddenly, from nowhere, a cat has leapt on the desk, landing itself on the keyboard, sending you pitching over backwards, before somehow managing to type 'YGGGGTfffffffffr % % % % % % % % % % % %**&p9audpoof' in an email to your boss. This would never happen with a dog. Dogs are, God bless them, deeply unsubtle creatures. You can hear a dog coming a mile off, clattering and jangling down the corridor, all but chatting out loud 'HERE-I-come-hello-HELLO-how-jolly-EXCITING-that-I'm-coming-to-see-you-how-MARVELLOUS-what-a-lovely-time-we-shall-have-ooh-HELLO!-are-those-biscuits-I-*love*-biscuits-*HELLO!*' A dog is a merry-baker-touting-his-wares type of creature. Whereas a cat is a spy. A hovering spy who takes a sly pleasure in surprising you, sending tea and biscuits flying as it descends unseen from a light fitting, before stalking away from the carnage with nothing more than a disdainful sniff and a cursory shake of their back leg. In itself a weird manoeuvre.

vi. Catnip. Very weird, this one. The way they go nuts for catnip, and only for catnip. Dogs, in a more logical fashion, are delighted by a range of smells: food, other dogs, meat, bones, home, crotches, seagulls, owner. Cats, just catnip. Everything else – meh. And there is no indication as to why they are so keen. You can't eat it. It does not signify safety or affection or nourishment. It is basically a fetish.

So, yes, cats are weird. I think I've argued the case convincingly enough. I have considered overlooking this, bearing in mind that if 'being deeply weird' were an obstacle to a loving relationship, then 95 per cent of humans would be devastatingly lonely; if only they showed some desire to bond. But they don't, which means that a relationship with a cat can never be more than a one-sided thing, a fake relationship at best. Dogs are desperate to co-operate, to help their friends the humans out wherever they can. Of course you can bond with a cat – like I did with my beloved Casper – but I now believe that the dog–human bond is infinitely superior, because it really matters to both of you. And that's what I want from a relationship – any relationship – as an adult. A partnership in which both parties really care, both parties want to be involved. Both parties have the emotional presence and strength to admit they need each other. And that, my friend, is what you get from a dog. And I knew that the minute Peggy leapt into my arms away from that scary wave.

Are you convinced? As convinced as I am of the essential superiority of the hound? Not quite, you say? Well, I was prepared for just this eventuality, MDRC, and have armed myself with a few compelling 'no, really, dogs are better, come on now, face it' parting shots. If you're still sitting on the fence (which is another weird thing cats do for pleasure) in the great Cats versus Dogs debate, then have a choke on these apples:

Hospital Visiting. When a dog visits a hospital, it isn't weird. Not in the slightest. A dog is a lovely thing to have in a hospital, a cheering presence, a canine Patch Adams, if you like. A cat visiting a hospital is deeply, profoundly creepy. If you saw a cat on a ward, even a cat wearing a collar with a big shiny bow on it and a sign reading, 'HELLO, I AM MR JINGLES, YOUR HAPPY HOSPITAL CAT', you'd assume that it had snuck in via the bins to cause trouble. And you'd probably be right. Dogs sit quietly by hospital beds, lowering blood pressure and reminding patients that there's a good and happy world out there. Cats would maraud around, knocking over the drip stands and pouncing on people's arses through their open-backed hospital gowns as they wandered by, like some furry pervert.

Telepathy. OK, so maybe dogs aren't *quite* telepathic. But I do think they can read one's moods and needs so accurately that it often veers into spooky. In a good way. Peggy always knows when I'm ill. If somebody comes to walk her on my behalf when I'm stuck at home sick, she'll have to be hauled out of the door whining desperately. Her bottom firmly planted on the road; the poor person having to drag her as her nails scrape along the tarmac like a child having a tantrum, and usually having to resort to picking her up and carrying her to the park. And if they make the mistake of taking her off the lead, she will hurtle out and rush back to help her owner – well ok, sit at the end of the bed asleep, but it's the thought. She genuinely believes she has to be there. And I couldn't be without her when I'm ill. There is nothing more comforting than the feeling of a little creature pressed gently and cosily against your back or leg when you are alone sleeping off some grim bug. Once, during the writing of my sitcom, I rented a cottage in Cornwall for a week to knuckle down, and succumbed to a severe bout of tonsillitis. I went to bed that night assuming I had shut the door to my bedroom, and left Peggy in the sitting room. However, in the middle of the night I woke to find her nestled right next to me on the pillow, ready to be of service. Sure, I thought I was hallucinating and needed immediate medical attention, but it didn't go unappreciated; she must have pushed open that bedroom door to administer necessary morale. Spookily

Peggy seems to know what part of my body is suffering and will lie next to it – hence right by the pillow for the tonsils.

What's more, she always leaps in to help when she senses that I might be in some sort of danger. It's very endearing, even when her sense of what's dangerous is comically misguided. I once had a sports massage in my home (I know, call me David Beckham), which involved a brief moment of pain, at which I let out a small cry. Peggy interpreted this scenario as someone making an attempt on my life, and jumped up on the massage table to rescue me from my assailant and to lick me back to health. She also enjoys 'helping' when I do a Pilates Plank – for the uninitiated, a slightly precarious-looking stationary press-up designed to increase core strength. Peggy thinks this looks terribly dangerous and stands right by me on high alert, whimpering, as if poised to call 999 at any moment, occasionally licking a small bead of sweat away. And don't tell me I am the only dog owner whose dog rushes to their side when life has meant a good cry is needed. Peggy will leap on to my lap and lick the tears away and it will often be what can slowly bring me around. She also hates it when I'm angry. Something must have happened to her as a puppy because if I ever utter the F-bomb – which obviously I seldom do and if I do swear I simply say bottomsticks; but, you know, if I do occasionally get fiery – then she looks genuinely frightened and leaps up to me, tucking her face into my neck. I hate her being scared but it's a brilliant anger-diffuser.

Also, and we're about to get even more spooky here, I had an operation on my knee a couple of years ago, during which I left Peggy with my sister. At 3 p.m., the *exact* moment I was wheeled into the operating theatre, Peggy jumped up on to my sister's lap, and didn't get down until my operation was finished. What makes this extra spooky is that a) Peggy is not a sitting-on-lap kind of a dog, which is why it was brought to my sister's attention, and b) not even my sister knew what time my operation was, yet somehow Peggy knew. Coincidence? I think not.

No cat would do this. If you were doing the Plank in the same room as a cat, it would either ignore you in an 'oh-no-you-are-so-*embarrassing*' sort of teenager-to-mother way, or it would deliberately pounce on your back (from nowhere because it's been spying and laughing at you) and send you crashing to the ground. In the presence of a masseur, a cat would simply judge you for being so stupid and non-Zen-like and human as to need a massage in the first place.

Dogs will go the extra mile. OK, we've touched on this already, but in extremis dogs will do really, really unimaginably bizarre and wonderful things in an attempt to look after their owners. Freaky things. For example, the spaniel on the farm who saw its owner hand-feeding lambs from a bottle during a particularly busy lambing period, and eventually picked up a bottle between its teeth and started feeding the lambs itself. What's that I hear you cry? 'Aaaaaaaaah, that's the cutest thing I've ever heard. There's no way a cat would ever do that because it would have already drunk all the milk itself.' Exactly. Thank you.

Dogs will – very often – save you from extreme danger. Get a load of this. In 2005, a stray dog came across a newborn baby wrapped only in tattered clothing and a plastic bag. The child was alive, but alone, in a poor neighbourhood in Nairobi, Kenya. Witnesses said the dog carried the abandoned child across a busy road, through some barbed wire, and into a shed where her litter of puppies were living. While further details are sketchy, it seems that the man who owned the shed later noticed the baby, who was then taken to the hospital. Health workers said at the time that though no one had claimed the baby, it was doing well and responding to treatment. People were also donating goods to the child. A – MA – ZING.

Dogs have six different kinds of bark they'll use to communicate with you. Whereas cats have only three settings: meow, purr, and that weird chirruping thing they sometimes do when there's food around. Unless you count 'dribbling while purring' as a valid means of communication. Which I most definitely do not. (Although I must confess, when tired, I've been known to partake in a little dribble 'n' purr.)

Dogs will never, ever leave you. You see posters everywhere for missing cats, and nine times out of ten you just *know* they've wandered off for a mini-break two streets away, probably with a kind family who feed them five meals a day because they bat their eyelids and pretend to be a stray. They are happily moonlighting with another family. UNACCEPTABLE. If a dog runs off, it's only ever because it's got no choice. For example, it smelled something so unimaginably marvellous that it simply had to sprint across three fields in order to investigate. And it always comes back, tail between legs, genuinely very sorry and sheepish and desperate to make it up to you.

If you're not now convinced that dogs are the superior beast, then you most likely never will be. But I have done my best, and I have done it out of a sense of duty, pure and simple.

For I am a Dog Person now, and must do all I can on behalf of my team.

And I can't wait to continue to tell you tales of Peggy and me, as we become more and more inseparable as the years go by. Here really begins the story of a loving woman–dog relationship. And the wonderful thing is, MDRC, all you need to do is turn the page or swipe the Kindle and there we will be. See you soon!

CHAPTER 6

Working Nine to Five

After my pre-interlude explosion of sentiment and the declaration of love, I feel this next chapter should be about our engagement, the big splashy wedding, Peggy serenaded up the aisle by an enthusiastic choir of dogs harmonizing to 'Who Let the Dogs Out', and a honeymoon somewhere drizzly with lots of seagull carcasses to roll in, possibly Ramsgate. But as I hope we've firmly established, This Is Not A Romantic Comedy. Oh no. This is Real Life (said in a gritty police-drama voice – though I just sound like Joanna Lumley with a mild hangover). And in Real Life what happens most often, for good or bad, is work.

And, MDRC, after my wonderful jaunt in Devon, I found myself both knee-deep and face-down in the most intense splurge of work I'd ever known. It was – let's not be coy – my absolute dream job; a once-in-a-lifetime opportunity. The BBC had, after deliberating over the pilot we gave them, bravely commissioned me to write a whole series of my own sitcom, the sitcom which would later become *Miranda*. It was what I had dreamed of since I was a child, and what I'd worked for over the previous fifteen years; but never really believed a possibility. And here it was, a rare chance – my own show on the hallowed BBC. I am still surprised it ever happened. But enormously grateful. So, please bear with when I tell you that writing a sitcom of any kind, alone, from scratch, is blooming hard work. I have never shied away from sharing how difficult I find the writing process. For me, most of the time, the experience is at once lonely, frightening, exhausting and boring. Not the barrel of laughs some might assume. After a month or so of loafing around celebrating having got the commission in the first place, the pressure of actually sitting down to write the thing felt enormous. Enormous-er than enormous. Positively elephantine. I had never written a sitcom before so there was a hell of a learning curve to face. Plus it niggled away at me daily that whatever I was writing was going to be broadcast. Actually ON the television. This was akin to settling into a six-to-eight-month stretch of homework, but homework that will be paraded and judged by a population who know, love and fiercely judge their comedy. It was a hefty weight of responsibility, and if it wasn't for my newest and bestest friend Peggy, I think it might actually have proved impossible.

Writing

She was a wonderful writing partner. Absolutely wonderful. The only thing that stopped Peggy from being completely perfect was her inability to perform straightforward domestic tasks such as preparing light meals and going to the Post

Office. And she can't really be blamed for that. Although there were an uncanny amount of times I would get the dreaded Post Office 'you were out, ha, ha; you're going to have to come and collect your parcel from a remote industrial estate three hours from your house' chit during walks around the park, and I did then apportion blame. So let's say she was 99 per cent perfect. She was just lovely. She'd doze respectfully a few feet away from me, then leap to heel whenever I summoned her, seeming not to mind I was only calling her because I was so desperate for distraction that I'd have paid money to watch someone elderly trying to parallel park. A couple of times a day she'd spring into life and shoot back and forth across the room for no reason, like a furry little pinball; or suddenly find a ball, make it move with her nose, then run after it, in effect playing throw and catch with herself, both of which made me laugh far more than anything I was writing at the time.

Sometimes, in low moments, I'd allow her to sit up on my desk, where she'd rest her chin on my wrist and gaze up at the screen with what appeared to be doggish devotion and admiration for my fine comedic skills. She was a treasured creative companion. And she was a vitally necessary companion, too, it turned out. The words I'd whispered in her ear – 'it's you and me against the world' – that day on the beach, had turned out to be quite prophetic. Writing that first series was an enormous mountain to climb, grapple and mount (pardon), and there was only Peggy to climb, grapple and mount (pardon) with. You see, I'm not one of those people who can write in Starbucks, or in a production office, or in a busy family kitchen filled with bustle and chatter. I need silence, and solitude, and space. I find I need twenty-four free hours in order to get six good hours of writing done, so I had to completely clear my diary, both professionally and socially, in order to give the sitcom a fighting chance.

And that's what I was absolutely going to give it. There is no point doing anything like this unless you give it your all, and truly know it's had the best shot. Fear of failure is probably something we all recognize, isn't it, MDRC? And the thing is, subconsciously or otherwise, we can avoid that fear by not doing our best to protect ourselves. I knew if I did that, I would then have to sit with the thing I fear way more than failure – regret. No. Thank. You. I had to work as hard as I could and park fear of failure at the top of the multi-storey of niggling anxieties that made up my mind at the time. This was a little easier for me to do than it might have otherwise been, because I was utterly convinced the series would be a failure anyway! I assumed very low ratings and I assumed those ratings would be made up by a few members of the WI and the odd gay man who had seen me guesting in *Absolutely Fabulous*. And I was totally on-board with that. I could befriend my tiny, niche audience, and we could become a sort of salon. I could go to bars with the gay men (only two or three of them, so we wouldn't even need to reserve a booth). Then, in the mornings, I could bake cakes with my WI mates, most likely called Marjorie and Cynthia. I was looking forward to it. My expectations were fully managed and I buckled down knowing that when it flopped it would be because it was culturally not the right climate, and not for my lack of trying. Yeah, in your face, regret, suck on that there, apple o' wisdom.

But this degree of solitude – as generations of stories about people on desert islands will tell you – can send you a tiny bit tonto/bananas/STARK RAVING CRACKERS. Had it not been for Peggy keeping me vaguely connected to the world of other living breathing creatures, and demanding that I take her out amongst them twice a day, I feel sure that by day six of the writing process I would have somehow grown a mad wiry beard (think Tom Hanks in the second half of *Cast Away* but, you know, a bit prettier . . .), developed a hump and a wild facial tic, and be swigging my urine from an old shoe, firm in the belief that doing so would 'drive away the devil'. As it was, during my writing process I stayed relatively sane.

Peggy charges in 'Sane?' SANE? *slides past on the wooden floor unable to get a purchase to come to a stop* Wooohooo . . . ! Sorry, PDRC, slid out of the room there – she polished the floor to avoid writing this morning . . . Back to the point. She says she stayed relatively sane? AHAHAHAHAHAHAHAHAHAHAAAAAAAAAAAAAAAAAAAA! So I've told you already about some of the things she does when she's writing. Frankfurter Olympics, acting out her sitcom doing all the voices and stuff (she IS silly). But for some reason she was really, really way more stressed than usual this time.

Me, I have no idea why sitting still writing jokes about farting might be stressful. I am more of a Brecht girl, if I am honest. Lest you be surprised by my intellect, I have to tell you shih-tzus were bred to adorn Tibetan palaces, and to even sit in the large sleeve of a king or queen, so farce, well . . . it's not really me.

Anyway, so she got at least nine million degrees madder than she's ever been before. I might just be really really cheeky and describe a typical day of Miranda writing when things are getting a bit stressful. Naughty Peggy. Tee hee hee. Ok, why not, so, this is what I have to put up with.

0700: Alarm goes off. Snoozes. Every seven minutes that

thing goes, for nearly two hours. The alarm noise is the theme tune to The Flintstones. *Terrible. Very hard work on my refined ears.*

0845: Looks at clock. Panics. Gets up. Puts on entirely random selection of clothes, e.g. pyjama trousers, duffle coat, baseball hat, one walking boot and one fluffy animal slipper.

0855: Picks me up and sings a rendition of 'Peggy Sue' at me. Pre-teeth brushing. I can't begin to explain the breath. I am a fan of smells but this is . . . as her mother once said, a cross between digestive biscuits and Brie.

0900: Lets me out. We both do a lovely, long morning wee.

0930: Eats breakfast. She was told that protein in the morning is the way to go (tell me something I don't know), but although I understand most humans would have eggs, she goes for 2 x frankfurters 3 x fish fingers (I KNOW), 1 x bottle of Lucozade Sport and 24 x spoonfuls of Coco Pops – 'because every meal should have a pudding', eaten with miniature spoon from a McDonald's Happy Meal which makes her look like a giant. Tee hee hee.

0945: Puts on Dolly Parton's 'Nine to Five'. 'Dances' – or rather does some moves that look like a newborn foal's first attempts to walk. Just saying it how I see it. Gets excited that this is going to be a good day. Apparently the creativity is going to really flow.

1000: Sits on swivel chair at desk and goes round and round and round and round and round until she falls off the chair and says a word which even I know you're not supposed to say.

1001: Writes 'falling off an office chair' on the ideas wall.

1003: 1 x frankfurter. (Sometimes we share the frank-furter. I like it when we share the frankfurter.)

1004: Already starting to fear that it's NOT going to be a good day. Prays to the God of Comedy.

1005–1055: Sits at the computer and writes at great speed, whilst mumbling out loud in funny voices. (Funny weird not funny funny, in my opinion.)

1055: Walks around the room shouting 'IT'S NOT FUNNY IT'S NOT FUNNY IT'S NOT FUNNY!' which ironically is the one thing I do find very funny.

1130: Opens the fridge door, stands in front of it, eats a piece of Cheddar cheese which she gnaws straight from the block as if she's a giant mouse.

1135: Burps. Laughs.

1205: Switches on the TV. Says 'hello, you lovely silver fox' to someone called Phillip Schofield. Switches it off again.

1230: Takes me to the park. HOORAY HOORAH IT'S TIME FOR THE PARK HOORAY HOORAH! (Though some-times mumbles out loud things she's just written, which is massively embarrassing.)

1315: Says rude words about a card that has been posted in the letterbox – something about having to collect it and why couldn't postmen deliver at a respectable morning hour any more and why do they wear shorts, even in the winter.

1316: Writes down 'anger at the Post Office chit' on ideas wall.

1330: Simultaneous typing, eating and murmuring.

1430: Does a 'loo dance'. Because needing the loo is a real reason to break off from writing. Spends as long as she can on that weird white bowl.

1500: Makes up an alarming dance routine to a Billy Joel song.

1520–1700: Nap on sofa. I generally like to lie on her tummy during these times and nap myself. We both snore. She wakes me and her up with a fart. I leap off and get as far away as possible.

1701: Looks at clock. Panics.

1702: Picks me up, looks me right in the eye and sings the whole of 'You Are My Sunshine' to me, slightly slower than it's usually sung, and in a minor key, so it sounds a bit scary. Puts me down only when I start to tremble. We can turn on the tremble, I hate to break it to you.

1735: 1 x frankfurter.

1740: Second walk. YEESSSSS! Takes frankfurter with her and eats it on the street. NOOOOOO! How old is she – eight?

1800–2100: Repeat of earlier typing/mumbling/shouting horrors, only this time with a bit of looking at the clock and shouting, 'How is it 9 p.m. ALREADY!'

2100: Watches Big Brother.

2205: Reads over all the things she's written that day; decides 80 per cent of them are rubbish.

2210: Wonders whether you could eat a fry-up in the bath.

2215: Has a bath. With a cupcake, having declared, 'Everyone, it's bath and bun night!'

2230–1130: More mumbling and typing.

1200: Crawls up the stairs crying and passes out in bed.

0800: Wake up. Repeat cycle.

Don't ever say I don't give you all the goss. Oh, hang on, garden door is open . . . CAT! CAT!! I don't know whether I am chasing because I am scared or because it's *fun. *cat hisses and spikes up like a hedgehog, Peggy spooked and runs back into her basket* Cats Are SO WEIRD.*

The only time we left the house or park during that long, frantic period was to make trips to the late lamented BBC Television Centre. During the week we'd pop in for the occasional meeting with my series producer, and at weekends I'd sneak into the deserted building and use the quiet, almost holy, steeped-in-television-history space to write. Having a peep at the iconic studios where my heroes Morecambe and Wise, to name but two, had recorded was inspiration enough to keep me going for another few weeks. For I am a writer who principally writes to perform. (I won't lie to you, during this *Peggy and Me* process, I have been imagining a book signing to keep me going. Or, rather, a nice cup of tea, bun and chat with Marjorie and Cynthia. Hello ladies.)

Dogs weren't really allowed in Television Centre, so initially I would lie to the security guards and pretend that Peggy was taking part in a programme of some kind: 'Oh, yes, she's expected; they're looking for a canine co-presenter for Crufts and she's top of the list.' 'It's a prank show for BBC3 online called *Crotch Invader*. She's got a tiny camera up her nose and she's going to ram it into the crotch of fashionably dressed men in the sixteen to thirty-two age range to decide which one of them gets to date Miss World.' Actually, if anyone working for BBC3 is reading this, then you can have that, that's a hit right there. The lovely security guards eventually became accustomed to Peggy and me, took kindly pity and waved us through.

Thankfully. Because as the intense and solitary writing stretch went on I found I needed Peggy more and more. She was reminding me it was essential to connect to others to be really alive and to function fully as a human. And I had stupidly, imperceptibly got myself more than a little lonely. As a single woman living alone, it was Peggy that was shouldering the burden of my key relational connection. It was her who I felt knew the ins and outs of my fears and my dreams during this self-imposed isolation. It was looking into her eyes that calmed me down and made me feel loved and loving. I know some of you might think 'bit desperate, Miranda', but I can't shy away from how important Peggy started to become.

Oh, well now I am feeling really guilty about the writing process gossip. Coz actually I do wish I could help her. I would do ANYTHING for her. I wished I could get to the

Post Office. I love her so so so much. Warts and all. And don't get me started on the warts. JOKE. TEE HEE HEE.

I really really wish that I could lick all her fears away. I can't but I do the next best thing. I sit, and watch her, and send out 'Powerful Love Vibes'. I hope she knows how much I care. And I REALLY hope she expresses that knowledge by stopping eating my oat-and-honey biscuits. Because they're mine. Not yours. PEGGY's biscuits. *goes to bury a bone in Miranda's new bedding*

Peggy really was essential comfort. And I finally decided to let her cross the sleeping-on-the-bed line. Before, this had only been allowed during bouts of illness. But I felt more secure with her little presence at the end of my bed.

PDRC, I did not feel secure, but I knew she needed me, so I took a deep breath, grinned and braved it. I mean, no one likes a show-off but . . . I AM THE BEST DOG EVER.

And she is – wait for it, utterly fascinating canine fact coming up, MDRC – hypoallergenic. As in, does not moult. Brilliant. For two reasons. Firstly, no dog hair anywhere, ever. One of my greatest fears is becoming a 'pet-hair-everywhere' person. You know the sort; you open the door and the whole house just smells and appears . . . matted. You can't get into their car without developing a TB-like cough as the hair settles to the bottom of your lungs, or retching from the overwhelming aroma of 'wet dog'. You ask them, 'How many pets do you have, exactly?' And they answer, 'Oh, plenty plenty!' Because the fact is they don't actually know how many pets they have any more. The answer is probably 'six, but eight if you count the two dead cats mixed up with the sofa cushions and nine if you count the shed hair which has gathered to become essentially a bear'. So hoorah for the fact that Peggy does not shed. Secondly, she cannot bring on any sort of allergic reaction, even in one as asthma-prone and wheezy and problem-chested as myself. She's the dog equivalent of an almond milk, kale and pumpkin-seed smoothie, or really posh linen (probably gluten-free) from Harvey Nichols.

With Peggy helping me slumber better, time moved on, and soon enough and thank God, the tortuous writing process came to an end and it was time to film the sitcom.

Acting

As I've said, the performing, the acting, the doing, is by far my favourite part. My raison d'être, if I may be so bold. From writing to acting is like stepping out of a dank, dripping cave into a glorious playpen full of friends and lights and costumes and laughter and a handy canteen. Made more marvellous this time because Peggy was allowed into the rehearsal room. I felt it was only fair, given that she'd suffered so nobly alongside me through the writing. Plus this was the only time I was going to have my name in the title of a show, so it did warrant at least some kind of J-Lo-esque behaviour. Generally I am way too 'British' to carry off any kind of starry-ness. It took me a good few weeks to allow a runner whose job, amongst other things, it was to make me a cup of tea to . . . well . . . make me a cup of tea. I insisted she took the weight off for a bit, as I stood over the steaming tea urn, desperate for the sit-down I was giving the woman who was meant to be giving me a sit-down.

Peggy in the rehearsal room balanced out a little this fear of being demanding. I was grateful for her breed in this instance – a dalmatian, or collie, or german shepherd wouldn't have been right to pop quietly in the corner of a theatrical set-up. A bichon-frise cross was just the ticket. Not too ridiculous, i.e. not a chihuahua that might get mistaken for a joke shop prop, but not a bigger working dog unsuited to lying about looking pretty for most of the day. And she was quite a hit. As I made friends with my new colleagues, my new sitcom family – so did Peggy.

She was a particular hit with Ms Sarah Hadland (perhaps prophetically indicating to me that best friend in sitcom world would end up being best friend in real world). Then her attentions started to stray to Patricia Hodge (my, what I call, sitcom mother), for perhaps a slightly more grounded energy in the rehearsal space. (Sarah and I had the tendency to manic.) This attention to Dame-to-be (surely) Hodge brought out in Sarah a surprising competitive streak. *You see*, Peggy's greetings to those she fell for became notorious. She would run up and down and around you in crazed, energetic spurts, making bizarre love noises that sounded like a dog doing an impression of a mouse, and it would culminate in her bringing you some kind of present. If a bone wasn't available, people have been known to be awarded asthma inhalers from my bag, socks, a polystyrene cup from a bin and – in one particularly bleak instance – half a stranger's burger. Sarah was determined that Peggy should give her a better and more enthusiastic greeting than she gave anyone else, and was willing to go to quite frightening lengths in order to make this happen (I daren't go into detail, but suffice to say that *someone* might have taken to smearing chicken on their neck in order to encourage certain dogs to 'jump up' in an enthusiastic manner).

You are extremely honoured if you receive such a spontaneous greeting from the Pegster. She is very fussy as to who she lets in the Miranda-and-Peggy inner circle. To her mind, her job is to protect me from anyone who might be a threat, which often leads to some embarrassing aggressive barking at people who enter the house that she has decided (99 per cent wrongly) give off a bad vibe. None more embarrassing than when she accosted the BBC's Head of Comedy, who had popped down to inspect rehearsals and meet us all one day. Unfortunately and obviously unbeknown to us, it seemed he had quite a severe phobia of dogs, particularly yapping ones that look like they may take a chunk out of your ankle. And so followed a cringe-worthy concoction of the Head of Comedy running around the room clearly terrified, but trying to keep his executive status and pass off the fear (it didn't help when he stood on a chair); me going into middle-class overdrive pretending this was actually a sign of love and affec-tion ('She loves you, sir, aren't you special ha ha'); and Sarah Hadland trying to roll on the floor so Peggy could smell the chicken on her neck, lick it and stop barking. When things finally calmed and we had all sat down for introductions, Peggy decided that actually the Head of Comedy was someone she wanted as a BFF, sprung on to his lap and began to lick his face off. This was equally terrifying to him, the poor man.

We all started a kind of crazed group laugh to try to diffuse the situation, although I think he was pretty close to escaping to his boss and asking for a few months' gardening leave. And then came the 'Peggy present' that gave the whole debacle an excruciating denouement. She had taken out of my bag – wait for it – not an asthma spray, not even a used tissue; no, a sanitary towel. Yes, a feminine hygiene product OF ALL THINGS, and placed it at the feet of my new boss, who, before he had seen what it was, picked it up whilst thanking Peggy, nobly attempting to control his fear, and was left addressing the cast and crew of his new sitcom with a sanitary pad in his right hand. I might just as well have said, 'Good day to you, I am the woman you have risked hundreds of thousands of production money on, I am menstruating, have an assistance dog who provides me with sanitary towels when she thinks I or my friends might need one, and this is my tiny co-star who has chicken all over her neck, I do hope you are looking forward to working with us!' How we ever got a second series, I don't know.

By the end of the filming process I was knackered. Gloriously, happily so – it was worth it – but knackered nonetheless. It had only been eighteen months since my chronic viral fatigue and my doctor definitely didn't prescribe not only getting a puppy but 'write and perform in your own sitcom thereby inducing high levels of stress' to fully recover. I needed a holiday. I considered a trip away with friends – pop off somewhere hot, rent a house, all that jazz – but it felt like an organizational hassle. Plus, I realized that after the hurly-burly of scries-making and all the attendant larks, the person, if you can call her that, who I most wanted to spend time with was, yes you guessed it, Miss Peggy Sue Chef Hart The First. Friends and family understandably thought this a little mad, but I knew what I needed most of all was quiet simplicity. Gentle company, without the need to chat and plan jaunts and balance my needs with theirs. I realized that, although Peggy via the Dr Hunky-Viking-Vet episode had taught me I should let go of other people's approval, I hadn't yet been able to put that into practice. On a holiday I would be concerned that I might be getting in the way or annoying someone or not being jolly enough or not being interesting enough. It's different now. On my last holiday, if someone attempted to talk to me before lunch, I would simply say, 'No thanks, go away, see you at 1 p.m.' All done lightly and kindly but you can find a depth of confidence in friendships that is so freeing. Anyone under twenty-five, or even thirty-five, reading this – there are pluses to getting older, that being a perfect example. That and a 'clubbing night' simply means a twenty-minute after-dinner bop in the kitchen to Take That's *Greatest Hits*. So me trying to relax around people on holiday post series one, still not fully confident and free, exhausted, was not going to work. I needed someone who'd contentedly fall in with any plans I cared to make and just jog alongside me wherever I went (which could have been Sarah Hadland as, by nature of our differing length of strides, she would oft have to jog as I walked). I knew that the one person who fulfilled this role perfectly was my Pegaloo. Better than perfectly. She was, at that time, my ideal travelling chum.

Of course, Peggy's presence somewhat narrowed down my choice of destination. I wondered about a trip abroad. Nothing arduous, you understand, no trekking through Nepal or lolloping up Machu Picchu (are those really holidays?), just something small and manageable. But I was taken aback to learn that in order to take a pet abroad I would need to get a pet passport. A passport, MDRC, for a pet!

I sometimes wonder if, in addition to there being passports for pets, there's also a whole alternate airport universe for them. I've imagined this – the 'PetPort' – in quite some detail, actually, usually when waiting at airports while trying to distract myself from my own fear of flying. And, more to the point, fear of airports. Dreadful dreadful places. Airports are places where I go 'sod it, I'm going to die soon, I might as well spend £250 in Ted Baker and then eat a Garfunkel's

Full English Breakfast at two in the afternoon' whilst compulsively checking the departures board because I'm convinced I'm going to miss this flight even though it's almost definitely going to kill me. Madness. And madness which happens while you feel vaguely violated from having had to take your shoes off in public (why does that feel so intimate? You're only showing off your socks).

So I imagine a PetPort. The animals clear security, dogs and cats have to take off their metal tags and collars and put them in a litter tray; hamsters have their cheeks patted by security guards (who are lions); kangaroos open up their pouches; before they all pass through an enormous cat flap into the main terminal building. There they're free to browse an array of tempting perfumes in the Duty Free Store – 'Piss', 'Shit', 'Skip' and 'Anal Gland' – before enjoying a light yet overpriced meal of jellied meat and tripe rings in a miniature branch of McDOGNald's (thank you). There's a 'smoking area' full of miserable-looking Staffordshire bull terriers (only Staffies really smoke these days) who blow smoke at the judgmental rabbits who hop past daintily, on their way to their little rabbit yoga holidays in the South of France.

I enjoy the idea of a PetPort because the stark reality of travelling abroad with a pet seems to me unutterably tragic. The thought of putting Peggy in a cage and seeing her wistful eyes as she moved along the travelator to the no doubt terrifying cold hold of an aeroplane. Actually, I heard (no idea if it's true) that a famous pop star is so scared of flying that he had to take his dog into the cabin with him to calm him down. He gets a note from the doctor claiming that his dog is a much-needed 'emotional assistance dog'. I hereby declare that my prime professional aim is to reach a level of celebrity where I can pretend that Peggy is an emotional assistance dog and take her into the cabin with me (presumably wearing sunglasses and feeling terribly excited about sitting next to all the other celebrities and their dogs which for some reason I imagine would look rather like them. Tom Cruise and a beautiful, sleek, nicely muscled collie/staffie cross with perfect teeth. Jennifer Lawrence with a lovely Lhasa apso. Anyway, that's my dream. If I can briefly go Kim Kardashian on your arse. There's a phrase.

But in the absence of a PetPort and lacking the fame to take Peggy with me wherever I chose to go, our holiday choices were restricted to the UK and indeed to hotels that allowed pets. In the end, I opted for a tour of Wales, the Lakes and Yorkshire. And I was glad I had been restricted thus. I mean, bar the obvious weather problems (anyone else got a fifteen-year-old unused barbecue rusting away outside?), Great Britain's countryside and heritage does make for the most marvellous travel. And it was going to be wonderful. Peggy and I were now the very best of chums, she was fully house-trained, she was used to the car and petrol stations. We'd be like a far happier, more professionally fulfilled *Thelma and Louise*, barrelling through the National Parks singing along to a hearty combo of Smooth FM love ballads and the *Latest and Greatest Musicals* three-disc set and have the time of our jolly old lives. I hoped.

I hoped so too. I was really nervous when I first saw her packing suitcases, I thought she might be going somewhere without me. I didn't want to sit in the suitcase like I know some cats do to tell their owners not to leave them because that's just rude, someone has just washed and folded that jumper and doesn't need cat hair all over it, property should be respected (cats are IDIOTS) – but I did roll out 'Peggy's repertoire of cute poses and positions'. No one can refuse such delight, such charm, such beguiling wiles as the Peggy repertoire of cute poses and positions. NO ONE. Eventually I heard her say 'you're coming', which I understand because I am very very clever.

I was SO SO SO EXCITED. A holiday with my mummy. I sat on the map on the passenger seat to see where we were going. WALES? My first holiday and we were going to WALES?!

I mean, look at me. When you look at me and think holiday destinations, you don't think Wales. You think Le Touquet. You think Monaco. You think St Lucia. WALES?!

First Holiday

Wales was the first stop and I checked into a lovely hotel overlooking Lake Vyrnwy (I have no idea how you pronounce it either). I found it a little weird checking in with a dog. They were allowed with an extra twenty-pound charge, but in my head there was something peculiar about saying that myself and my dog were needing a room for the night. I assumed people were looking me up and down thinking 'woman/dog freaky honeymoon couple alert'. As I filled in the 'Name of second guest' section on the hotel information card with 'Peggy', in brackets, 'a dog', I thought right, first stage of the holiday we can chalk up as 'bit awkward'. But I soon settled into the hotel room (and lest you forget, I LOVE a hotel room), making sure I experienced all facilities to the max. Bath: check; tiny impossible kettle: check; drink sachets: drunk; complimentary biscuits: eaten; towelling dressing gown: adorned; spare pillows in cupboard: strewn all over bed; trouser press: used just for the hell of it. And I cosied down for the first of what I hoped would be many long recovering sleeps.

Alas, it was not to be. I woke up after about two hours due to . . . a smell. Pet owners amongst you will be with me, I'm sure, when I talk about the horror of *A Smell*. That unwelcome, unexplained scent which comes with no obvious visual clue as to its source, but which sends you off on a terrible half-asleep treasure hunt, where you know that the grandest prize on offer is a grim, steaming pile of . . . excrement. I am so sorry to do this to you, MDRC, but we are indeed here again. In Peggy's defence this was only the third time in her life she had suffered from a loose bowel but why oh why save it for a hotel room? She was once again shitting over my best-laid plans.

After I found and gathered up the offending substance, Peggy and I were forced to make perhaps the ultimate walk of shame. And just so you have the full picture: wearing pyjamas, odd socks, no shoes, middle of October, rural Wales, hair unbrushed, mascara as far down as my chin, carrying a stuffed bag of several scraped-together liquid poos. Yes, I was bewitching. Down I went, through reception, preparing to head out into the autumn chill. Peggy looked jolly excited at the prospect of a mega-fun midnight jaunt, head held high and prancing, while I kept my gaze fixed firmly on the floor and tried to avoid eye contact with the receptionist on night duty. Until I heard a surprisingly jolly 'oh hello . . . ' Then a more surprising 'wow'. I looked up and at the desk was a very dishy nineteen-year-old male receptionist (think Hugh Grant, the early years) sort of checking me out. And not in the 'pay your bill your stay has come to an end' way, in the, you know . . . sexy way. I mean he had given me an actual 'wow'. I thought maybe there is something about the tousle-headed odd-sock midnight-roaming look that is nothing short of full-on cougar. Then I remembered I was carrying a bag of poo and quickly hid it behind my back.

Awkwardly attempting to deflect from my being in reception in the early hours I proceeded with a dollop of youthful badinage and a topping o' flirting: 'Hi, I am like totally such a night owl . . . I mean like us young people hardly need sleep right . . . sleep is for babies . . . and old people . . . so yeah thought I would see the moon . . . the moon is just so like . . . great . . . isn't it, the moon . . . ' With the badinage-flirt heading perilously close to a weird waffle about the moon, I shuffled hastily outside. But before I got to the door I was stopped dead in my tracks on hearing, 'Umm . . . do you want me to show you the stables . . . ?' URH EXCUSE ME, WHAT NOW PLEASE?! Was this some kind of Welsh youth euphemism? It turned out, absolutely not. As you will discover in a moment he was talking about Peggy, but I TOTALLY misread. I thought gosh . . . perhaps the bit of flesh now appearing through the hotel dressing gown that didn't quite meet around my middle (one size does NOT fit all) was sure-fire alluring. 'We've got some spare stalls up there . . . ' he continued. As someone educated at an all-girls boarding school in the 1980s I learnt most of my sex ed from Jilly Cooper (thank goodness she rewrote *Riders*), and the offer to see a spare stall in the stables could really only mean one thing. I replied, 'Umm . . . goodness, young sir, are you suggesting . . . well, a quite literal "roll in the hay" eh?, which rhymes . . . ha ha ha.' Thankfully, before I uttered anything too shaming, he added, 'There are a couple of other dogs staying up there too.' The penny dropped. 'Oh for my DOG, I see . . . yes . . . not us, for the . . . shenanigans . . . ' 'What was that?' he asked. 'Nothing.'

I gathered myself and agreed to him showing me to the stables at the top of the hotel's driveway. As we walked he said, 'It IS you, isn't it?'

NOW WHAT?! What does he mean this time? There was no way I could ever consider a toy boy, I don't understand 'the young'. How am I supposed to answer that? 'Yes, I THINK it IS me, I am alive, I am me . . . WHAT?!' And then it hit me. Somewhat embarrassingly, this was the first time I'd ever been recognized as a person 'off the telly'. I'd been appearing on *Not Going Out* for a couple of years by now. Hence the initial 'wow' when I first entered his reception (definitely not a euphemism). I was tempted to lie in order to preserve the dignity of Lee Mack's fine sitcom (poo in a bag, ladies and gentlemen, please remember I was *still* carrying a poo in a bag), but I opted instead for a polite 'thank you, yes, it is'. And in a moment of panic flung the poo bag as far away as possible. However, my fling had not flung correctly. I had flung high, not wide, and the bag o' poo landed on a branch in a tree practically in front of us. I felt that there was no way to reconcile these precise circumstances with my new status as 'someone-who-very-occasionally-gets-slightly-recognized-because-they-have-a-supporting-part-in-a-sitcom'. So I tried to make an endearing 'joke'. 'Interesting. Bag of poo in the tree. You might have thought that was me but actually I heard about that on the news . . . birds have started copying humans and bagging up their poo after they've finished doing it. Amazing, isn't it?!' I turned to him hoping we'd both laugh and connect but unfortunately he seemed to think I was being completely serious. We walked in silence to the stables. I reflected that the being recognized thing, instead of making me feel more positive about myself, just heightened any sense of my own eccentricity. I was now

170

an actress, sort of known to him in some way, and I felt horribly conspicuous. I realized any kind of fame would be a minefield.

Peggy bounds in Ooh! Ooh! I need to get something off my little furry chest. Now I have recovered from remembering the horrors of the 'assuming the nineteen-year-old fancies you night'. I was on the lead, I had nowhere to run. I just had to sit back and watch the horror unfold before me, PDRC. I mean, I think Miranda is probably a uniquely attractive human, but NOT the kind that is going to attract a nineteen-year-old hottie. I could date the winner of Crufts himself, but you see, I AM a hottie. I just say it how I see it.

Sometimes I think Miranda assumes she's in with a chance to date a member of One Direction. But that might just be because she is always bouncing about in the kitchen singing 'you and me got a whole lot of history' and other very basic lyrics they sing.

But, PDRC, this whole strangers coming up and talking to Miranda thing It is SO WEIRD. We'll be walking along, I'll be about to chase a squirrel and then somebody will wander up and give Miranda a little piece of paper to sign, which they'll then take back from her and walk off. Or sometimes a loud brazen woman will come up, and stand very close and ask her to open a fête or speak at a charity luncheon. And sometimes, the weirdest of all, funny men sit in the back of cars or in bushes, and they very quietly take photographs of Miranda when she goes past.

Well, I don't like it AT ALL. I can tell when she is anxious and trying to get away from someone and that happens every time a stranger like this approaches. And if *she gets anxious then I get anxious. And I do NOT like feeling anxious. I know no one likes a show-off but I am not anxious, I am actually a really jolly, springy pup bringing light and life to everyone wherever I go.*

But more to the point, why on EARTH is she so popular? I mean no offence, but she's really really über-ordinary. She's from the Tesco Value range of human beings.

I'm pleased to say that I have a theory as to exactly why this might be happening. You see, when I was a tiny little, well, frankly PERFECT puppy on the set of Not Going Out, *and Miranda first got me, no strangers EVER spoke to Miranda. I mean no offence, but even charity muggers avoided her and taxis would hardly stop for her. I just say it how I see it. Then, a few months after I arrived, people started to pop over, and now . . . now that she's been my owner for a few years, you'll notice lots and lots of people want to introduce themselves to her, and hundreds of people come into big dark rooms called 'studios' to watch her messing about in costumes. (Honestly, it's so not a job. All she does is mess about putting on clothes which are someone else's but which look a bit like her own. Or she stands around for up to five hours eating biscuits and chatting, saying three lines then getting driven home in the back of a car like she's the Princess Royal.)*

What I am saying is, PDRC, all of the attention has happened in the time she's had me.

So, I can only assume that . . . People KNOW. People know that this strange tall friendly Hart-lady is the owner of the best little dog in the world, the amazing, prancing Peggy the Pegalicious light of life, and they REALLY want to be her friend because of it. They're hoping they will be given access to glorious marvellous ME! And those little pieces of paper that she signs are, I have worked out, 'promises'. They will be things like 'Peggy's far too busy and important for you to give her a pat right now, but I hereby sign this document declaring that at some point in the future I will grant you five seconds of interaction with the glorious Peg, Warmest Wishes, M. Hart.'

It all makes sense to me. It's like so SO obvs, isn't it? Now I have worked all that out, do excuse me. *takes five minutes to find the right way to curl up in her basket*

We arrived at the stables. A few concrete-floored looseboxes, quite big, quite chilly, but almost definitely a safe and reasonable place for a dog to spend the night. They were probably only about 500 yards from the hotel entrance, but in the dark and cold they might as well have been Siberia. Lit by a single bulb, the stables looked vast and frightening, a terrible chamber of horrors into which I was deciding to decant my poor, vulnerable, trembling little dog. I knew she'd be fine. I was going to leave her there with a cushion, a blanket, a toy, some food, even a sodding hot-water bottle. But MDRC – please know, I am not proud of this – I stood there for a full half an hour trying to decide what to do. Was this a terrible abandonment? Could I leave my poor little fluff-ball all alone overnight? What if she felt scared? She doesn't know when I am getting back. What if she fell into an emotional decline and gave up on life and quietly expired, all because I wanted eight hours' sleep? If that happened, I'd probably never sleep again. I pulled myself together – she's an animal, a wild animal – slammed the door shut, and strode off, doing all I could to ignore the yelps and wails and whinings coming from within the stables. I managed to make it a full three paces away from the door before swinging round and darting back into the box to retrieve Peggy, with an agonized cry of 'I LOVE YOU I LOVE YOU I LOVE YOU I LOVE YOU I'M SO SO SORRY I LOVE YOUUUUUUUU, PEGGY!' I took one last glance round the chilly stable, tucked her under my arm and moved on. This sort of set-up might be all right for a working spaniel or a sheepdog or some sort of foxhound, but Peggy was very much a mummy's dog. She needed more convivial, human spaces.

The car, I thought. I'll bung her in the car. She's used to it, likes it even, and I'll retrieve her before sunrise so as to avoid any of the terrible scenarios I've been warned about by all those 'DOGS DIE IN HOT CARS' adverts. I shoved her in the back seat with her blanket, closed the door, locked up, made it all the way back to my room before closing my eyes briefly and imagining her sad, hopeful face pressed up against the window, wondering if I'd gone for ever. That's the awful thing; animals have no sense that difficult circumstances will pass. This in-car everlasting purgatory has replaced the wonderful life they used to hold so dear, and this will never, ever change. And I couldn't bear to have Peggy thinking this for a moment, so I galloped back down through reception, past the by now completely baffled hottie of a receptionist, and collected her. Goodness knows what he thought of me, an indecisive madwoman marching back and forth through reception in the middle of the night, putting her dog in different places.

Here I was again; it seemed my Peggy and me journey was giving me another chance to free myself from the drug of approval. But I wasn't there yet. I was embarrassed by what hottie receptionist was thinking and simply judged myself unkindly as some kind of dog-owning loser. Peggy spent what was left of the night on the bed and cosied up closer than

ever before. No doubt sensing I needed her love and valida-
tion. I calmed down and chalked up the whole event simply
as: Irrational love for dog: 1, Common Sense: Nil.

*Oh Peggy's Dear Reader Chum. I can't begin to explain how
happy I was to cuddle up next to her that night. I found
myself really really trembly and scared at the possibility of
her getting some sort of boyfriend and having a grown-up
relationship. What would happen to her doggy? I'm scared.
Would we still do the night-night nose lick and the dancing
to Andrew Lloyd Webber? Oh golly me. I know she isn't
ready yet but what with trying to get off with the receptionist and the vet incident *paw instinctively goes over
eyes* it's obviously on her mind. It could happen coz she
is LOVELY. Oh golly GOLLY me. *settles down in new
position. Sleeps fitfully**

Despite that first troublesome night, my holiday with Peggy
ended up being the best possible tonic for the post-work
blues. I had got to know her even better and began to notice
tiny things about her. I was still feeling a little stressed from
the series, a little bit discombobulated by my shifting status,
wondering which way it would go. Once the show aired I
might never work again, or end up being recognized more.
Neither was a natural or welcome situation. And then I
noticed how Peggy, when she lay down, always let out a long
exhale, a sigh, a statement of intent: 'Tension be gone, I'm
in the relaxation business now.' So, I began to do the same
thing; to breathe out long and low, exactly as Peggy did. Best
relaxation tool I've ever learnt, and I learnt it from a dog. I
know it's obvious stuff – breathing slow and deep induces
calm – but she was the best friendly prompt for it. Previously

I had gathered the notion from a pink-Lycra-legging-clad woman in a yoga class saying patronizingly 'remember to breathe'. WELL OBVIOUSLY. How about 'remember to put some proper trousers on! TIGHTS AREN'T TROUSERS! And the colour makes them look like they're your ACTUAL LEGS! I might not be able to breathe but at least my pants are fully concealed.'

As my connection and feelings for my dear Pegster deepened I was segueing naturally on this holiday to a 'proper dog owner'. The sort of person who's never not owned a dog, and who will have one by their side, always and for ever. This was reinforced by two particular incidents. The first happened about two-thirds of the way through the trip, when my mother phoned me and the first question she asked was, 'How's Peggy?' not only before she asked how I was, but as if Peggy were very much a person. Then a few more specific follow-up questions. Has she made any friends? (No.) Is she enjoying the scenery? (She hasn't painted a landscape but seems to be yes.) Is she eating properly? (She just stole a packet of Softmints from my handbag, so yes and no.) Why hasn't she sent me a postcard? (Because she's a dog.) Odd as it was, I sort of liked it. I was glad that the world was beginning to see Peggy and me as a unit. A duo. A pair.

After Wales, we headed up to Lake Windermere, which for those of you who don't know, is slap-bang in the middle of some utterly tremendous walking country. Another wonderful thing that Peggy did for me was to reignite my love of walking. When I was younger, I loved nothing more than to fling a cheese sandwich in a backpack and yomp off up a hill, but I'd somehow lost sight of that in the hurly-burly of urban living. And bearing in mind we are still in the fat years at this point, albeit the tail end of them, I had needed to put quite a bit of effort into lying about watching telly with a variety of fatty takeaways to gain heft. But Peggy got me right back on track; her straightforward enthusiasm for the outdoors reconnected me beautifully with my own. Yet another spiritual lesson from my hound. This time reminding me of the beauty of beauty. The importance of nature. The feeding it gives the soul. The sense it gives of a whole world out there reminding you that you are but a speck, so pop your worries back into the futile box.

The only downside to reconnecting with the outdoors was that it also reconnected me with cows. MDRC, I try not to go in for feuding and animosity – life's tricky enough as it is – but if forced to nominate a nemesis of some kind, I would have to choose The Common Cow. I am completely, irrationally terrified of cows; even more so herds of cows. I feel that all cows all over the world are just waiting for me to lumber into their field with an Ordnance Survey map, so they can gather into a tight group and hurl themselves towards me in a manner more commonly seen in cavalry charges. I fear this to the extent that I will go to quite considerable lengths to avoid having to be near them. On one walk near Lake Windermere I ended up taking a two-and-a-half-hour detour to avoid a field of the beasts (I jest ye not). And Peggy was so obedient throughout this lunacy; so loyal and so sweetly trusting of me. She followed me uncomplainingly on my long, exhausting, neurosis-driven walk, as if she just knew that wherever I took her would be good, because I loved her and had her best interests at heart.

I was deeply moved by this, moved by how tremendous it felt to be so simply trusted, and I found myself thinking about the notion of God. I know this is all getting a bit . . . well, deep, but I really thought – if there is a God, this is how he'd want humans to behave. He (or She, or It) would want us to really trust, to stay close, to have faith in our instincts, to go where Life takes us, even if at times it felt dark and difficult, all in the sure and certain hope that we're being taken somewhere good. OK, I'd just been on a baffling two-and-a-half-hour walk with nothing to eat but half a manky banana from the bottom of my bag, but on reflection, it still feels like quite an insight. And one that hasn't left me.

It was the first time I got to grips with the notion of that kind of trust and, more so, of relinquishing control. Giving myself to something bigger that might have a purpose for my life. Certainly not an easy concept, but it suddenly seemed more sensible and more humble than thinking it was all down to me; that I had to make sense of all life's twists and turns and downward spirals and darkness. That I had to grip on, and it was all my fault if it didn't work out, even if what I did was my absolute best. That hadn't been working out for me in the past. I wanted what Peggy had. I wanted my existence to be one of purpose and with discipline over my choices, following as obediently and calmly as I could a thing which I believed had my best interests at heart and loved me unconditionally. The latter being the crunch point I suppose. That if a God is 'up there' loving me unconditionally (as Peggy knows I love her), I would rather believe that than not. I immediately felt more connected, more real, more peaceful. Wow, this dog-owning lark was becoming quite the unexpected life-changer. Perhaps you could say that God was talking to me through my Dog. God/Dog, sort of the same.

Shortly after the crazy-cow-avoidance walk, I experienced the second incident which marked me out in my mind as a dyed-in-the-wool dog person: I bought Peggy a coat. Yes, I became one of *those* people, one of that strange breed who think it perfectly reasonable to dress their dog in a garment of their choosing. Now, as a rule, I'm no fan of dogs in clothes. Have you ever seen a dog, or indeed any pet, in an outfit and seen them look joy-filled. No. They always look, at best, mortified. I was concerned that the simple canine raincoat was going to be the thin end of the wedge – that before long I would be dressing Peggy up as Wonderwoman, or putting her in a Lady Mary Crawley costume and shoving her behind the wheel of a miniature vintage car. But, in my defence, it was raining. Properly chucking it down, and Peggy, as I've said, isn't a dog who does well in rain (imagine a mop that's been left in a puddle). And it felt like the sensible option. She didn't appear to agree and had to be wrestled into the coat and looked furious and disgusted with the whole business.

EXCUSE ME! It wasn't having to wear a coat that I objected to. I'm not an idiot, I really really don't like to get wet, though I do love a leap in the odd puddle, especially if there is a bird in it to chase, but it was the CHOICE of coat! Peggy's Dear Reader Chum, it was a canine Puffa jacket in two shades of blue which poppered shut under the belly and under the chin. Do I LOOK like I want to walk round Lake Windermere dressed as Tinie Tempah? I am a classy bird; if I had to wear a coat then it should be a chic belted trench coat. The rule when dressing me should be 'whatever Joan Collins would do'. *trots off, indignant, tail held high, walking in a slight mince*

Towards the end of the Peggy and Me holibob, we visited Beatrix Potter's house. I loved her stories as a child (still do), and it was inspirational to see where she had worked. The place had been preserved exactly as it was when she left it (well, you know what I mean – they'd emptied the bins and things but her pens were still laid out on her desk, and her letters; it was like stepping back in time). It was reassuring, too; this little isolated cottage in Cumbria, where she'd written all alone, seeking solace in animals and in nature. It comforted me to think that the path of solitary creative endeavour could bear such marvellous fruit.

On the last day of our trip, I took Peggy up a hill to look at what I'd been told was the most beautiful view in the area. I let her off the lead, and she trotted off ahead of me. Whenever she got too far ahead (in her view), she'd stop and look back anxiously and wait for me to catch up. I loved feeling so needed. I felt so happy being on the receiving end of such loving, diligent attention that it made me feel that perhaps I ought to be giving it a bit more. Perhaps things would be more enjoyable and life would go more smoothly if I gave more time to my friends and family, my loved ones; to let them know that I really did love them as Peggy loved me. The last few years had been very much about work, which was all well and good – opportunities to be seized, once in a lifetime stuff – but perhaps it was time for a change; time to become a bit more of a people-person again. To balance out the recent loneliness.

Oh golly me, help, she IS thinking about other relation-ships . . .

When I reached the crest of the hill, Peggy jumped right up into my arms. 'It's you and me against the world.' Whenever I stop to admire a view she always does this. It's very sweet.

I like to think it's so she can see the view from my perspective, wants to enjoy it with me, but I suspect it's just habit.

It's not habit. I just want to be close to her. Oh golly, is she really thinking about MEN.

I'll leave you here, MDRC. Peggy and me, Peggy in my arms, enjoying the scenery and wondering what's coming next.

CHAPTER 7

Crazy Dog Lady?

Iknow that we have touched upon the phenomenon of the Crazy Dog Lady. And of course I'm not denying that there is many a Crazy Dog Gentleman to be found in this world; a quick turn around any urban park on a Saturday morning will doubtless remind you of this fact. But I am a, what I call, female – despite what various shopkeepers, pub landlords, clothes-shop proprietors and roaming gangs of teenage boys might occasionally say to the contrary – so the female archetypes bother me a tad more. As you'll know if you've been paying any sort of attention to this tome – and if you've not then perhaps take a little break? Bake a cake, snooze, visit a botanic garden? – during the last chapter, enjoyment of a smashing holiday was slightly tempered by the fear that I was at high red-alert-level risk of turning into a 'crazy dog spinster' of the highest order.

Now, if this were a fictional account of a lanky, but

sensational, woman called Miranda and her hilarious-yet-inspirational life with a naughty little dog called Peggy, then this chapter would probably be devoted to me telling you how very wrong I was. How the second after I had that thought, some sort of King Charming ('Prince Charming' doesn't quite work when you're over thirty-five, does it? Sounds a bit cradle snatch-y. Like I'm rambling around Chelsea in a tube top trying to get off with Prince Harry) strode up in a Barbour jacket and whisked me off to an affair more full of love and joy and surprise and tenderness and beauty than anything I'd ever known. However, as we're in the realms of non-fiction, I must come clean and tell you the sad truth that almost immediately after Peggy and I arrived home, my slide into what felt (and probably looked) like crazy, barking, Bonio-chewing dog spinsterhood continued apace. It was most worrisome. We are fast-forwarding a few months here, MDRC.

The sitcom had aired and to my utter shock was deemed successful enough for a second series. There was the odd job offer coming in which served as welcome distraction from the trappings of sudden 'success'. Namely the being recognized awkwardness, the increased chances of career failure (further to fall and all that), the being judged and, way worse, misjudged. But the pertinent point as regards our little story: my continued need and reliance on my hound. I could not have been more grateful for our woman-dog family unit. Slightly eccentric, sure. A near five-foot-ten-inch height difference. Differing levels of furriness. Different backgrounds. One from a show-biz dynasty of hyper-talented fur-balls, the other – let's be frank – a bit suburban. To the onlooker we would have looked a fright. Pottering around unwashed to various degrees, one of us passing little pieces of cheese down to the other, them offering oat-and-honey dog biscuits upward in return. The odd bickering fight, 'Peggy, that's a nice family having a picnic, will you put those mini-sausages DOWN, no, not carry the whole box away to that tree, PEGGY! I am so sorry . . . Peggy, come HERE.' The odd random cuddle, her chin on my shoulder, me whispering, 'You are the most beautiful doggy in the world, oh yes, the most boootiful doggy, yes you are.' But hey, it was what I had and it made me secure amongst all the other life changes. Secure, until I was suddenly forced to take stock and wonder if I had slipped close or into Crazy Dog Lady.

It all kicked off with a phone call from my mother, asking if I'd like to go away on a little holiday-ette for Easter with my sister and her husband: 'It'll be me and Dad, Alice and Christopher and you and Peggy. I've organized a dog-friendly hotel!' Nice as this was, my stomach lurched a bit; at some point, without my even noticing, we had become 'Miranda And Peggy', an old married couple, never apart. I caught a brief glimpse of our future social life, my friends debating whether or not to invite us round. 'Shall we have Miranda And Peggy?' 'Oh, maybe. But she always clambers on to the sideboard and licks the joint clean before everybody's finished eating.' 'Mmm, and Peggy's table manners aren't great either.'

Worse, my mum said, 'Perhaps you could both drive down on the Friday?' And out of nowhere I found myself responding, 'Yes, good idea. We'd like that.' Did you hear that, MDRC? 'We.' *We'd* like that. I mean, *really*. That's annoying enough when ordinary human couples do it, isn't it? Let alone growing-crazier-by-the-minute dog owners, projecting creepy personalities on to their unwilling pets. Please say I'm not the only one who gets driven nuts by couples who start '*we*-ing' (as it very much were) when they're newly together and in the first flush (oh dear, now I've we-ed and flushed). A time when, logically, they don't know very much at all about what makes the other one tick. Yet they've decided that they are, on some biochemical level, one and the same, incapable of having divergent views. 'We loved that film.' 'We weren't so keen on the popcorn.' 'We *do* like aubergine *parmigiano* but other than that we tend to find aubergines a bit greasy-tasting, unless they're served mezze style with a dollop of minty yoghurt! Yes, that's *exactly* what we *both* think about that! Crazy, huh?' If I wasn't constrained by polite societal convention I would shout in their faces: 'Oh do SHUT UP! You CAN'T both think the same thing about everything! It's impossible. WE ALL KNOW that you only THINK you think the same thing because you're drugged off your tits on sex-chemicals! And I think YOU know that as well, but you're just yammering on to show off about your fabulous . . . intercoursal relations. So please stop it because I'm seeing right through you even though I'm obviously not bothered and you're not getting to me IN ANY WAY!'

But I can't get on a high horse here. I myself had just 'we-d' (don't). Was that what lay in store for Peggy and me: a lonely, bickering, dog-woman life of communal 'we-ing' (again, stop it) until one of us died and the other one dropped off the twig days later, unable to face life without her dearest chum. I was, to say the least, concerned.

'Miranda And Peggy'

Despite all the signs pointing me very firmly in the direction of CrazyDogSpinsterVille, the family trip was a welcome break from second series writing. (Which was proving same-old-same-old with a dollop of extra-tricky second-album pressure.) I sensed that my family was actually rather relieved that I was finally one half of a 'Miranda And Someone', even if the someone in question was less than a foot tall, hairy, let out frequent high-pitched noises and had to be strapped down and forcibly bathed from time to time to stop her smelling like a decade-old drawer full of rotting vegetables. (You're right, MDRC, I'm sure I've had far worse relationships.) Our Easter jaunt was the sort where the various family units went off and did their own thing during the day – so Mum and Dad, my sister, her husband and their then toddler son, and . . . me and Peggy. And I do think that Peggy being there made the whole business considerably easier. I had a default somebody to go off and do things with, which spared any 'oh, should we ask if Miranda wants to come too, we wouldn't want her to be lonely' sort of hideousness. And, I suppose, my family were able to shift me out of the 'slightly baffling and problematic conundrum of an older single woman' category, into 'creative single woman with a *lovely* dog – isn't it marvellous how she channels all her energy into her love for animals, she'll probably be head of the World Wildlife Fund before you know it, ha ha! . . . ' category (which may be a new category I've just invented, but parents with single offspring around the world, feel free to use it at your leisure).

While the others were off being couple-y and family-ish one day, Peggy and I went for a lovely long walk on the beach. It was a proper wild, English day on the coast – bright sunshine, intermittently overshadowed by majestic scudding clouds casting heavenly patterns of light across the wind-whipped sand – all that sort of loveliness. Against this backdrop I took a few photographs of Peggy (by a few, I mean about 150). This was too beautiful an opportunity to pass up. They were wonderful photographs. One-offs: beautiful carefree Peggy bursting out of the surf, gazing moonily at the camera, then frolicking wild and free. I was entranced.

I was entranced. I was entrancing. I am SO entrancing, I entranced myself. Yours, Peggy the entranceress.

I wondered why my family were slightly less entranced when I sat them all down that evening for a slideshow. Not only didn't they seem to share in my wild photographic joy, but were giving each other sidelong 'I don't know whether she needs match.com or a mental health team but I know she needs it now' sort of look.

It was here I learned that taking many photographs of your dog frolicking on the beach = an enjoyable and daft pastime. Spending two hours forcing your family to look at said photos = the behaviour of a madwoman. And it shows, at best, a lack of humility. Yes, dog ownership was presenting me with my next 'spiritual' lesson. This time about how to go about being a bit more humble in life. For during my dog-photo exhibition there was no 'how are you?' Not much of the listening, of the stepping back and putting your own issues to one side and let someone else feel interested in, listened to and nurtured. I vowed to be less, well, all about me, a bit more humble. Wow, Peggy really is the Eckhart Tolle of dogs. (Who, as an aside, I always think looks like an adorable, friendly pug!)

Much more importantly, it got me thinking about where one has to draw the line as far as dog photographs are concerned. It is yet another veritable social minefield of dog ownership. Here follow my findings, please do enjoy: General snaps are fine, more so if there's a friend or family member in shot. Photographs of your pet in small novelty costumes (hats, bow ties, *but never swimwear*) are absolutely fine, as long as it's Christmas or a child's birthday party, and as long as the animal in question is cat-size or larger. No one needs to see a hamster in a little knitted hat, that's just degrading. Commissioned photographic portraits of dogs and horses are absolutely fine – aristocratic, even – but an elegant, posed black-and-white photograph of a cat will never not be weird. Painted portraits of your dog are only acceptable if a) they are done by a child of primary school age, or b) you are a duchess or an earl and therefore actually need portraits painted to cover the acres of bare wall in your twenty-bedroom country pile. It's only OK to frame photographs of your dog if they're of a very high standard, ideally professionally taken; framing a bad, blurred snap of your hound marks you out as the sort of person who takes your pet to nice restaurants for 'date nights'. Please send me any further thoughts on a postcard, though ideally not a postcard featuring a picture of your gerbils dressed up as the Von Trapps.

As a postscript to this – because you know me, MDRC, I like to get to the very bottom of all these essential life issues – I do believe the sharing of dog photos has become socially more acceptable in recent years. The snaps on that family weekend were taken in 2010. Five years on I found myself at a dinner party (I know, hark at me!), and the minute there was talk of somebody's dog, out popped a number of iPhones and then at least half an hour of having people's dog photos thrust in one's face, occasionally being forced to zoom in on a particularly cute shot, or made to press play on the twenty-second hilarious video of the family dog humping the ageing grandmother. We were all fairly sane people at the party – professionals, sensible mothers, a fine and noble actress who I couldn't possibly name (Sarah Lancashire) – yet here we were pawing over dog photos (as ever credit where credit is due, pun-wise). I then realized what was actually happening. We were simply wanting an excuse to look at pictures of *our* dogs. No one gave a monkey's about the other people's dogs. Not after the first glance anyway. We would all much rather have taken ourselves off to a quiet corner of the room to scroll through photos of our beloved pets.

Two things struck me here. *Firstly*, the calming influence of a dog photo. Looking at pictures of our human loved ones more than likely just reminds us of the stresses that go with living with them. You'd look at a picture of your husband and think, 'That shirt AGAIN! If I'd wanted to marry a tramp I would have done.' Or, 'Why's he cut his hair so short, it's spiking up, he's not in a boy band, he KNOWS I don't like it short,' and 'Why can't he chop lemons on a chopping board, there's always a sticky patch on my kitchen island!' You'd look at a picture of your teenagers and think, 'Why do they smell quite that much, I'm retching just remembering when I last risked entering their room,' or, 'I think I'm actually scared of my daughter. Shall I follow her on Facebook as me or set up a fake account?'

Nothing like this with a dog. No, no. Just unconditional love. Just calm. Just caring. Secondly, it's another nod to the winner in the Dogs versus Cats debate. We were at a social event sharing photos of our dogs. Guarantee you if someone had piped up with a picture of their cat amongst some daffodils in the garden, or asleep in the laundry basket, we all would have looked politely, said, 'Mm, gosh, lovely', then subtly glanced at each other with 'oh my word, nutcase' eyes (a very specific facial expression I recognize well, having been on the receiving end of it more times than I care to admit).

I've talked about the mishaps, travails and intermittent joys of going on holiday with one's hound, but may I just say that no matter how strange or embarrassing or awkward or poo-ridden or crazy-dog-spinster-making our trips *à deux* have been, they are as nothing compared with the horror of leaving her behind when I go away by myself. I find myself weeping like a mother sending her son off to war. Before I started writing the second series of the sitcom, I went to Australia for six weeks to get some much-needed fun under my belt with my friends, and to keep some perspective on my dramatically changing life circumstances, to remember the world is a bigger place than your personal career niggles. So I left Peggy with a friend's mother in Epsom . . .

I would have preferred Mayfair . . .

. . . an eminently safe, responsible and kindly person with whom I knew she would be perfectly safe and well cared-for – and nearly had a breakdown in the process. Golly, I hope I am not the only dog owner like this. I took absolutely ages to say goodbye to her. It went like this: Long cuddle, say goodbye, explain how long I was away for, put her down, try and leave, rush back in, pick her up, long cuddle, tell her she was going to be totally fine in Epsom, put her down, pick her up, twenty-five kisses, put her down, pick her up, squeeze her a bit too hard, put her down, walk away, turn back, sit her on my lap and look her directly in the eye and tell her I love her so much, ten kisses, put her down, pick her up, final cuddle, five kisses, leave, start weeping, start wailing. I got in the car and cried all the way to the airport (funnily enough this isn't one of the airport scenarios that Richard Curtis saw fit to cover in his *Love, Actually* airport montage), then spent the first three days of the trip quietly muttering, 'Sorry, Peggy', so racked with guilt was I.

From time to time on the beach in Oz I'd catch myself wondering, 'What's she up to?' What was I expecting her to be up to in Epsom? Needlepoint? Placing bets on the horses? Getting really stuck into series two of *Breaking Bad*? Occasionally I'd be sent a photograph of her in the snow as I basked in the heat and I'd feel a maternal pang of longing. And I wondered: is this normal? I didn't voice my concern to anyone. I suppose I was afraid that they'd turn grey-faced and shocked and say, 'Actually, mate, that is bloody weird. Like, a feature in *Take A Break* magazine level of weird. I suggest you call the Samaritans pronto before you end up in bed with a goldfish or something.' So I kept schtum. The stronger my own suspicions that I was sinking irrevocably backwards into crazy dog spinsterhood became, the more this felt like a sort of dirty secret, and the more I felt I had to keep it hidden from the world at large. Life had other plans, however.

Shortly after the Easter family trip I was dispatched to the local nursery to pick up my nephew, only to find myself met with a few odd looks. Mothers and children in the car park pointing at me and laughing. I was unfazed by this. You can't get your skirt stuck in your knickers as often as I do without becoming pretty much immune to the old point-and-giggle. Until someone shouted out, 'Hello, Aunt Pussy!' directly at me. Now I was fazed. It turned out that my dear nephew had been required by his school to give a presentation that day at nursery: 'What I Did On the Holidays.' He had produced a (by all accounts excellent) photo-board presentation of our recent trip, featuring Granny, Grandad, Mummy, Daddy and . . . Aunt Pussy. Yes, MDRC, I am, as they say, Pussy. Bear with. It was the nickname my sister gave me when we were children, before an understanding of what else it might mean, I hasten to add. The joy of an innocent age. Sadly, it stuck, really quite firmly, and however hard we try to call each other by our actual names, Pussy just comes out (that sounds all kinds of wrong, forgive). And now, thanks to my nephew and a veritable committee of gossiping nursery mothers, the world knew it. I might have got away with it but unfortunately there was an incriminating picture of me on his photo-board under Aunt Pussy. Mortifying. But worse . . . and you may say, really, what is worse than your family nickname being Pussy? Well, for my shame, the following. You see, my nephew had also introduced my dog to the world as 'Cousin Peggy, Aunt Pussy's daughter'. Cousin Peggy, apparently, 'doesn't speak' (she's probably too embarrassed by her association with Aunt Pussy), but is otherwise the best cousin he could possibly hope for. My nephew had made it sound like I go around insisting that people recognize Peggy as my ACTUAL DAUGHTER. Although this was a dollop of double mortification for me, I felt it was testimony to the wondrous Peggles, who was placed in such high esteem in my nephew's affections he would consider her some kind of actual cousin.

Strangely, it all marked a bit of a happy turning point for me. I decided that if others thought (or, more accurately, knew) that I was a crazy dog spinster of the highest order, then I might as well embrace that and be one. It felt like an exciting step. A step away from fearing what nineteen-year-old

Welsh receptionists might think of me and a step closer to self-acceptance. And it seemed that there was a positive to fame at last. It gives you a bit of a licence. I mean, by the nature of the beast you are going to be misjudged, so you may as well let go of the trying to present 'right' and just be completely yourself. It's well known we have to be able to accept and love ourselves before entering any kind of meaningful human relationship. My key 'Peggy and Me' lesson was once again rearing its beautiful head.

Oh, no, no, golly, no, I'm panicking, she is talking about human relationships again. *randomly rolls around on back, yelping, returns to upright*

I just really really don't want to share her, PDRC. That would be even scarier than the time I put my head in a cereal box because I thought there was still cereal in there, and got stuck and reversed round and round in circles with Miranda laughing at me till the box came off. That was AWFUL.

Oh, but hang on, if she is talking about accepting herself first . . . oh well, I should be fine then. OK, fine, and relax, because that will take a really really REALLY long time. Tee hee hee.

No but seriously, PDRC, it will, because this is a woman who, for example, makes 'boats' out of cold meat then eats the boats shouting, 'I am a great white shark!' A woman who has to stand and sing the special 'Putting Out The Bins Song' (and do all the actions) before she puts out the bins. A woman who props her bananas up against the wall in a row then bowls tangerines at them for UP TO THREE HOURS AT A TIME on a NORMAL WORKING TUESDAY. This is, you could say, a woman who has more than most to accept about herself.

*OK, chill, Peggy. Chill, PDRC. PHEW! As you were . . .
*in Peggy's case removing mud from between her paw pads
and spitting the mud on to Miranda's recently washed
tiles**

'Miranda And Peggy' At Work

This new sense of self-acceptance meant Peggy became more
a part of my public life than she had been. I took her with
me filming every day I could, and allowed us to be seen as
Miranda And Peggy. If by some weird chance she couldn't
accompany me, people would ask, 'Where is she? Is she OK?'
And you know what, I didn't mind it in the slightest. Because
film sets, it turns out, tend to be stuffed full of proper, crazy-
and-I-know-it animal lovers. Dog lovers, particularly. Once I
began to open up about Peggy, I was astonished by the response
I got. People joyfully chimed in with wonderful stories about
their own embarrassing hounds and hound-ettes. The set of
Call the Midwife was a particular goldmine; Pam Ferris loved
to regale us with stories about her rescue lurcher Stanley at
any given opportunity and, in a break between scenes one
day, Jenny Agutter informed us that her dachshund, Tufty,
was almost certainly Princess Diana reincarnated. Her evidence
for this was as follows: if she, the dachshund, ever saw the
Queen on television she'd start growling ferociously; she hated
blue Queen-style handbags; she had a fringe of hair that she
would shyly glance Diana-like through; and – get this – if
Jenny ever got into a car for work that happened to be a
Mercedes, Tufty would start shivering and absolutely refuse
to get into it. I believe this story categorically proves either
Jenny's dog is in fact Princess Diana reincarnated, or that I
am by no means the most dog-mad person in the world.

Helen George had two dogs (one of whom, little Yorkshire terrier Lottie, Peggy took an instant dislike to – we think she was intimidated by Lottie's miniature feminine wiles) and Judy Parfitt, inspired by the love for our pets, ended up acquiring her now-inseparable-from miniature poodle Freddie. A miniature poodle who, I would tease her, looked just like her. There was no getting away from it; someone had to say it as they pranced around set with an identical shock of strawberry-blonde curly hair/fur.

It wouldn't be an odd event to see me, Jenny, Helen and Judy in a row in the make-up trailer with various mutts on our laps. Pam sensibly decided her lurcher was too big to be placed on her lap. Nothing stranger than an enormous dog sitting atop and dwarfing its owner. The presence of our hounds made the set a happier, jollier, livelier, friendlier place. While we're here on the set of *Call The Midwife,* it might be worth a quick paws for thought (the fact that I haven't extensively employed that pun suggests that I'm a writer of great elegance and restraint), for reflection on just how far and how fast things had moved, professionally, in the time that I'd had Peggy.

A coincidence. I think not.

I suppose all due to a mix of good fortune, hard work, and a willingness to follow my ridiculous dreams despite all the doubts and fears and knockbacks and naysayers along the way.

Oh.

And it really felt as if things were turning out beyond my wildest dreams, if I may be a bit cheesy for a moment. All those lonely frankfurter-snaffling hours spent bashing out the first and second series of my sitcom had paid off; I'd been commissioned with a third series, this time for BBC One, and now had the opportunity to go to work on the set of a big period drama, where I got to swap dog stories with the likes of Jenny Agutter and Pam Ferris. I mean, Mrs *Railway Children* and Mrs *Darling Buds of May*, for goodness' sake! Some of my wildest youthful dreams were meeting heroes, and even this was becoming reality. Almost the best thing about my job I would say. I shared a curry with Ronnie Corbett – I know, quite the sentence. Unbelievable to have met a Ronnie. French and Saunders were now Dawn and Jennifer, and mates. I had auditioned for Emma Thompson, I didn't get the part, but hey, I auditioned. And I had been introduced to Dame Judi Dench. And cried. I cried in Judi Dench's face, well, over her head, such was our height difference – salty droplets landing on her elegantly placed pashmina. Even with that mild embarrassment, it was all utterly thrilling. Most of these encounters were at work, but strangely enough one or two did come to me as a direct result of my having Peggy.

She proved to be an unlikely gateway to random celeb encounters including, The One And Only Mr Michael Ball. BallGate, as I'm now choosing to call this incident, took place at BBC TV Centre, where I'd popped in for a morning meeting. Just as Peggy and I were entering the building, that oh-so-familiar golden-voiced curly-topped gentleman was on his way out. I was about to beat a hasty retreat before he and I could make eye contact. I'd not met him before and I often find myself reduced to a wibbling heap of jelly in the presence of anyone I admire (if I'm honest there was also a bit of a dribble on Judi Dench's head, please don't tell her) – when he stopped, crouched down and said to Peggy, 'Who's this lovely little thing, then?' He was quite smitten with her.

He's only human.

He was fondling her head while she preened and fidgeted and stuck her tail in the air and whined and generally made a bit of a spectacle of herself. Only after a full minute of this mutually swooning disgustingness did Ball notice that there was a human attached to the dog. He looked up at me and said, 'Oh hi, you're Miranda Hart, aren't you?' I blushed a deep, deep shade of puce, almost purple, the kind of skin colour which on medical dramas causes fifteen doctors to run into your cubicle with a crash cart. I couldn't believe he knew who I was, so I replied with something along the lines of: 'Hrrrgpprrrmmmmmmphhhh, you're Michael Ball, Michael Ball! Michael Ball you are, Ball, Michael Ball . . . lovechangeseverything hahaha.'

Ever the gentleman, Ball responded with a kind, 'Well, lovely to meet you. And I can't believe you own this *gorgeous* dog!' I met His Musical Theatre Majesty, The God O' Love

Ballads, and he complimented me on my *dog*. There's something not quite right about this picture. No compliments about *my* acting skills, or liking *my* sitcom, or perhaps noticing that he could just tell I had some latent dance talent such was the length of my limb and general air of coiled-spring poise. No suggestion of dueting with me. What I was really touting for was an invitation to record an album of 80s classics together, then tour the world for the rest of our lives singing said 80s classics in arenas, stadiums and opera houses (not that I'd given it much thought). But Ball and I parted company with no such plans to hook up (funnily enough). Still, what an encounter.

Indeed it was, PDRC. And all thanks to beautiful me. And now he has fondled my head with his big, warm, generous hands I await the call from Cameron Mackintosh offering me, at the VERY least, the job of understudying Toto in the next revival of The Wizard of Oz.

Although I fear I might have been let down by Miranda for that thing she said to Michael Ball, the 'hrgggrrr-rmmmmmmph' thing. It was actually really LOADS worse than that. She actually made that noise whilst eating a mouthful of a ham and tomato sandwich. WHO takes a bite of a sandwich when they've just met one of their heroes? WHO?! And what happened was that tomato pips came out of her mouth and were sprayed on to his lovely blue shirt. SO EMBARRASSING.

It baffles me, this whole walking while eating thing she does. She is a professional of some standing who could absolutely afford to pay for a little sit at a table and chair if she wanted. I mean, even if I find some sort of old kebab at the side of the road, I will make the effort to sit down *and eat it properly, with some respect for its magnificence. But here Michael Ball's shirt suffered, and that is really not a trivial issue AT ALL. * trots off doing vocal warm-up exercises**

I thought that BallGate was about as good as it could get, dog-induced-celebrity-encounter-wise, but I was wrong. Not too long after BallGate I took Peggy to Richmond Park for a change of scene and to enjoy a larger expanse of countryside. Sometimes the smaller urban park makes me feel like an animal prowling the fences of its cage. I saw a man approaching with a bit of a crazy-looking springer spaniel. At once adorably full of *joie de vivre* and an immediate and terrifying threat to public order, in that very special way that only springers can be. The spaniel was frightening Peggy (imagine a randy runaway Premiership footballer bursting into a prefect's school dormitory or the boudoir of a prim ingénue, and you should get the picture), and its owner was rather desperately calling it back. I geared myself up for one of those nightmarish, über-British, over-apologetic dog-owner conversations; 'Oh, I'm *so* sorry,' 'No, *I'm* so sorry,' 'No, really, I honestly couldn't be sorrier,' 'Well, I promise you that if you *could* be sorrier, then you still wouldn't be half as sorry as me.' 'Let's just both lie face down on this patch of grass for a bit of gnashing and wailing about how sorry we are, shall we?' 'Yes, let's, good plan.' 'No, you first.' 'No, please, you first, I'm so terribly sorry for my forwardness', and on and on and on, until the sun sets and the temperature drops and you're spitting chunks of midnight ice out with each sorry apology you make (your dogs have long since found their way home of their own accord, and are enjoying a lovely casserole in front of the fire). Anyway, all revved up was I for this monstrosity, taking a deep breath and doing my special 'humble' eyes, when the man arrived and I found myself face to face with the one and only Tom Courtenay. Whom I've admired for eons, literally eons (not that I know what an eon is, to be fair, other than knowing it's about the amount of time I've admired Tom Courtenay for). Tom Courtenay! SIR Tom Courtenay, a knight of the realm, no less. He was impeccably polite and kind, and mentioned that he and his wife enjoyed my sitcom, which was, frankly, one of the most marvellous moments of my life. And all because of Peggy being completely irresistible to an over-enthusiastic springer spaniel.

AND can I just say, I think that Sir Tom Courtenay is MUCH more the sort of celebrity I should be spending time with. There's proper dignity with Sir Tom, majesty even. One could argue that the likes of Michael Ball are a bit . . . light entertainment

I know I was born into the world of sitcom and comedy, but I really need something much more 'me'. I was hoping Sir Tom and I would become friends and I could sit in theatre dressing rooms in the West End. That's where I belong. In and out of a stage door. Sherry in paw, head-fur dyed blue and set in rollers, a robe, on a chaise, never more than ten feet from Helen Mirren. Ah, the theatre!

Because I am an easily swayed super-fan of the highest order, I must say that the affirmation of Michael Ball and Tom Courtenay, coupled with the combined mad-dog-lady experiences of Ferris and Agutter, did do a fair bit towards my feeling even more comfortable as an out-and-proud, crazy dog lady. In fact, it had started to feel as if I was pretty much the least animal-mad person in show business. Did you know that Paul O'Grady hand-rears lambs? That Ben Fogle has claimed he has never felt grief like it when his Labrador died because she entirely moulded his life? And that Boris Johnson has a 'secret parrot' sewn into the lining of his suit jacket, which he has little chats with when he thinks nobody's looking? (One of those examples is made up.) It all made me feel much better about some of the deeper routines I had got into with Peggy. I feel a list coming on. I hereby announce **Miranda's Cray Cray Dog Love Displays**:

- I often call Peggy 'my little girl'.

- My command to get her to come to heel in the park is 'What's this?' (as in what treat is she about to get) which she only understands if spoken quickly and at a high pitch so it sounds like I am screaming 'horses' as I pound around the park, for no good reason.

- Sometimes, when she is sleeping in another room, I like to suddenly shout 'what's this?' because I love watching her bounding towards me with expectant joy of what I might be offering her.

- I have been known to give her a bone, follow her to her basket and lie down, my head on the edge of the basket, to watch her excitedly burying or chewing upon said treat.

- I have also been known to wind down before bed by putting my head entirely in her basket, lying right next to her, holding her paw.

- I oft do a very much what I call, Peggy-Poo-Dance. I had noticed that whenever she passed a motion she did a celebratory skip and run, I suppose due to some sort of relief and/or feeling of lightness. It amused me greatly and I felt it only right for me to join in with her, a little skip and a few celebratory free-of-poo manoeuvres (think contemporary dance with a hint of jive).

- In the spirit of full disclosure I sometimes do a Miranda-Poo-Dance at home, post a trip to the toilet. Try it. Puts a bit of jollity into an otherwise mundane moment.

- And due to urgent circumstances beyond my control I have been known to put Peggy in a taxi across London in order to deliver her to my sister's house. And I mean alone in the back of a taxi, with no human companion, just her fare, which led to much confusion with the taxi driver whose English unfortunately wasn't the best. 'You come with, no?' 'No,' 'No?' 'Yes.' A pause as we stare at each other. 'You lady, get in with dog please.' 'No, I don't need to go, just the dog.' 'Just dog? No no!' 'Yes, yes, just dog. My sister will get her the other end, she isn't off on a mini-break on her own.' Something in Polish. We stare again. 'Yes, dog, with you.' 'No, just dog.' 'No!' 'Yes.' And then something further in Polish. 'OK, because you funny lady, it's fine.' I don't know whether that was because I was funny weird, or funny funny. Either way, the dog made it safely to her destination.

All in all, it did feel like my work had led me to my kind of people – all fellow animal goof geners.

Dog-loving eccentricity – indeed all eccentricity – is nurtured and encouraged in the theatrical world. It is undoubtedly one of the things which first drew me to it, and a large part of the reason I feel so at home doing what I do. There is an openness, a silliness. Weirdness thrives. But I worry sometimes that that's making me a bit strange, unable to function in the 'normal', perhaps slightly colder and less tolerant, world. The necessary at times more formal and respectable world. I'm already in a theatrical cocoon, and then there's a dog-lovers' cocoon within that cocoon. I am double-cocooned. I think it's fine to embrace this cocoonery – it's fun, why not?; the arts are as vital, if not more, frankly, as politics and commerce – but I worry about the bonkers-ness it engenders spilling out into my 'real world' encounters, when I'm away from work and work people, out living my day-to-day life. Is it OK to be 'the bonkers actress with the dog'? I suppose what I am really wondering is, does my attitude towards my dog mean that it will always be *just* me and her? Will people think that my being one half of Miranda And Peggy means that I'm not interested in romantic relationships? If my heart is now fully healed from the break-up, am I choosing craziness over romance?

Uh – oh.

Also, aren't I a bit young for all this? Isn't this whole me-and-the-dog business a bit, well, ageing? Even just cycling around Hammersmith with Peggy in my wicker bicycle basket adds fifteen years at least. I should really be blasting out some Bieber on a ghetto blaster (I mean MP3 player) to counteract.

Not that there's anything wrong with ageing, of course. As you know I love many of the things that being in my forties has brought me. Like being able to engage in conversations which would have bored the twenty-year-old me witless, eg., what's the best way to dry a pair of jeans (tumble drier, banister, or outside line?) or, what to wear to an event in order not to cause a fuss ('smart, smart casual, or smart smart?' 'Smart smart, but not, you know, smart smart'). But all those bonuses notwithstanding, where does all this leave me? I'm exhibiting definite signs of turning into a crazy dog spinster, but apparently I have enough self-awareness to recognize that it's happening, and to rein in my behaviour appropriately. I am falling ever more deeply into my role as one half of Miranda And Peggy, but know perfectly well that what I can get away with in the make-up trailer with Pam Ferris et al. most likely won't wash in Tesco. MDRC, it was really 'all going on', as they say.

Whilst I was mulling and chewing all this over, and generally getting into a bit of a stew, I had a fun life occurrence, which was a catalyst to my decision on where I finally stood on this whole 'to be or not to be dog loon' debate. As a part of my encroaching crazy-dog-ness, I once took Peggy swimming! (A private pool, I should add, not to a public baths to join in with the toddler group or OAP water aerobics, with dog.) I thought it was terribly sad that she couldn't enjoy an activity I loved so much, so I carried her into a swimming pool with me and began to lower her gently into the water. She somehow knew how to doggy paddle, despite never having been in the water before; nature had told her exactly what her brain and legs needed to do in order to survive this water business. So I let go of her, and off she swam, her little nose poking out of the pool, front legs paddling desperately onward.

I was shocked by my surge of love and maternal pride as she doggy-paddled so perfectly. She soon scrambled out and spent the next fifteen minutes zooming back and forth up and down the lawn trying to dry herself, as if someone had given her a line of cocaine. It was genuinely laugh-out-loud funny, a sight from start to finish, my companions (not dog people at all) seemed to agree, and Peggy was happily unharmed. My act of dog-spinster bonkersness, the eccentricity of my relationship with Peggy, was bringing people pleasure. And that, to a certain extent, balances out any weirdness. But not completely. You've got a normal life to live, I reminded myself. Things to do, places to be, and the option to be considered a romantic possibility.

With that, I had made my decision. And it was simply this: Rein it in, Hart, rein it in. I knew this could be treachery to accepting myself fully, but perhaps you need to present as a little, well, presentable, in order to be accepted? Make the effort to appear like a regular functioning human, at least until you've extracted some kind of commitment from your significant other. As I had just been swimming, I likened this conundrum to choosing to purchase a swimming costume with an inbuilt bra at the risk of feeling 'elderly'. Or go *au naturelle*. Not nude, just let the 'puppies' be their unruly selves within a standard costume. I appreciate only women with a large upper circumference may fully understand this analogy. Suffice to say, if you go with the built-in bra you are presenting the world with something that is certainly improved, perkier. But not entirely your reality. But it's better to give yourself that chance than introduce yourself to someone whilst your bosoms look like a pair of melons lumbering about in tights. If you get me.

Oh, Rein it in, Hart, rein it in.

CHAPTER 8

'So Embarrassing'

What was that? What did I just say? 'Rein it in, Hart, rein it in.' Ah, yes. Sage advice there from the Chapter 7 me. Far from reining in my dog lunacy, I immediately plunged straight back into some intensive, locked-up, one-on-one time with Peggy, during which my eccentricity not only thrived but, frankly, blossomed. Had I owned an enormous pair of Y-fronts, I have no doubt that at some point during this period I would have put them on my head, worn a bra on the outside of a jumper and run burbling through a shopping centre throwing Coco Pops at people shouting 'hello, everyone, isn't it marvellous being bonkers? And how bonkers is the word bonkers, bonkers is just bonkers', so bonkers did I go.

But, MDRC, it was a good kind of bonkers, the kind which gets things done, the kind of bonkers (I've said bonkers way too much now, it's sending me . . . bonkers) which is a direct result of a very happy circumstance; I had finished work on *Call the Midwife*, and was writing the third series of my sitcom. I've said this before and I'll say it again, but I couldn't believe my luck to be doing the work that I was doing. It felt like only last week I was praying for series one to work out while simultaneously praying and hoping against hope that my new insane little ball of fluff wasn't going to stage any more poocalypses for as long as she lived. Life was moving on, as it inevitably does, and now I couldn't imagine it without a) my being in regular work, and b) my being the owner, mother, best friend and major life-companion to my marvellous little Peggy.

I'd got a tad more confident in my writing process, and no longer felt the need to pop into Television Centre for meetings quite as often as I did. So I was at liberty to roam. One of the enviable things about writing is that if you really want to, you can do it anywhere. Which as a London-dweller is fantastic. I find London hard to write in, really. Sitting at home alone all day, when everyone else is jumping on the tube to work, and going for lunch with colleagues, and generally being more in the swim of things than I feel I am. I find my imagination tends to run riot, and I weave rich fantasies about how completely fabulous everybody's lives are, how they're all barrelling towards jobs in laugh-a-minute joyful creative offices with 'chill-out areas' and ping-pong tables and a lavish, complimentary canteen (is there anything better than FREE FOOD?) serving cuisines from around the world – a cross between the breakfast buffet of a luxury hotel and the toy shop where Tom Hanks runs up and down the huge piano in *Big*. In this office, it's *always* someone's birthday, and a cake is trundled out at 4 p.m. every day, which is washed down with fistfuls of (calorie-free) M&Ms in big glass bowls, which are magically refilled every night. And everyone emerges at the end of the day feeling happily tired and exhilarated, safe in the knowledge that the work they're doing really matters. They delight in their lives, these blessed, golden commuter-people I see going past my window at eight o'clock every morning.

Of course, I know from my years spent working in offices that this is total rubbish. The majority of office life consists, in my experience, of sitting under strip lights with a vague sense that one should be anywhere else in the world, doing anything other than this. Also, obsessing from 8 a.m. onwards about the hoisin duck wrap you're going to have for lunch from Pret, only to find when you get there that they're all sold out and you're lumbered with a floppy hummus and red pepper from the back of the fridge which, as every meat lover knows, is The Devil's Sandwich. That is the reality most people face. I will, however, always be grateful to my office life for providing me with my love of stationery. I would say it now classes as an actual and official hobby. What Post-it notes can I collect? (Currently using small ones that serve as bookmarks with a dog's head at the top of them. Brilliant, your book or notepad now has little doggies peeking out at you.) What novelty Sellotape holder can I find? (I have one that has a man sitting on a loo and the Sellotape is his loo roll. And the cistern of the loo is a pen-holder. Seriously. It's genius.) I sense I have lost a few of you. Back to my point – stationery aside, I know office life isn't all larks, and calorie-free M&Ms simply don't and won't ever exist. But urban isolation – even with dog – breeds extravagantly delusional trains of thought. And I was jealous of everyone going to work. So I thought it best to get out of town. Mix things up a bit. Roam.

I opted, as it was to be a long-ish period, to do a little house-sitting. Over the course of my writing life, I've become rather partial to a good old house-sit. (Arranged with the owners, I should add – that sounded a bit 'squatty'.) You get to stay in houses way way lovelier than your own (though always a bit of a downer as it makes your home feel like a shit-heap on return), in places you'd never choose to live in permanently but which will do very nicely indeed for a bit of a treat. Also, you get a vague sense of being helpful to the house's owner, and – joy of joys – you get to nose through their cupboards and drawers and learn all about their long-forgotten hobbies (set of scuba-diving equipment, anyone? Hunting rifle? Bowling ball?). Although it can back-fire if you happen upon a stash of fungal infection ointments. Information you didn't want about your friends, thank you. And information that you will now never not think of when you see them. 'Hi, darling, want some fungus . . . hummus . . . hummus, and there's Twiglets although they're quite yeasty . . . I mean . . . cold out, isn't it? Cold sore . . . cole-slaw, let's make some coleslaw . . . !' Nosey-ing never pays, people.

House-Sitting

So off I went, initially to a little cottage in a forest in the middle of the countryside. It was lovely and peaceful, and absolutely perfect for writing. The only downside of such obvious solitude was that, in the middle of February, when the days are short and the winds sharp, my mind began to wander unavoidably in the direction of ghosts, ghouls and other spooky beings. Mad, I know. I'm not a ten-year-old girl; but you try it, before you scoff. You try sitting in a cottage surrounded by pines in the middle of a power cut when your phone's run out of battery and the floorboards make a creaking sound which, late at night when your imagination's beginning to go a bit, sounds slightly like there's a tiny little person underneath them, begging for mercy. But at least I had my faithful friend, Dear Little Peg, to keep me grounded and sane and to keep my spirits up.

Until one night, one dark and stormy night, when I couldn't seem to find her. I looked here, and I looked there, and there she wasn't. It was most disconcerting; all the doors were closed, she couldn't possibly have run off. I sat down for a little nip of something to calm the nerves and gather my thoughts, when the living room curtains suddenly billowed out towards me. I properly jumped out of my skin, screaming, a lot, certain that the flock of fanged ghosts that had clearly eaten Peggy was on its way to get me too, when out burst . . . well, you guessed it. The blooming Pegster herself. I was enormously relieved, and actually ever so slightly cross. Because besides her being a creature I simply loved and adored and loved and adored to look after, she had become my rock. Really. Whatever emotion was rearing itself on any given day, Peggy would be there to help. A bit anxious and lying down next to her, hearing her sleepy little breaths would calm me; a bit blue and a tight cuddle would lift the spirit; happy or excited and picking her up and dancing around the kitchen with her meant I was gleefully sharing it; lonely and I would sit next to her and hold her paw. Peggy and I paw in hand. My rock. During GhostGate, I needed her, next to me, to stroke her soft, reassuring coat. Yet she was not only absent but the cause of the commotion.

Tee hee hee.

213

I decided that my next house-sitting gig should be done in the company of a friend. So I joined forces with my chum, the actress and comedy writer Emma Kennedy, and we went to house-sit for mutual friends together in Henley. Emma was also in the thick of a writing project, so I thought we'd be a good match for one another. What's more, she was also with dog – Emma is the proud owner of a beautiful beagle, Peggy's best friend Poppy. We were both in an incredibly busy patch with our writing, and so when we learnt that the weather forecast for one Thursday was good, we declared it a holiday-day and set off on a grand river adventure: Me, Emma, Peggy and Poppy.

We hired a small but sturdy boat, heaved the dogs on board, and ceremoniously christened ourselves Captain Hart, Lieutenant Peggy, Commander Kennedy and First Seaman Poppy (much to the bemusement of the man we rented our vessel from). We then set off down the river, making sure we were travelling in the opposite direction from the Henley Regatta, which was on during the week of our stay. I don't know if you're familiar with the Henley regatta, MDRC, but it seems to be populated only by the seriously posh (in a red-canvas-trousers-from-Savile-Row-and-a-Mini-Boden-romper-suit-for-the-toddler-sort-of-way), and the seriously sporty – two groups of people I instinctively shy away from on the grounds they make me feel utterly inept on both counts. I end up nervously spitting salmon-and-cucumber canapés in their faces whilst lying about how much exercise I do. I once got in a terribly muddled conversation with a budding Olympian about Kettle Bells, as with no gym-culture references (because gyms are evil and SMELL OF CROTCH), I thought he was talking about a new cheese-based snack to go with Kettle Chips. And the one time I poshed up for a similar kind of summer do, my tiny kitten heels kept getting stuck in the lawn. I would move off, and they would remain. Lazy shoes; very very lazy. Regattas were to be steered clear of.

So off we pottered down the river. And very merrily so, free from the shackles of our laptops. It felt all rather glorious and English. *Swallows and Amazons* meets *Tales of the Riverbank*. It felt the perfect thing to be doing on the one summer day of that year (anyone reading this outside of the UK – as you probably know, our summers last forty-eight hours). And boy was it hot. We were rather worried about the dogs in the hot, shadeless boat, to the extent that I let Peggy have a drink from my water bottle. (I didn't use it again myself, I promise. I realize that doing so is only a few notches down from sharing ice creams with one's pets, or trying to breast-feed them.)

Aside from the heat, the principal challenge seemed to be dealing with the locks and lock keepers. Lock keepers on day-tripper-friendly stretches of the Thames are to me some of the most patient people in the world, faced daily with scores of tourists down from London for the weekend who've most likely never experienced anything more nautical than a bath, yet are now in sole charge of a half-tonne vessel containing their entire family, several litres of barbecue lighter fluid, a toolbox full of dangerous implements they don't know how to use, and anywhere between eighteen and fifty bottles of local real ale. These people (I am afraid that in my experience they're most often male) will stand in the cockpits of their boats wearing 'Captain' hats which their wives bought them from Crew Clothing as a joke, and will sound the horn of their vessel often and seemingly at random, in order to display their mastery of the river. When approaching locks, these men will be desperate to be seen as the lock keeper's equal, so they'll wave extravagantly and bid him a hearty 'ahoy there, fellow mariner' (this guy is actually called Duncan and works in IT, what IS he doing?). This momentary distraction will cause them to mistake the boat's accelerator for some sort of brake, and they'll shoot forwards into a queue of similar boats, causing several families' picnics to fall overboard. They will blame this on 'terrible swells' even though the water is flat as a pancake and there hasn't been any wind for a month. They're a deeply alarming breed.

To freak Duncan out as we queued behind him, Emma googled 'knots' and we proceeded to talk very loudly and assertively about nautical knots, me holding a piece of rope as if I were about to tie a Running Bowline or a Sheepshank. But to the lock keepers we were anxious to show we were different from the macho hordes, so we navigated the locks in a state of constant apology for what terrible seamen we were and how we were probably going to crash into the bank any minute now, sending our poor dogs flying, which lowered the lock keepers' expectations and made it clear that they had to be kind to us. Which they were. We made it through several locks without incident, and cruised on down the river in an elegant fashion. I was rather proud of us. We were beginning to feel at home on the water and I secretly hoped we looked how Maggie Smith and Joan Plowright might have done in the film version of our day out – beguiling, elegant, yet very approachable. I may have been overthinking our look.

Talking of which, quite early on, Emma suggested I put on a hat and big sunglasses to stop myself getting recognized by revellers (good word, 'revellers'; bit medieval, I think) so we could have a complete day away from it all. I was surprised; at this point in my career, I still hadn't quite got the hang of being someone who gets recognized. Whenever people approached me in the street, my first thought was never 'oh, they must have watched my sitcom', more, 'oh no, I've probably got something stuck on my shoe, or in my teeth, or tucked into my pants, or all three'. I heeded Emma's advice and put on a baseball hat and Ray-Bans which made me look a) slightly like a man in a sports inspirational movie who's been brought into the scary local school to rescue the children by starting a softball team, and b) instantly ten times more recognizable than I had been a minute ago. Literally, the second I put on the hat and glasses people started shouting, 'Oi! Miranda! Ahoy, Miranda Hearty' (yes, very good). And then . . . in terms of fame and boating jaunts on the Thames, the very worst thing happened. A full-on Party Boat chugged past; it was mid-afternoon by this point and the Party Boatsters had clearly been at the rum and cokes for a good few hours. One of them recognized me, and alerted her friends, and they all began to chant a wild chorus of 'Such fun!' 'Such fun!', until I was forced to throw a jacket over Peggy to protect her privacy and to protect me from accusations of being the sort of mad person who takes her dog for a day out on a boat. This wasn't an activity that could be classed as 'reining it in', dog-love-wise. I instructed Commander Kennedy to put her foot down and get us into clear water. I was erotically authoritative as Captain Hart – there's an image and you're welcome. Coming across a friendly Party Boat is definitely the celebrity-having-a-quiet-day-out-on-the-river equivalent to being attacked by pirates. I have never known the phrase 'Such fun!' to be infused with 'such menace'.

We reached a quieter stretch of water, and plodded along very happily. Concerns of recognition, work or dog-bonker-ness falling behind us with every beautiful stretch of Thames we passed. Until I started to desperately need a wee. Commander Kennedy, as authoritatively (and erotically) instructed, brought the boat over to the bank, but we couldn't find anywhere to moor up. So – and please bear in mind before you judge us that we are both comedy writers, not masters of reason and logic – Emma gripped on to the grassy bank with her hands, trying to get a purchase on various twigs, stumps, clumps and daffodils. Once she had a daffodil in one hand and molehill in the other, Commander Kennedy declared it safe for me to disembark. Ever the trusting ship-mate, I placed one foot on the bank and lingered for a moment, half on the boat and half off, at which point Emma's daffodil (shockingly) gave way and the boat began to drift away from the bank, forcing me to do a sort of desperate mid-air splits. Fearing for my safety, Peggy panicked and tried to jump out of the boat to rescue me, upon which Emma grabbed her, in the process relinquishing her grip on the bank, which allowed the boat to drift back out into the river. I, of course, fell into the Thames with a substantial splash and squeal. Not only was I shocked to find myself IN the Thames – not ON, but IN; I was also shocked that Emma Kennedy, my supposed friend, saw fit to rescue Peggy, even if that meant my tumbling into a freezing cold, fast-moving river.

Adorably, though, Peggy was completely terrified by the prospect of my being decanted into the foaming deep, and barked hysterically in an attempt to summon up a rescue squad. She was right to be scared, frankly, as I'd only been in for thirty seconds when I found myself face to face with an angry swan which, when one is bobbing about at sea level, is as horrifying as being confronted by a dinosaur who hasn't eaten for a week. I was in a heady state of combined panic and hysterics as I swam away from the hissing swan – why is a swan hiss quite so sinister?! I sensed the situation was hilarious but could only half go there – was I going to get recognized, was I going to get bitten by a swan, was I going to die of Thames water poisoning, was I going to get sucked under the boat and – more to the point – how ON EARTH was I going to get from the water back on to the boat? The makers of small pleasure craft do not consider this when manufacturing their boat-lets. These vessels are almost impossible to mount from the water, and I can't have been the first person overboard. I simply couldn't heave myself up.

The hissing swan then started to come for me at quite a pace, which in turn caused such a burst of adrenaline that I found myself scrabbling up the riverbank to safety like a Ninja. Commander Kennedy was now without a skipper and had to navigate solo back to the bank to pick me up. A tricky manoeuvre, but it gave me the chance to do the wee I still so desperately needed. There wasn't the cover of a tree or bush, and by the time Emma and I had discussed whether facing the river or mooning would be less horrifying if I was spotted, I just had to go. And indeed, as I did – you guessed it – the boat of aforementioned revellers loomed into view. Cue a massive but sarcastic cheer. The sort of cheer you'd give a footballer scoring a spectacular own goal in the final thirty seconds of the FA Cup final. And of course, once you start weeing you just have to stay there and keep going, there isn't much you can do about it. I was giving them, shall we say, an eye-full, whilst sporting the drowned-rat look. By which I mean a drenched woman whose wet white T-shirt was clinging to her nude day-bra. The only way I could now resemble Maggie Smith would be as a more dishevelled and stinking version of *Lady in the Van*.

I was less worried about the smell and more worried about the look. I know a nude-coloured bra is sensible under a white outfit, but when it clings through a wet T-shirt and you have large female human orbs . . . PDRC, it looked like she was hiding two leather footballs. I had to stop Poppy tackling her because she really wanted to play with Captain Miranda's 'balls'. Tee hee.

I had to really calm Poppy down quite a lot on the trip actually. She had never dealt with such levels of embarrassment before and kept trying to throw herself in the river, shouting 'I need it to end, please let it stop.' I stepped up my duty as Lieutenant Peggy, told her I had dealt with way way WAY more tricky situations, and reminded First Seaman Poppy that the Captain and Commander needed us. I have said it before, I will say it again, without us, they are nothing. *attempts to salute with paw but falls over*

Once back on our humble vessel we became completely hysterical about the whole shebang, which meant before long
Commander Kennedy wanted a wee. I refused to let her. I
had had enough of these shenanigans and knew that the next
boat that came along would invariably have a paparazzi
photographer in it. Plus I didn't deem Emma's legs long enough
for the task. We considered me planking betwixt boat and
shore and Emma crawling across me before we thankfully
rejected the notion as INSANE. As we calmed down, I reflected
on what had happened and I turned to my supposed friend.

'Hang on. You chose to save Peggy over me. I repeat – you
chose to save Peggy, the *dog*, rather than Miranda, the *human*.
You left me in the river to get murdered by a swan.'

Midshipman Kennedy – I'd justifiably demoted her –
shrugged.

'Welcome Miranda to the ultimate, albeit slightly irrational, world of dog ownership. We should all really be
awarded a badge.'

I understood. I would've proudly worn the badge of the
ultimate dog-ownership bond. The level at which the bond
is so strong you realize that you might actually jump off the
back of that moving ferry to save your dog-let. Those little
doggy eyes are a drug. Those 'what's happening? I'm scared!'
eyes, which force you to do whatever it takes to help them,
at whatever cost (best friend being murdered by a swan).

We arrived back, mightily proud of our day out on the river,
and glad that it was over. As if the Party Boat and dunking
humiliations weren't enough shame for one day, we took a
slight, accidental detour on the way home and found ourselves
perilously close to the area where the Henley regatta was taking
place. Our strange, awkward little put-put boat with two dogs
on the stern deck and me at the helm, green and slimy with

Thames water, juddered past rows of sleek wooden vessels, complete with deckchairs and men in Panama hats and women smoking cigarettes through slim black cigarette holders, like ladies in a Noel Coward play. We managed to turn around mere seconds before we crossed the start line with the Olympic rowers. If this were a film, we would have triumphed against the odds, winning Olympic gold, and been hailed as national heroes, but alas all that actually happened is that Commander Kennedy swore a lot and we safely if inelegantly navigated our way back to shore, where we recovered with a nice quiet sit-down, a sandwich and a bottle of wine. Each.

I wish I could say, MDRC, that that incident was the last time I was ever put in the position of compromising my dignity and safety for the sake of a dog, but alas, that would be a lie. Days later something arguably even worse happened. The house we were staying in was rather swish, to say the least, and at the bottom of the garden was a bridge you could cross to a little island in the Thames; on the island was a small pool and a Jacuzzi. Embracing the glamorous LA feel of the set-up, one evening, alone and feeling a bit summer holiday-ish, I went down for a Jacuzzi wearing just my pants. (Less of a glamorous LA look.) It was a private island surrounded and sheltered by high reeds; there was no one around . . . what could go wrong? Mid-soak, I realized that Peggy wasn't with me. Not that I was going to bung her in the Jacuzzi, but she's always around, follows me everywhere. I switched the Jacuzzi off and heard some frantic barks. I was worried. What if she'd fallen in the river, or got trapped in some sort of sucking mud?

The barking got louder, more intense. Panicked, I got up – topless lest we forget – on the edge of the Jacuzzi and bellowed, 'PEGGY! *PEGGY!*' like a bare-chested Amazon warrior-ess. No sign. I leapt out of the Jacuzzi and rushed back over the little bridge. Unfortunately, and sadly I can say typically, I heard a ripple of suppressed laughter as a party of twelve-year-olds in canoes paddled under the bridge, no more than twenty feet away from my bare bazookas and oh-so-startled face. I like to think the teacher took the opportunity to educate them, something about anatomy/eccentric people/the lengths that women will go to shield their dogs from harm, but this may be wishful thinking. I simply thank God that they were in kayaks so hadn't brought their camera-phones. Hopefully they assumed I was some sort of cool tribeswoman doing a *National Geographic* photoshoot. Possible. Peggy, it turned out, had not been able to follow me over the bridge as the little gate must have shut behind me before she had the chance to follow. She was safe. Her barks were simply the worry of not being with her owner.

Peggy opens her eyes from the tight sleepy ball she was in, on the inside of Miranda's discarded coat Oh, Peggy's lovely lovely reader chum, I do so hate being separated from my owner. I mean, I really really really properly hate it. I just feel completely lost. And really really scared. I always dread the moment she gets her house keys, puts on her smelly trainers and her too tight leather jacket, and then turns to me and says 'stay there'. More words I understand due to the super cleverness that is the Pegsteroo.

Whenever we are at the front door my little heart thumps really fast in my chest because I so so SO hope I will be going with her. But there is always the chance *those two nasty words come my way, and then I know I can't go adventuring with her.*

It's why when she does get the lead out or she says to me 'yes, you're coming' with her silly gummy smile (have you noticed how much gum is revealed when she smiles or laughs, as much as a baby, tee hee), I go really majorly hyper. I know I am meant to be sitting still for her to put the lead on, but I am SO wound up, with joy and relief and excitement of where we might be going, and I just HAVE to move. I can't help it. Even if it's sort of on-the-spot pick up and put down of my pawsies, like a kind of dressage move! My tail ends up in complete control of me too; it not only wags, but goes in sort of really massive circles. I actually find that a bit embarrassing. It just won't stop. I look like a toy that has been wound up and like my tail is a helicopter.

And, PDRC, I can't tell you how sad I feel, I mean really really sad, when I have to stay at home on my own. Not only because I will miss her, and I worry when she will come back, and I don't like being on my own and often can't move from the door mat, and because she sometimes leaves 80s power ballads on and a girl can only take so much 80s music, but because I worry about her. I really really do. She needs me to protect her. I like to keep an eye, AT ALL TIMES.

But actually if I am really really honest, I just miss her. I feel like a part of me is missing when she isn't around. Like my whole reason to be just vanishes. It's really horrible. Sometimes it's OK if I go with the dog walker I now really like, or Miranda's sister – she has children who secretly give me bits of their food at mealtimes – but I always always always really really much prefer being with my tall-lady-owner-who-sometimes-gets-mistaken-for-a-man. *buries head in paws, slightly embarrassed*

So, there I was, pretending to rein myself in, trying to conceal from the world at large that I was a full-on crazy dog spinster. And yet somehow I found myself plunging head-first into the Thames, and standing wet and topless on the riverbank bellowing my dog's name at a party of children in canoes. 'As long as I keep my insanity hidden from the public view, then it'll be fine. It'll be a secret, between me, Peggy, other dog owners, and a handful of extravagantly eccentric, animal-loving members of the show-biz community.' That's what I thought. But it seemed circumstances were conspiring to push my dog madness out into the open. I wonder if a lot of dog owners feel like this. And by dog owners I mean otherwise normal people who have a strangely intense bond with their pet, not the sort who wear T-shirts with their animals' faces on them, for I think that's crossing a line. I wonder if they feel that they're a bit odd, and need to hide it. Pretend that they don't really care for their dogs, or that they just care about them the normal amount, just enough to stop the RSPCA getting involved, when really they know full well that they'd throw themselves off battlements if it meant getting home in time to give Bowser the bulldog his tea. That they really are no different to children in our affection.

Are we all like this? And are we all, perhaps, pointlessly fighting the same battle in trying to hide it? Should we just give up and let it all out in the open, and wander round with our dogs in slings, talking loudly about feeding schedules? Are we all, underneath, exactly like the extreme dog owners, the dog-T-shirt-wearing nutters? Do we only judge them because we can see ourselves in them, and fear the truths they show us? I was stewing again: was I hiding my true self and trying to conform? How free should one be?

Back Home

Back in London, seemingly aware of my growing public profile, Peggy went out of her way to embarrass me. Even more so than usual. Her greatest crime was attempting to follow a strange man home from the park. I shall repeat this, MDRC, a strange MAN. Because she thought that he was me. A man. Admittedly, he was wearing very similar jeans and jumper to the ones I was wearing, but really. As she trotted alongside him, I could see he was becoming confused, cross and a little bit frightened by this bichon frise following him out of the park. I finally caught up with them and said, 'I'm ever so sorry, I think she thought that you were me', and the man had the balls to look mightily offended by this. HE was offended! I think any sane person would agree that I am the wounded party here. Particularly as he was the most hirsute man I think I've ever seen: 'tache, full beard going down his neck to join his chest hair. Oh yes, he basically had a hair snood and Peggy thought I was he. The pitfalls of being six foot one. Plus side – I can reach high shelves, and if I wanted to play basketball I would be a sure-fire hit at it, so in your face, petite ladies, who would never be mistaken for a hairy gentleman!

While I'm on a 'oh my giddy aunt, you are so embarrassing' rant, Peggy has a dreadful tendency to get bored of games before I do. She has often made me look like a fool in the park as we (I) enjoy a bit of throw and catch with a stick or ball. She will do a couple of turns with contagious glee, then I will make some animalistic high-pitched whoop as I throw it again, start running after it, only to see Peggy has declared the game over, and begun washing her paws. Making it look as if patient dog has been throwing stick for idiot owner. Any chance I could have of connecting amorously with other park-goers = over. Then there's the food-stealing incidents. I have previously mentioned the mini-sausage thefts from a family picnic. But there was also the removal of a Tupperware box of chicken drumsticks from the open rucksack of one of the lads playing basketball at the hoops. I saw it happening and simply fast-walked away like a baddie in a silent film. A fellow dog walker shouting 'isn't that your dog?' after me as I played deaf, my fast walk getting more and more mincy as I attempted 'stealth'. Of course, once Peggy had finished her drumstick, she ran straight after me for everyone to see she was indeed mine. I considered continuing with the pretence, maybe handing her over to the park police as lost property, but I couldn't see where it would end.

Mind you, this was a notch down, embarrassment-wise, from Peggy stealing a soft ball. From a toddler. Peggy loves toddlers, for they often drop food and generally smell of rusks. She'll hover around and follow them in the hope of a treat. But in this instance it wasn't food; she decided the bright squeaky squishy ball this toddler was holding must be hers. She jumped up to try and remove it from his little hands. And cue crying. I rushed up to apologize to mother and son and, as I was about to secure the peace by handing the ball back, Peggy weed on it, thereby marking it very much as her own. Like you might lick a cupcake at a children's party. (Not that I have done that. I have.) Incidents like this were now rendered a gazillion times more embarrassing than they would otherwise have been by the whole getting-recognized situation. Having a dog was a flag of conspicuousness I was still getting used to, let alone fame.

Right, I might have to get off my high horse here. Metaphorical horse. Imagine a dog actually on a horse. Though Miranda did once place me on top of a Great Dane which I didn't find funny AT ALL. And I also don't like it when she puts me in swings; it is also really NOT FUNNY. She thinks I like it but I think my scared face obviously looks like my happy face, because I find it TOTALLY TERRIFYING.

But, to get off the metaphorical horse, it turns out, PDRC, that fame-wise it IS Miranda who people want to see, not the amazing Pegaramer, the best dog IN THE WORLD. It makes no sense to me whatsoever. Who would want to spend time with someone so disappointingly un-fluffy?

It's all really very peculiar. I don't get it. If I met Beethoven or the dog from The Artist *I wouldn't scream at him. I mean, we are all just dogs. Miranda is just a normal – well, you know, normal-ish – person and very very embarrassing to be around. What IS the fuss?*

And can I just say it may be difficult for her to get recognized in public but I bear quite a brunt. Do you have ANY idea how annoying it is to be stopped on the way to the park when you've heard that the poodle-who-looks-like-Michael-Ball is going to be there and you're keen to get a bit of flirting in? Or how very embarrassing it is to be photographed in the basket of Miranda's bicycle when one is three weeks from one's last visit to the groomers' and looking a little bit tufty around the edges? The other dogs never have to put up with this. And a bicycle basket – the INDIGNITY. A side car, maybe, but not a basket. *trots off, does a delicate little burp*

Despite how massively embarrassing some moments with Peggy were, and how nuts I was becoming as her owner, letting her go, giving her up, having her whisper it – *rehomed* just wasn't going to happen. Never. No way, siree. I feel shame that at the beginning of our story I even considered it, considered I might have made a bad decision. First of all because, well, please turn to any relevant pictures in this book and look how lovely she is, and second, she was teaching me so much. Pumping me full of the sort of life lessons which people probably spend years in therapy trying to figure out.

My next Peggy lesson was one of the most important and, for me, one of the most challenging: Simply – to live in the moment. To let go of any attachment to the future – anticipation, fear, anything – and appreciate the present. Dogs are so fiercely in the moment, and so ready to delight in it, that I found I couldn't help but learn from mine. Around the time of the Henley trip, I was deep in anxiety about series three; what if it was awful compared to the other two? What if it finished me off, career-wise? What if it just plain wasn't funny? What if the move to BBC One put it under too much pressure? I was tumbling down this neurotic rabbit hole once while on a walk with Peggy in West Sussex. I'd deliberately chosen a route that took in a bluebell wood. My secondary school was surrounded by bracken and bluebells and I was hoping that the smell would conjure up my schooldays and jerk me back into gratitude, remind me how many of my dreams had come true since that time, and just how fortunate I was to live the life that I was living. Plus, I love bluebells and all the spring beauty they stand for. But I couldn't manage it. I couldn't get out of my own toxic head.

I had brought my phone with me to take photos of the bluebell carpet, but became a slave to it instead, replying to emails head down, fretting. Then I caught Peggy out of the corner of my eye. I saw how she was behaving; completely absorbed in her surroundings, responding sharply to everything around her, every smell, every sight, every new and wonderful sound. She was so committed to the landscape that she almost became a part of it, and I *knew* that the only way I could be happy was if I did the same; forced myself to be where I was, relax into the now. I realized I had been shuffling along emailing and missed the best bluebell wood. What an idiot. It dawned on me then how much I have missed in life. Truly. I have missed so many moments and memories by being stuck in my head worrying, 'what if this?', 'what if that?' What a BIG FAT WASTE OF TIME. For a big old worrier like me, this was huge stuff. Huge and gentle and wonderful, and all from Peggy. All before I had heard the now known and accepted word 'Mindfulness', which is essentially to what I refer. I can still see the detail of those bluebells now; the smell. So strong. All because I watched Peggy, saw her in-the-moment-ness and copied. Well, not literally copied. I didn't get on my hands and knees and start marking my territory by excreting on tree stumps.

For all my neurotic overthinking of 'crazy dog spinsterhood', the fact was that my relationship with Peggy had deepened as we'd shared experiences and grown up a bit together. You see, what was happening was I was wanting to connect with someone deeply. Share life. I had to admit it, I was wondering, for the first time in absolutely ages, whether or not I might be ready to be with someone again. And by 'someone', I mean a male someone who is definitely not a dog, someone who would be interested in me in a romantic sense, if you catch my drift (and if you don't, then HOW ON EARTH COULD I MAKE IT ANY MORE OBVIOUS, GUYS?).

What clued me up as to the fact that I might at last be ready for a bit more activity in that department was bumping into an ex in, of all places, a shoe shop. I was in that oh-so-strange condition unique to the shoe shop of wearing two completely incongruous shoes. The shoe I'd walked in in – in this case a sturdy walking boot – and the shoe I was trying on, an oh-so-dainty ballet pump. Good word, 'pump'. Hard to say it without going slightly overboard on each 'p'. 'PumP'. So, yes, I was wearing one ballet flat and one walking boot. And to test the possible PumP out I was walking up and down the shop practising a strange, rolling stride that the three-inch height difference between them demanded, when I glanced to my right and saw . . . my ex.

Rather than just quietly accepting that this is a bit undig-
nified, but never mind, it happens to everyone, nothing to
get in a flap about, I decided to 'improve' the situation by
slipping into what I can only describe as a highly stylized
'rap walk'. The sort of rolling, edgily lolloping gait so beloved
of men in cheesy 1990s hip-hop videos. Goodness only knows
what was going on in my head; I think it must have been
something along the lines of 'oh No, NO NO, there's my ex,
and because it's my ex it's essential I have to portray that my
life is perfect and wonderful and cool and carefree, so I think
the only way to do that is to do a humorous "rap walk", oh
No, NO NO, this has gone really wrong but I'd better stick
with it, HELP'. It's human nature, isn't it, to make sure you
present as beautiful and alluring and essentially miss-able as
possible to an ex-partner? For some reason, even if you like
them, you still want them to go home and cry their eyes out
because − naturally − you are the only woman they, nay
mankind, could ever love. With that in mind, I was determined
to make something of the different-height shoe walk. And
because I was a bit well known by now, I thought somehow
I could endear and get away with it. So I . . . wait for it . . .
I rapped. Yup. Yes. Uh-uh. I rapped. I freestyle-rapped in a
shoe shop, doing crazy 'hip-hop' hand gestures and spitting
out rhymes like 'Hey hey trying on a shoe/While I'm getting
over you/Skip skip skip to the loo/Need a poo . . . '
Horrendous. Beyond horrendous.

My ex watched me through the glass with the expression,
I imagine, Victorian people had on their faces when going to
visit Crazy Uncle Kester in the asylum. Sorrow, bewilderment,
pity. A small crowd formed around him. Weirdly buoyed by
this, I could have gone on for hours had the shop manager
− a kind lady, just doing her job − not dragged me away from

the window display. I was glad she did, although she manhandled me a bit and I became stuck to her. Now, I don't know if this is something which just happens to me, but I have been stuck to people more than once or twice. Or rather, something I'm wearing gets stuck to something they're wearing until there we are, locked together in a terrible embrace. In this instance, my necklace got stuck to the sleeve of her woolly cardigan, leading to huge mutual awkwardness, me with my face nestling in her armpit – never good, face in a pit – and both of us trying in vain to free ourselves. I ended up using this incident in the first finale of my sitcom and remember an awkward conversation with the director who asked how she thought I could make it believable considering it's highly unlikely to happen in real life.

Anyway. That was where my ex saw me: in odd shoes, in the window of a shop, nose nestled in a stranger's armpit, having just given one of the top five worst hip-hop impressions in the history of the genre (I'm sure that there've been at least three worse performances on *Top of the Pops*; don't forget, we have lived through the 8os). Instead of feeling scarred by the public humiliation of the situation, I felt a wave of sadness, aloneness. I felt somehow lost. I didn't want to get back together with my ex, but I knew I was finally ready to consider a relationship with a two-legged creature. I knew I was ready because, I had finally, MDRC, despite all, accepted myself.

Peggy leaps up on to Miranda's lap, nestles into her armpit as she writes This was NOT what I wanted to hear. Well, all right, I have to say I do really want it for her if she really thinks it would make her happy, but I did think it would take a lot lot lot longer than that.

Because now that means that some sort of BOYFRIEND might appear. I will REFUSE to share her. I will sit between her and her yucky boyfriend at all times, on the sofa and on the bed, and I will growl if he ever tries to sniff her bottom or whatever disgusting things it is that humans do to show affection. And I will try and spook him out of the house by barking suddenly whenever he moves, and I will plant half-chewed bones in his clothes. Tee hee hee. He won't last long . . . I might even wee in his shoes. NAUGHTY PEGGY. Tee hee hee.

I was happy if people labelled me the crazy dog lady. Or, if you remember my unusual analogy, and frankly, how could you forget: I was happy to be seen in a swimming costume without an inbuilt bra. We all seem to assume we need to try to fit a mould of what we think we ought to be to attract someone. But of course it's the opposite. It's being our true selves that makes us lovable. That way there are no surprises and no compromises and no fears when you enter a relationship. You love yourself. You have an inner confidence. But it makes us vulnerable; someone might not be able to accept the bonkers bits. It's worth the risk, though. If I am meant to meet someone I will. I was still trusting of a higher power who had a plan for me.

But hang on, the good old stress voice chipped in: if it wasn't meant to be, would Peggy be enough?

WHAT?! Would I be enough? HOW RUDE! OF COURSE I would be enough.

Oh Miranda, I love you so so SO much, don't leave me or share me. I am enough. I PROMISE I am. Quick, do something, Peggy. OK, here are the top five reasons why I am enough:

1. Beautiful soft curly coat which makes me look as if I'm surrounded by a light, pretty cloud.

2. Amazingly cheerful personality to counterbalance your negativity, ooh, ooh, and my ability to live in the moment.

3. No poo apocalypses since 2009. And I put up with your wind.

4. UNSWERVING loyalty, to the point that I am even loyal to people who look a bit like you (I promise not to mistake you for a man again).

5. Michael Ball thinks I'm pretty.

See? Miranda, are you listening? MIRANDA! I am SO TOTALLY enough. Miranda. . . ?

CHAPTER 9

Enough?

Well, MDRC, we really are wrestling with the big questions, aren't we? There I was, promising you a jaunty romp through the world of dog ownership – leads, poop-a-scoops, sitting and jumping and the like   and here I am addressing the sort of questions that The Great Philosophers themselves were unutterably stumped by. What is love? What is 'enough'? What do we need from others in order to be happy? What's the jolly old meaning of life, eh? And just as the great Aristotle did before me, I'm addressing them through stories of getting my face stuck to a shoe-shop assistant's armpit and inadvertently flashing to twelve-year-olds on a canoeing trip. Which is a damn sight more than Aristotle ever managed. So I left us hanging with the conundrum, 'If I never fall in love again, might my relationship with Peggy be enough?'

After posing that, I went for a walk (twice round the park

then home, via a quick petrol-station pause for some fruit pastilles), had a meal (jacket potato and greens, I share because I am quite the sweet-before-savoury maverick), and gave the whole business of the dog-human bond versus the human-human bond a proper mull-round in the old Hart head. It was a thorough old mental ramble, I'll tell you for nothing. I even got to thinking: what's the purpose of relationships? *Those* kinds of relationships, I mean, the ones which get people chasing each other through airports in the closing minutes of romantic comedies. Putting the whole notion of (mouth it please, we're British) S-E-X to one side for a bit, what do we *really* gain from the old lifelong companionship, love'n'marriage business? And could you – perhaps – just perhaps, MDRC, get an almost-adequate substitute from an excellent relationship with a really really great dog? A dog like, say, Peggy?

Oh my golly golly me. Humans are ALL OVER THE PLACE. Relationship this. Self-acceptance that. Live-in-the-moment the other. Aristotle my arse. *licks arse*

If I am really honest (because remember I am a classy theatrical of a dog), I think this book is the equivalent of Pets Win Prizes, *with a couple of lines from* Eat, Pray, Love *thrown in. Vaguely amusing, bit uplifting if you're into that kind of thing. The perfect stocking-filler for a premenstrual pet owner in the throes of a mid-life crisis. Just saying it how I see it.*

If I am even more really honest with you, PDRC, I am actually beginning to feel a bit cross about this book now. Even if it might be my launch into celebrity. I have been planning a reality show. If anyone is going to be the Kim Kardashian of the dog world, it is I.

But I feel a bit cross because we still seem to be harking on about whether I'm 'enough'. I am MORE than enough. I mean, who else could she give little bits of digestive biscuits to in exchange for a paw-to-hand high-five which I took three goes to get because I am SO CLEVER. She wouldn't get those kind of laughs with some horrid two-legged boyfriend thing.

And if she did get some sort of horrid two-legged boyfriend thing, then I just KNOW they'd be curled up on the sofa feeding each other marshmallows doing that RIDICULOUS thing that human couples do where the women are all lovely and kissy and fawny to the men, who are so odd-smelling and lazy and car-obsessed and DO NOT DESERVE SUCH FAWNING – while poor little Peggy is shut in the garden, little shivery nose pressed up against the glass, whining, unheard, unloved, cast aside and left to pine alone. So, yeah, urh, NO THANKS. I'll be keeping a really really beady eye on the outcome of this chapter, PDRC. Excuse me whilst I settle right down to do so. *gets up, runs in several small circles, sits down, gets up again, runs in one final circle (her tiniest yet and going in the opposite direction), and sits down again. For good this time. Honest. Oh no, hang on, a final circle. Plomp. And exhale*

Human-Human Versus Dog-Human Relationships

I thought best to frame my 'are relationships worth it?' rumination by spelling out the pros and cons of human-human relationships, and dog-human relationships. I'm fascinated to tell you, and I hope you'll be fascinated to hear, that with the notion of (mouth it) S-E-X quite firmly disregarded, human-human relationships and dog-human relationships seem to be almost level pegging (or should I say pegg-y-ing). In many respects, dog-human relationships actually seem superior. I shall explain forthwith via a natty vertical verbal storage system. Otherwise known as a list.

1. **Dogs don't talk back.** And they listen for as long as you need to get it all off your chest. They don't make annoying suggestions to fix it. And most importantly they don't pretend to listen whilst actually dreaming about being friends with Jeremy Clarkson and Chris Evans and going on a driving holiday together in Eastern Europe for hilarious laddish adventures. When dogs are listening, they are just listening. At worst they may have a quick scratch down below. If your partner does that, you KNOW they aren't listening.

2. **They never roll their eyes at you.** For example, when you describe last week's episode of *Strictly Come Dancing* to them in loving detail (with actions, of course). Nope, they think everything you say is valid and interesting. They never roll their eyes at all, in fact, unless they're having some sort of quite adorable rolling-around-on-the-ground-trying-to-scratch-a-difficult-itch festival. And no one wants to see a human partner doing that.

3. **You can put them in the garden when they smell.** You can also do this with a boyfriend, I concede, but they have a habit of climbing over the back fence and running off to the pub, where they'll get

drunk and phone you and shout, 'Why did you shut me in the garden?!' before staggering home smelling worse than they did before.

4. **You can shove a dog in the front basket of your bicycle.** Very useful if you want some company on your way to the shops. Try this with a human and you can get arrested. Plus taking your partner shopping is an absolute no-no. It's not a bonding experience to watch your partner changing outfits under strip lighting. It is an experience likely to end in you having a half-naked shouting match in front of strangers. Which is fabulous if that's what you're into, but please count me out. And sadly you can't tie your boyfriend up outside a shop and tell them to stay there whilst you go about your business.

5. **You can put a dog in the back seat of a car without it criticizing your driving.** It will only make a sound if it fears that it's in immediate, mortal danger. It

doesn't question the route you have chosen, or shout at you for not taking those lights, and it doesn't say things like, 'Mind that woman', AS IF YOU HAVEN'T SEEN HER. 'I have seen her, I have OBVIOUSLY seen her.'

6. **You are able to forgive their bad breath.** Or even don't mind it at all. They are a dog, you expect their breath to be a little on the stinky side. If a human partner's breath smells, then unforgivable. Total deal-breaker. Inconsiderate. And unnecessary. They have access to toothpaste. Mouthwash! All the dentists they can handle! Their breath ends up being beyond irritating. Much like any heavy breathing or chewing at breakfast. Peggy doesn't even annoy me when she loudly slurps water from her bowl; in fact, I find it utterly charming and cute.

   There are three more and I have left the best till last. For these are the *key* reasons for the brilliance of a dog-human relationship.

7. **Dogs are genuinely thrilled by the sight of you first thing in the morning.** And not just because they want you to make them a cup of tea. They wake up and are little bundles of joy, straight off the blocks. They leap up to give you a kiss, not fazed by any sleep dribble or kebab in your hair – actually they are delighted by any dinner that might happen to still be adhering to your person. They are beyond excited to spend another day with you. They don't need three cups of coffee before they

stop stomping and grumping and consider giving you a tired, slightly limp wet peck on the cheek to avoid your breath (I know, I am a hypocrite and I of course also sometimes fall victim to 'Breath Of Hell').

8. **Dogs only ever follow you around in a non-annoying, actually quite sweet way.** When a bloke's trailing you round the kitchen because he's bored, it's generally so irritating that you want to hit him in the face with a saucepan. With a dog – adorable.

9. **You can stroke a dog without it misconstruing the physical contact as an offer of (keep mouthing) s-e-x.** Let's say no more.

10. **I've got nothing left to say but it's annoying not ending a list on number 10.**

On an emotionally meatier level, a dog can only break your heart so much. In fact, it can only really break it by dying. As far as I'm aware, dogs lack the capacity for betrayal. I am the only person Peggy wants to spend all her time with. Me and the odd person who looks freakishly like me (I'm talking to you, hair snood man in the park with what must be brilliant legs). You'll only ever have to compromise so much with a dog. You might have to move its basket into the conservatory or make room in the cupboard for a box of Bonios, but you'll never have to trade up to a Ford Escort and move to Buxton to be nearer its parents. You'll never argue in John Lewis about what tog duvet you should get. There'll be no, 'You say you want a thicker tog but then you complain of being hot in the night.' You'll never argue about who has the car keys. 'You were the last one to use the car, where did you last put the keys, RETRACE YOUR STEPS', and get short shrift in return. You'll never have to have a difficult conversation with a dog. You can lie to a dog without it being any kind of moral issue: 'Yes, Peggy, we're going for a lovely walk, NOT to the groomers'.' You never expect too much from them. You never get let down. With a dog you can experience affection, fun, the sense of being absolutely needed by a creature you've chosen as your own, whilst bypassing the sharp end of human relationships. It's win-win.

But, I wondered, does avoiding the sharp end of human relationships mean missing out on the really good stuff? Intimacy, emotional connection, the thrill of being really known and accepted by someone else? Authentic emotional depth, MDRC. I didn't know. I was especially confused by one particular incident from my time with Peggy, which seemed to prove to me that the bond I feel with her runs quite cavernously deep; that I feel things for her which never in a million years did I believe I could for a mutt.

*Who is she calling a mutt? *looks behind her, no dog there* ME?! How completely and totally ridiculous. LOOK AT ME! I come from a long line of pedigree bichon-frise theatricals. I mean, REALLY.*

I call this tale The Terrible Tale of the Thames Near-Miss. If this were to be filmed it would be a redemptive Sunday afternoon sob-fest, in which I'd be played by Meryl Streep, wearing grey and keening.

The Terrible Tale Of The Thames Near-Miss

So, please again make yourself comfortable – tea, coffee, kale smoothie, Quality Street, steak; literally whatever floats your comfort-boat – for The Terrible Tale Of The Thames Near-Miss. One brisk autumn afternoon, Peggy and I were out on a walk by the river in Kew. Every Monday, after a studio sitcom recording the night before, I chose a different place to take her for a walk. It would not only burn off some adrenaline still latent in my system after a physical three-hour record the night before, but also distract me from thinking of all the things I felt I could have done better, or indeed what tomorrow was bringing as regards the next episode.

This particular Monday I had chosen Kew Gardens, where I had never been before, I am ashamed to say. Sadly they don't allow dogs, but I found a lovely section of the Thames towpath nearby to stroll. All was well; we were enjoying the path, mindfully observing the little ecosystems in and around the river. Dear little birds nesting on islands here and there, the leaves on the trees just beginning to turn. The gentle glories of nature. We were walking in unison, cherishing the deep understanding between owner and beloved dog. Then, suddenly, Peggy saw a duck in the river.

I'd forgotten that Peggy was so very fond of ducks, and indeed that proximity to ducks might be any kind of an issue. But all of a sudden Peggy darted away from me and leapt down the bank of the river in keen pursuit of one of these waddlers. Please bear in mind that this is the London portion of the Thames, so the 'bank' consisted of a steeply sloping concrete wall leading to a tiny strip of muddy, gravelly 'beach'. The sort of 'beach' you'd go on holiday to if you were a character in *Trainspotting*. Initially, it was pretty funny. Peggy on the grubby little beach barking at the duck, me laughing at Peggy from twenty or thirty feet above. I assumed that Peggy would climb back up in a minute, and we'd continue on our merry way. Then I realized that Peggy *couldn't* climb back up the concrete bank. It was steep, it was slidey, and she had no way to get any kind of purchase. Starting to worry a bit, I walked on along the towpath, calling to her so she would follow below, hoping we'd find a nice muddy verge for her to scramble up.

MDRC, we didn't. Instead, we found that as we travelled further along the river, the big concrete verge continued – imagine the downward-facing portion of a forty-foot ski jump, grey and dirty – while the little strip of beach got progressively narrower and narrower, until it was less than a foot wide. Water lapped at Peggy's feet. I remembered how strong the Thames tides were. If she didn't get back to the towpath soon, she'd be swept away down the river. And I don't think she would survive that. She was still following me faithfully, evidently completely convinced that I'd lead her to safety. But I could tell that she was in distress.

A few more strides on with no sign of this concrete wall ending and I was equally distressed. Her panicked little face looking up at me as she bravely tried to follow me as the Thames lapped at her paws was too much to bear. The tide was literally coming in before my eyes. And HER eyes, MDRC. Imagine. She was giving me the saddest doggy eyes there are – the desperate, lost 'oh I am so frightened and helpless' eyes. It was all too awful. I suddenly saw some people walking along the towpath towards me. I was so relieved, and called out to them, crying by now, 'Help! Help! My dog is down there, she's going to drown!' They ignored me. Normally, this is the point where I'd say something like 'of course they ignored me, crazy lady shouting at her dog, etc' but actually, to be serious for a moment, how dare they? How dare they just ignore a fellow human, clearly in genuine distress? Would a word of comfort, a small gesture of solidarity, have been so difficult for them?

Just as I thought humanity was irredeemably broken and Peggy was lost to me, our white knight approached, in the form of a very kindly gentleman. He wasn't riding bare-back or bare-chested upon a horse as you might have ideally liked your white knight to have presented himself. If I am perfectly honest he was wearing grey flannel trousers, a sort of plastic shoe and had a carrier bag with three Pot Noodles in it. But I cared not a jot; he was my knight. He not only stopped to sympathize with my plight, but discovered a bit further down the path a very rickety old ladder attached to the concrete wall that led directly to Peggy.

We had to move fast; Peggy was now shivering against the wall, at times the water swelling right up above her legs, nearly carrying her away. I tried to climb down the ladder but, even with his help, pretty quickly succumbed to vertigo, proper vertigo of the wibbly-legged, whole-world-spinning panic-attack variety. Our white knight, whose name I don't know but he looked to me a bit like a Colin, bravely went down in my place. Time was of the essence. I knew that one big surge of water and she would be gone. And I was experiencing one big surge of love so intense for this animal that I just could not let this happen.

Thank goodness for 'Colin'. He reached the bottom and stood in the water – *in,* he really was a hero – but Peggy, damn her, wouldn't let him pick her up. She barked at him, terrified. Clearly she'd trusted quite enough for one day, what with all the following me blindly along an ever-narrower beach to what must have felt to be an almost-certain death. She looked at him and barked and yelped and I screamed down at her from the bank with serious desperation, 'Peggy, you have to let him hold you because you're about to be swept away!' This went on for what felt like an eternity – it really did look as if she was about to be drowned – and then Colin manfully threw his leather jacket into the water over her, scooped her into his arms and carried her up the ladder. When he passed the shivering bundle to me I burst out crying. The thought of losing her had been too much to bear.

Honestly, I can't remember a time when I've felt the intensity of dread that I felt on that horrible day. The notion of life without Peggy . . . well, it was a notion I couldn't entertain. It would be simply – an empty life. And, grim as it was, the pain I felt when I thought that I was about to lose dear Peg is testament to just how good our relationship is. How, despite her being a dog, how real and meaningful it really is. I had the thought, during this awful drama, 'It's better to have loved and lost than never to have loved at all', as they say. I saw that, hard as it would have been to lose Peggy, it would be much, much worse never to have had her at all.

Perhaps not surprisingly, it got me thinking about Peggy's inevitable death. Don't worry, this isn't going to descend into a meditation on mortality and the ultimate silence of being, I'll leave that to the Booker Prize long-list, thank you very much. But this is a book about a dog and I did promise we'd explore all key areas of dog ownership. Which, hideously, must at least nod to the inevitable end of dog ownership. It's a sad fact that dogs simply don't live as long as humans. Science may one day find a way to change this (urh, imagine how a seventy-five-year-old West Highland terrier would smell), but for now it seems that I am likely to outlive Peggy by a (hopefully) considerable stretch. Of course, I thought when I first sat down to mull this over, of *course*, horrible as losing Peggy would be, it won't be a patch on the grief you feel when you lose a human companion, will it? Surely not. But I imagine the immediate grief, the first few hours, days, weeks, are actually every bit as hard to deal with when it's a pet. Particularly when you are in a one person-one pet family unit and all your love is channelled to that animal. But – MDRC, please forgive me if I appear flippant here, I honestly don't mean to be, I appreciate that loss of any kind is confoundingly difficult, and my deepest sympathies if you're currently in the midst of it – at least with a human death you've got the funeral to organize. Something to keep you distracted in the initial stages of grief. With a pet you've got, well, nothing really. The vet might ask you what you want to do with the remains – incinerate, take home and bury or perhaps taxidermy. I think I'd quite enjoy Peggy looming over me for all eternity. But then, well, it's just a bit weird, isn't it? Where would I put her? Mantelpiece (or MENTALpiece as it would probably be known) or private shrine? And can a love survive the downgrade from living pet to ornament? Would I have to dust her? And what pose would she be stuffed in? Already this is getting too weird, and Peg is still very much alive and barking.

Of course, some people do hold funerals for their pets. But in my experience, pet funerals have a terrible tendency to become accidentally, side-splittingly hilarious, despite the effort one might make to the contrary. There's something about the funereal outfits, the tissues at the ready, the order of service, the carefully selected, suitably reverent outdoor space, the tiny coffin, the hush falling as the celebrant utters the opening words to mark the life of . . . Waffles the hamster. What hymns do you sing? The only one remotely appropriate is 'All Things Bright And Beautiful', and even that's borderline. And then there's the eulogy to be got through. With the exception of guide dogs, Olympic show-jumping horses and the odd miracle cat which calls the paramedics because it sniffs diabetes on its elderly owner, the life and achievements of any animal basically boil down to 'walk, sleep, eat, toilet, cuddle, eat, yap, scratch, toilet, sleep, eat, walk, OOH LOOK A SQUIRREL!, toilet, scratch, yap, eat, sleep, sleep, sleep, eat, sleep'. Not a bad list of achievements (indeed one I personally admire), but not a memorial supplement in the *Sunday Times*, either. And how do you play the whole guest-list business? Ask all the neighbourhood pets? Forty humans gathered round mourning the passing of a pet is scarcely less ridiculous than five cats, a handful of assorted birds and a horse in a smart black suit standing beside the open grave. No, it's too mad. No funeral, I'm afraid. It'll be straight to the taxidermist to have Peggy sewn into her *Strictly Come Dancing* outfit and stuffed into a tango pose. Sorry, what a thought. That's quite enough morbidity for one chapter, let's bring the focus back to good old life, the realm we're lucky enough to be inhabiting at this moment (unless you're reading this from beyond the grave, in which case HELLO! What's it like there? And could you please ask my Granny M to get in touch and tell me where she put the key to the Welsh dresser?).

In addition to teaching me just how deep my bond with Peggy ran, The Terrible Tale Of The Thames Near-Miss (starring Meryl) taught me the biggest of the big fat spiritual lessons I was gleaning of late. Faith and trust. Peggy had absolutely no reason to trust me that day in Kew. The beach was getting narrower, the river was coming in, and there was no help or hope in sight. But she blindly trusted me. There were so many unanswerable questions for her, yet she loyally and faithfully did what I was encouraging her to do. It got me thinking about my own faith in . . . well, I say God, but you may say Life, or the Universe, or the Fundamental Goodness and Purpose of Everything. Because often we don't know why we go through rubbish in this life, why we're lonely and confused, why things sometimes hurt or break and, more to the point, why things break when we have done all we can for them not to. But a faith that it's all to a purpose, that we're being led somewhere good through our struggles, that it can be redeemed even if we are the cause of it, would help so much with that. I think. And that day on the towpath at Kew, as I hugged a shaking Peg, I knew I would step back into having a faith at the centre of my life. I couldn't be bothered to question any more. I would rather have a Peggy-like faith than not. Simple. Forget theological debate, I'll just believe, because it makes me feel safer, connected, in purpose, loved, and approved.

Life and love can be pretty blooming messy sometimes. Humiliating even. And maybe that's the point. Relationships are meant to disrupt you, shake you up, cause upheaval. We're meant to love people, to be chaotically interconnected. It's what makes life worth living.

Trots in, yawning, savoury-breathed, somewhat shaken after a dream in which she pursued a duck through the sky on a spaceship made of Scotch eggs HANG ON. We're back to talking about stupid boring human relationships, ARE WE? I can't keep up. I'm emotionally drained. And I thought this book was meant to be entirely about ME. Well, when my reality show comes good I'll be the celebrity. And she'll be ten paces behind me on a lead. *trots off, arse as high in the air as is possible, poo hole a little too prominent*

These lessons and experiences brought me to the conclusion that while Peggy's a wonderful teacher and companion . . .

I knew she'd come to the right conclusion.

. . . whom I love deeply, alone she wasn't enough.

What now please, say again? *scratches ear*

I needed a person again. I needed to let someone in, and to risk all the heartbreak and chaos that doing so would entail. Yup, MDRC, I was finally ready to put myself out there.

WHAT?!

A wonderful thing to realize. Brilliant, vital, thrilling, galva-
nizing. But also, let's be frank, completely and utterly terrifying and confounding. Every time I ponder the world of
romance a giant sea monster of panic rears up out of the
calm water of life and threatens to swallow me whole. First
of all, what THE HELL does it mean to 'put myself out
there'? To telegraph my sexual availability to all passers-by?
This isn't *Sex and the City*; I can't just whack on a Wonderbra,
pay someone $200 to wax off all my body hair, then sit on
a barstool and wait for Kyle MacLachlan to come and drag
me up the aisle. I'm a shy, gangly, awkward Brit in Marks
& Spencer's clothing, who spends an awful lot of time with
her dog. Mainstream culture doesn't cater for the likes of
me, dating-wise. There isn't a template. I could start wearing
a short skirt and giving traffic wardens the glad-eye, but I
worry my neighbours might just call the police, assuming
someone was running an illegal brothel with me as the 'star
buy'. And what if I *do* end up snagging some sort of 'date'
with a gentleman caller? I'm afraid that just ushers in a fresh
hell of those first couple of dates. There is one thing
accepting yourself fully at home, at work, with friends, in
relaxed company, but when it comes to dating, for some
reason self-acceptance suddenly flies out of the window. You
start questioning how to be on an extreme meta-level. 'OK,
come on, Miranda, be erudite and cultured with a wide
range of interests, have lots of hobbies, but not too many
as you want him to think there's space for him in your life.
Don't be too keen, don't be too standoffish, don't eat very
much, but eat enough to help you not be too drunk; eat
seductively, but DON'T TRY TOO HARD' and on and on
and on and on, until I'm so anxious I smear butter up my
arms trying to 'sexily' eat half a bread roll, then sit in silence

for fifteen minutes before blurting out 'I love Badminton!' and bursting into tears.

I'm probably only so harsh on myself because I have to admit I am quite harsh on men. I find the smallest things off-putting in a first-date environment. For example, I once abruptly ended a fledgling relationship when the man turned up on a folding bicycle. I'd managed to get past the health-and-safety visor he was wearing (bit awkward but OK), and the bicycle clips (again, not massively sexy but not deal-breakingly so), but I abruptly balked when I saw the folding bicycle. There's not many things I know for sure, but I know that I could never, ever be S-E-X-U-A-L with a man who rides one of those. They look like little clown bicycles! With those tiny little wheels and that high wobbling seat. What next, a penny-farthing? Or a tandem, which he'll think 'romantic' for me to ride on the back of, even though really it's deeply creepy and embarrassing and disruptive to the flow of traffic? And like we are on our way to some kind of strange dressing-up show where we pretend to be Wartime People for possibly sordidly S-E-X-U-A-L reasons. No, I couldn't have it. The strength of my feeling around this maybe gives you a clue as to why I've spent so much time as a single woman. I think I may have created in my mind a Prince Charming, some kind of folding-bicycle-free, never-irritating perfect human with just the right level of sensitivity and humour and intellect, who of course doesn't even nearly exist. Or does he? I don't know.

*It doesn't matter! You've got me! I don't ride a bicycle. I can't! And I'd never even try, promise! *looks up with the most pleading endearing please-keep-loving-me eyes in the world ever**

During this exploratory, yes-I-think-I-would-like-to-be-with-someone-again phase, I did have one pretty successful evening, actually. I got as far as bringing the man in question back to my place, which felt like a big and potentially scary step. And no, not because I might be thinking about rampant bedroom shenanigans on date one, thank you. I'm very much of the 'let them wait and if they disappear because you wouldn't put out then they weren't worth being with anyway' school. But the chance for more intimate conversation and a kiss never hurt anyone. The scary step is, in my view, the showing-someone-your-house-for-the-first-time business, what a nightmare. What if they think it's a tip, and consequently write you off as a pig? Do you tidy the house before you leave as a precaution, or might that make you feel a bit slutty? But you can't risk somebody coming back and seeing the takeaway boxes and the *Riverdance* DVD (what? Just because Irish dancing went out of fashion, it doesn't mean it's any less entertaining). But what if you do tidy, and then he doesn't come home with you, and you end up going home alone to be faced with your über-tidy, man-ready living room? Depressing.

But at the end of one date, I did invite the man back to my (pre-tidied) house. The bins were out, the embarrassments were hidden, the toilet was scrubbed and sparkling. I'd thought of everything, except . . . Peggy. I hadn't mentioned her to my date and perhaps just as crucially I hadn't mentioned my date to Peggy. She took an instant and violent dislike to him, yapping and going on the attack. I had to scoop her up and physically restrain her to stop her taking a chunk out of the poor man's ankles. He was kind about it, and suggested that maybe she was behaving like this because he was a stranger in the house. To which I responded out of some kind of perverse urge to defend Peggy, 'Oh, no! That's not it. I've had lots and lots of men round.' Before continuing, unnecessarily and in a panicked manner, lest he think I was some kind of strumpet: 'I mean, not just *men*, ha ha, I mean plumbers and builders and gas men and . . . no, hang on, that sounds worse . . . I'm not saying I go about shagging tradesmen, no, just there have obviously been men here . . . not loads and only ever downstairs – and by downstairs I mean downstairs in the house not downstairs in the trouser department! Ha, oh dear. Good word, trouser. Trouser. That'd be a good name for a dog, wouldn't it? (shouting) Trouser. Come here, Trouser! Gosh. Sorry. Rambling . . . do you want to use the toilet upstairs? I cleaned it. Not that it was especially dirty or anything . . . oh golly . . . is a snog out of the question?'

It turned out that a snog wasn't totally out of the question. But before we could even get close to that happy outcome, Peggy had to be dealt with. I shut her in the bathroom, and joined my beau on the sofa. After thirty seconds, I realized that Peggy's whining would be too much to bear – it sounded like she was being murdered. I brought her out, and put her in her basket. I got back on the sofa, ready to crack on with the romantic fun-times. All went well, until he lunged in for a kiss and Peggy sprang into life and 'joined in', licking my face furiously, and his. MDRC, there's a reason that not one *Cosmopolitan* guide to dating recommends inviting a small dog to join in with the snogging element of things. It is the ultimate passion-killer. The gentleman, unsurprisingly, left.

Well, I thought she was for once letting me lick her lips! I thought it was a licking game. I don't see why everyone should get to play a licking game without me.

256

Still, there might be certain advantages to having an over-protective hound supervise my love life. Dating-wise, Peggy could turn out to be a pretty good wheat-from-chaff sorting machine, so to speak. For example, things didn't go much further with that particular man, and I'm not especially sorry about that. It turned out he wasn't remotely right for me. And I wondered if Peggy's response had been telling; perhaps this guy gave off some sort of bad-egg smell (not a literal bad-egg smell, that would be mega-grim and I totally would have noticed it – I mean, more the vague but definite air of not being the sort of person I'd want to get to know better). For a man to be a part of my life, he absolutely must accept Peggy. That was non-negotiable. That was the deal-breaker, and it's a good test of a fellow, I think. If I believed that Peggy was the reason I'd healed enough to be ready to date, then the men I went out with must love her, if not quite as much as I do, then nearly as much.

After the first guy that Peggy vetoed, dating got a little easier. I managed to bust through my folding-bicycle-style prejudices and fears, remembering the lesson that life and love aren't perfect. Everything's a bit jagged round the edges, a bit not quite how we'd like it to be, and we need to embrace that, enjoy it, learn to love it if we're going to lead full and fully human lives.

The wise lessons I was learning from Peggy were certainly enough, even if I now had to admit that – as far as relation-ships went – Peggy alone may not have been 'enough'.

'Enough' again! It's getting too much to bear.

CHAPTER 10

Famous Peggy

By this point, MDRC, I was giddy with self-acceptance, a desire for new adventures, and a happy sense that being a bit of a dog-loving oddball was going to be my lot in life, so I might as well get used to it. And while surfing the wave of this good feeling, I thought that it might be fun to let Peggy have a bit of the spotlight. Yes, she had been part of *Miranda* rehearsals, and yes, she'd mixed with show-biz dog royalty on *Call the Midwife*, but I am talking about the next step. I was ready to bring Peggy into the public eye. She'd sat so kindly and loyally alongside me as I struggled through the fear and mess of getting my sitcom written and made; and she'd stood unconditionally alongside me through the ensuing fear and mess of negotiating fame, the least I could do was allow her a bit of the sparkle. My personal life was a simple one, not full o' sparkle or glamour (feign surprise please), but the job did occasionally lend itself to heightened moments of both and I wanted to share those moments. Put simply, I enjoyed my life better when Peggy was around. She made me feel secure, connected, safe. It sounds odd, but after a particularly intense or fun experience it felt rather lonely to return to an empty house and only have a dog to recount the tales to. Whereas those times she had been with me and we returned home together, there wasn't a sense of needing to share the day's experiences with anyone. I had shared them already by a constant connection to the person – rather, animal – I lived with. The segue from show-business bustle to stark solitude wasn't felt nearly as acutely, or at all. It would be hard to suggest a 'bring-a-husband-to-work day' and insist they follow you ten steps behind, not get in the way, or not speak unless spoken to, and ideally wait in a shabby Portakabin ready to give a loving welcome every time I returned. That wouldn't do at all. A pretty little dog is far better suited to the razzmatazz of the situation.

Peggy enters, imagining herself wearing a pink silk bathrobe with a feather trim, sequinned slippers, false eyelashes, and enormous, rhinestone-studded sunglasses. Looks around imperiously Finally, Peggy's Dear Reader Chum, FINALLY she gets to the important part of the book. The beginning of my Elizabeth Taylor-like ascendancy to the exalted position I now hold, an icon of glamour and an inspiration to all. *sniffs bottom, likes it, farts, falls over (probably slightly like Elizabeth Taylor did in her later years); trots off in search of a Martini glass, even bigger sunglasses and a little folding chair with her name embroidered on the back*

The business of acting involves a fair bit of, what we call, publicity. 'Publicity' is, of course, a euphemism for 'shameless and compulsive showing off', and jolly good fun it is too. A few weeks before a new show airs I have to start tarting myself around town, chatting to journalists and popping up on chat shows. If you suddenly see me in *Garden Fancier* magazine giving a 300-word interview about 'My Very Favourite Spade', then odds are I'm doing it because I've got a show to promote. It's not everyone's cup of tea but I enjoy it, and not just because it's nice to be out of the house, with others, but because it's celebrating the work that is finally safely in the can and the months of hard slog are over. For me, publicity is basically a bit of a party, with a school's out vibe.

Peggy On Telly

It was via the sitcom series three publicity-splurge that I ended up appearing on *The Jonathan Ross Show*. With my dog. Yes, with Peggy, on screen. It was her first foray into the narcissistic bunfight that is the world of mainstream media and I must stress, MDRC, it wasn't my idea to bring her on with me. I've only just got comfortable with putting myself out and about. I still have to suppress the female urge to go about apologizing for my own existence, and the thought of my insisting that I turn up with a fully groomed bichon frise was far-fetched, to say the least. I was happy to go public with Peggy, be seen out and about, at work and otherwise; didn't mind being snapped with her, etc., but I wasn't suggesting actually working WITH her. I mean, what next, an end-of-the-pier act – Ms Randy Heart with The Amazing Peggy Sue Doggy! No no.

It was actually Jonathan's idea, and his concept for the Peggy appearance was quite a fun one. He knows that I absolutely can't stand dogs in costumes. As I've said, I think you can tell by their faces that they more than don't like it. I don't care how excellent a Captain Hook costume you've made for your dachshund, to me he'll always look like a prisoner of war. If you're not quite with me on this point, MDRC, try turning the tables and imagine how *you'd* like it if someone accosted you on your way to work – on a perfectly normal day, you understand – and said 'No! No! Sorry! You have to stop, I'm afraid. Today you must go about your business dressed as Chewbacca. Yes, in this costume which I bought online and which is actually made for someone with a completely different body type to yours. Why? Well, simply for my amusement, of course! Why else? Hurry along and change please. Now, thank you!' I think we can all agree that that would be horrendous, so I don't see why we should do it to our beloved pets. Mr Jonathan Ross is, I'm afraid, of the opposite persuasion. He is defiantly pro-dogs-in-costumes; he likes nothing more than to see a poor innocent terrier wearing a giant foam tomato outfit, or an Afghan dressed up as Darcy Bussell. He finds such things jolly. They tickle him. So his suggestion was that I would arrive on the show, alone, as normal. We'd do a bit of chitchat, and eventually he'd bring the conversation round to Peggy, specifically to how much I hate to see a dog in an outfit. Jonathan would then suggest that perhaps Peggy likes to dress up when I am not around, at which point the cameras would cut away to the green room and – tah-dah! – Peggy would be waiting with the other guests, wearing some sort of hilarious/abusive costume. And cue my shock, horror, surprise and spontaneous laughter. Ladies and gentlemen, the magic of television.

Cut to the night itself. It was the first time I'd done Jonathan, as it very much were, and I was looking forward to it. All the chat shows are filmed at the London Studios on the South Bank. Arriving there can be a bit of an 'experience'. You get a small slice of royal treatment as you're picked up in a big shiny black car, which I must stress is actually pretty rare in show business (unless you're Hollywood famous. I'm talking 'British sitcom show business' here, which is a pretty earthy, budget-constrained variety of show business). My experiences of show business are generally more of the 'standing in muddy car parks at five in the morning eating sausage rolls and shivering' variety, so the little bits of swish-ness are enormously enjoyable. There are sometimes crowds of people lining the railings outside the studios, hoping to get a glimpse of the guests. I find this quite embarrassing to deal with anyway, and clambering out of the car with Peggy by my side made it all the more awkward. In my mind I tried to pull off a look that was a cross between Audrey Hepburn and Paris Hilton, but more than likely I appeared as some doddery old opera diva who refuses to travel anywhere without her little dog. Peggy seemed embarrassingly, Justin Bieber-ishly keen to 'greet her public' at the railings, and I had to give her a pretty firm yank to get her into the studios.

Just inside the entrance to the London Studios there's a corridor lined with pictures of celebrities who've appeared, not only on *The Jonathan Ross Show*, but also on all the other shows filmed in the venue. Everyone from the Loose Women to Alan Titchmarsh to Bette Midler to Stephen Mulhern. And of course, Paul O'Grady and his dogs, Buster and Olga.

*Peggy, now positively loose-tongued on the Prosecco that
Miranda spilt, chimes in sniffily*:

GRIM little doggies. Common. Yappy. Look like they
ought to be chasing around behind a butcher in the 1950s.
Just saying it how I see it . . .

As I approached my dressing room, my thoughts were still
skittering about wildly in the vein of 'oh, gosh, I'm a middle-
aged-before-her-time freak on telly with her dog; what if
Peggy does something awful, what if I do something awful;
this isn't like Graham Norton where all the guests are on at
the same time, I'm going to have to go out there and be
entertaining ALL BY MYSELF'. The stressy voice was taking
a while to let go and allow the newly formed self-acceptance
to get a look in. But Peggy yet again helped me through as
I realized I *wasn't* going to be by myself. Eccentric as the
set-up was, it'd be very hard for me to be boring on the show
with Peggy by my side. Even if I screwed it up, she'd be there
for everyone to coo and aaaah at. I decided to stop worrying
and just enjoy it. After all, there's nothing quite like show
business to force you into the moment. No matter how hard
you work, your big moment could pass at any second. It'll
be someone else's turn soon. Which is sometimes frightening,
of course, but part of the natural cycle of things. Things are
born, rise, peak, fall away. And that knowledge forces me to
enjoy every last bit of it.

And there were some lovely things to enjoy that day. You
don't get paid for going on Jonathan Ross, or any chat shows,
but they make it up to you with some delightful freebies and
a bit of comfort. Towelling robe, cupcake, iced water and
the most brilliant goody bag: candle, face cream, and –
weirdly but delightfully on this occasion – a free night in a

B&B in Gloucestershire. MDRC, I'm only mildly ashamed to admit that I am a total fool for a goody bag. Like Christmas stocking presents all for you, bundled up into a delicious package for you to crack open at your leisure. Honestly, you could put a pair of crusty football socks and an orange into an old Tesco bag, tie it shut with some electrical tape and write 'GOODY BAG' on it in biro and I'd come running.

So caught up was I in the fun of having a chat-show guest dog-diva moment – mouth full of cupcake, emailing the free B&B via the in-studio Wi-Fi to see if they had a hot tub – that when the young, fresh-faced production runner nervously popped his head round the door and asked if there was anything I needed, I found myself looking him fiercely in the eye and saying, 'Yes, the six puppies I ordered for Peggy to play with don't seem to have arrived. Please get it sorted.' The poor boy looked absolutely terrified, mumbled, 'Oh, shit, right, gosh, sorry, let me look into that,' and scurried off. I had to chase him down the corridor to reassure him that I was joking. But, blimey, he must get some very odd requests if he considers six puppies to be a plausible one. I don't know how anyone feels comfortable asking for room temperature Aqua Libra and sixteen square inches of gluten-free Paxo cooked in an ice-bowl shaped like a llama, or whatever it is the kids are asking for these days.

After spending a little while in the dressing room getting myself nerved up, Peggy and I were led down the corridor to the green room. I was a bit nervous but basically shipshape and ready for the off, only to discover that the other guests were acting god Michael Sheen, and almost definitely the coolest man in the world, Noel Gallagher. And there was me, bumbling and trundling along with my dog – aka NOT cool.

My crazy dog-spinster fears reared up a tad at this point. I mean, for goodness' sake! Who wouldn't feel a bit frumpy in front of Noel Gallagher at the best of times? Our meeting felt particularly peculiar because it turns out he is very slight, both lean and small, and there can be no denying it, I made him look like a borrower. I launched into an 'oops, must try and salvage this' tirade.

'Hi, so just before I say even hello Noel . . . and hello . . . well there I've said it . . . but I just have to say that this dog thing was Jonathan's idea . . . nice to meet you by the way . . . I mean she is my dog . . . but I don't . . . hi Michael, by the way, sorry just explaining to Noel that this is my dog but not my idea she's here . . . we don't usually do appearances . . . or tricks . . . although she can, but I won't show you "play dead" . . . I just don't usually . . . anyway, hello . . . Noel, I'm loving Noel Gallagher and the . . . ooh I've forgotten the band name . . . Low-flying geese . . . no, what is it? Birds, high-flying birds . . . yes, sorry . . . ' I was verbally assaulting these men. Which was one thing, but made about 1,000 per cent worse because, for an unknown reason, I started to speak in a sort of Mancunian accent. Yes, I began to imitate Noel's accent. To Noel. Why, why, why did I do this? Particularly when my attempt at a Manchester accent goes into a very camp generic Northern which is not only offensive but makes me sound like I am preparing to play Widow Twanky for a six-month run in Scarborough.

PDRC, I would say it was worse than the Dr Hunky-Viking-Vet scenario. Seriously. She should have just let the attention come to me; it's where everyone wanted to focus anyway. I was the star of the show, I think you'll find. Because really, who are people going to remember, when

all's said and done? The so-called 'actor', or the 'pop star'
or the 'comedian'? They're ten-a-penny. No, they'll
remember the rare and generous appearance by the quite
staggeringly beautiful shih-tzu/bichon-frise cross. Won't
they? Yes. They will. Thank you.

Noel gallantly and graciously let me finish my tirade and
then said, 'Yeah, great, well I love dogs.' Just as I was about
to slip into a negative spin imagining what he must think of
me, he said, 'Me and my Mrs love your show.' WHAT?! Noel
Gallagher likes my brand of silliness. 'It's proper funny.' OH
MY WORD?! I have to say it was just the boost I needed as
the show began. As is the custom on *The Jonathan Ross
Show*, there were cameras in the green room and the audience
was given a quick peek at all the guests: Michael elegant,
erudite Sheen, Noel über-cool Gallagher, and . . . Miranda
with-her-dog Hart. Again, a pang of, 'Oh, golly me, what if
my Mr Right's watching this at home; what if he was entertaining the notion of me as a viable option only to see I was
"with dog" and renounces, Duncan Bannatyne-style, "Ooh
no, I'm out."'

I brought this train of thought to a close, sharpish. Nope,
I decided. Enough of this. I am in a brave new world now.
A brave new world, where I am unashamed of myself, my
dog and my public Peggy and me relationship. A brave new
world, where I am out and proud, and if you don't like it,
hypothetical Mr Right watching at home and judging me,
then you can lump it. It is, quite frankly, your loss. For I am
fabulous and Peggy makes anyone's world a fluffier, lovelier,
funnier, relaxed-ier (aware that doesn't work) place. I'm
going to be calm, and embrace this experience in all its
oddity.

I was the first guest on, and while Jonathan and I chatted, the props man sneaked Peggy off camera, put her in her outfit, and returned her to the green room under the watchful eye of Michael Sheen. As planned, we finally cut away to Peggy in her costume – an enormous Mexican hat and a sort of smock with fake hands sticking out the side.

Peggy stomps in with a towelling dressing gown tie draped over her that she can't shake off Oh, she's got to this bit, has she? This utterly hilarious (NOT) part of my Jonathan Ross experience? Miranda thinks I have gone all starry but umm, excuse me . . . *insists they play Classic FM not Heart at her next grooming appointment* . . . this was just really not how you treat a dog of my level . . . You see, PDRC, I was whisked out of the nice green room where I was really enjoying some Twiglets and swapping stories with my friend Noel Gallagher, when I was only jolly well KIDNAPPED and put in the worst sombrero hat anybody has even seen, and a smock which made me look DUMPY, and then plonked down in the arms of Michael

Sheen (who is NOT my friend because he allowed this situation).

Do you think this is any way to treat a celebrity because that's just what I am now, that's just a fact, a celebrity who not one hour previously had been cheered and fed chips by a crowd of admirers and given a cupcake to eat (OK, I might have sort of stolen the cupcake, but you know what I mean, PDRC)?

Would you treat Joan Collins this way? Would you kidnap Joan Collins and put her in a sombrero hat? Or Cameron Diaz? Or the Duchess of Cambridge? WOULD YOU PUT THE DUCHESS OF CAMBRIDGE IN A SOMBRERO HAT? NO? THOUGHT NOT! *drags bed into the middle of the room so she is the focus of all attention, wipes bottom along wooden floor*

And it worked brilliantly; she looked completely hilarious and massively put out by the whole business.

Um, yes – FAKE HANDS!!!!! There were FAKE HANDS!!!!!!! RIDICULOUS. This was end-of-the-pier stuff, which I rightly consider myself to be quite seriously above.

And thank God it worked brilliantly, because my big 'comedy entrance' had slightly backfired. You see, the previous week Lady Gaga had appeared on the show, and had insisted on the set being transformed into a farmyard – hay bales instead of sofas, that sort of thing. I jest ye not. Now THAT'S a lady who can go proper diva. Dress of meat, and all that. Not something you want to try with a dog around. Maybe I could vibe a small gilet of Quorn. Anyway, Gaga has no fear of whether she comes across gaga (do you see what I did there, pleased with self) and she walked on with a sheep (again, not jesting), a real live sheep as a 'gift' for Jonathan. So I thought it would be funny if I made a comedy version of Gaga's entrance. And chose to bring on a guinea pig. On a lead. But I'd failed to take into account two things. First, that the joke would only work if you'd seen the show the week before and, secondly, that Jonathan was massively allergic to guinea pigs. So I basically looked like a, what I call, prize tool, vamping on randomly with a rodent on a lead, bringing Mr Ross out in hives. So yeah, thank God for the successful Peggy-centred animal-costume humour to cancel it out.

It was a fun, daft old night, and on the way home I reflected how far I'd come in the last five years, since I'd had Peg. Not just professionally but emotionally. I thought back to those early days, when I was ill and heartbroken and about as wretched as I'd ever been, not even wanting to take her to the park for fear other dog owners would engage me in small talk. My sitcom hadn't been commissioned yet; there wasn't even much of an inkling that it was going to be. And now here we were, Peggy and me, together on a prime-time Saturday night chat show, promoting its series three, with Peggy acting as my comedy wing-man.

Actually, Jonathan Ross hadn't been our first public appearance as a duo. It was certainly the thing which thrust Peggy irreversibly into the public eye, in a no-going-back-now sort of way, but a few weeks before the Ross recording I'd had a photographer come to my house who'd become ever-so-slightly obsessed with Peggy, and for some daft reason I'd consented to the pair of us being photographed together. Thinking, I suppose, that there was no way the Peggy-and-Me shots would make the article. Cue a front cover of a magazine, me and dog.

Peggy's been on a number of photoshoots since. We've got a few 'poses' down pat! Peggy seemed to have become part of my 'brand'. During Comic Relief 2013, for instance, when I was completing a week-long challenge in the lead-up to Red Nose Day, BT, the sponsors, made a five-foot-high Peggy replica which people could put money in. I even started sharing the odd tweet about her. I'm not the most enthusiastic Twitter user, but even I couldn't resist sharing when I came downstairs one morning to find that Peggy had eaten half of a wooden spoon. She must have nosed the dishwasher open – admittedly carelessly and improperly shut by me – and pinched it. I was at once terrified (surely a dog could die from eating half a massive spoon?) and strangely proud (she clearly wanted fibre so she went and found it. Resourceful!). I decided that this was acceptable Twitter fodder, and my faith was justified by a vast number of tweets coming back accusing Peggy of being a 'shit-stirrer'. Very good, tweeple. Very good indeed.

Talking social media (I am so 'with it'), I had a YouTube near-miss around this time. That is, a Peggy moment so hilarious that, had I had a camera-phone to hand, I believe I could have generated an instant YouTube sensation. It was a moment when I accidentally dropped a wasabi pea on the floor and Peggy, thinking it was some sort of delicious treat, went for it. She got it in her mouth before I could grab it, and the reaction when she realized how hot it was, 'twas hilaire. She spat it out, then jumped spookily high with an air of 'OW, that's hot!' then sneezed, then had a little drink, then sneezed, then darted around perturbed, as if trying to come to terms with what she'd experienced. There was a brief pause – I thought perhaps it was all over – and then more sneezing, quite scared sneezing ('get this hot hot

hot-ness out of me type sneezing'), then some small skittish movements, some shaking, a pause, a sneeze, a drink, a pause, more sneezing, a run up and down the room until a collapse on the cool of the kitchen floor. Despite my initial concern it might have caused her damage, I was properly, oh-I-cannot-breathe doubled-over-on-the-floor hysterical. Which makes me think I must make a public disclaimer: MDRC, no matter how tempting it may seem, do not 'accidentally on purpose' drop a wasabi pea anywhere near your dog. No, stop it, back away now. You are NAUGHTY.

Despite no YouTube sensation, Peggy was now considered to be a part of me, in the public image sense. Very much a part of the Hart. Young girls started sending pictures of her for her to 'sign' (how, I wonder? Do they want her to lick them?). People would stop me on the street and ask, 'How's Peggy?', or comment on how cute she was. Being with Peggy publicly was not just fun and freeing but officially essential to my mental health and general wellbeing, as I was to fully understand when we went on tour.

Peggy On Tour

Peggy on tour sounds like it might be a section where I can regale you with ridiculous and hilarious anecdotes, hopefully this time without any kind of nudey flashing. I should have included some kind of warning upfront: 'If you are in recovery from any kind of bosom-flashing-related trauma please skip this chapter, and the next, and the next, and . . . oh all right perhaps just put this book down and go and read one by Clare Balding who is an altogether more dignified sort of lady.'

Perhaps, tour-wise, you were imagining Peggy hilariously

and inappropriately running on stage, desperate to find her lost mistress who had inexplicably been kidnapped by a crowd of 15,000 and was being forced to make a fool of herself in front of them. Or other such japes. But, no, I am afraid there aren't such tales to spin here, MDRC.

My overriding memory of Peggy on tour with me was simply how much I needed her. The more sober approach to what I want to share with you at this point indicates the depth of that need and how I really don't think I would have fared well at all without her. Also it perhaps indicates a more stressful point in my career. It was 2014 and the stakes had become rather high. I had thought a tour would be an amazing opportunity when I booked and planned it eighteen months before, but suddenly here it was. The reality of a one-woman stand-up tour set in. Me, on me tod, in arenas, for heaven's sake. The first woman comic to do an arena tour, if I don't mind saying so myself.

I hoped, of course, that audiences would enjoy it, that I would get laughs, hold my own, and that there would be moments when we laughed together, complicit, energized. And that was the case, particularly during any improvised, in-the-moment audience-participation stuff. Genuine love felt for the brave people who came up on stage to join me, and for the occasional magic that would pop up between us. But generally it was all pretty terrifying. Being faced with 15,000 people at the o2 was the biggest thing I think I will ever do. And Peggy became, well, more like the emotional assistance dog I had wanted to take on flights with me. A proper working hound.

I cannot imagine not having her in the dressing room. It was a great distraction arriving at new venues, as I put her little bed out, found a bowl to fill with water, and watched her settling into a new room, sniffing, barking at security men. Having someone else to think about took the edge off the impending, 'I'm going to be alone on stage for two hours in front of thousands of people' feeling that is quite hard to describe, frankly. Even as I try to write it down now, it goes beyond words, that feeling. Believe me, I needed that dog. I enjoyed walking Peggy into a venue – particularly the o2. It felt a bit Beyoncé. A bit pop star. A teeny-tiny bit A-list. And my tour was most assuredly NOT A-listy. I hate to disappoint you. It was just me and tour manager Barry turning up after a four-hour car journey made up of a three-hour-forty-five-minute discussion about crisp flavours. (In case you're interested – Prize for if you could only have one crisp flavour: Smoky bacon; Surprisingly delicious flavour: Worcestershire sauce; Unacceptable, should-be-banned, flavour: Roast chicken.) So Peggy did definitely give the whole arriving at a venue a bit of pizazz. Gave me a bit of status. I won't lie; I often pretended (quietly, to myself) to be a pop star on arrival at the bigger venues. It was the closest I was ever going to get, why not enjoy it? But more to the point, there was something so lovely about seeing little Peg running up and down the cavernous backstage areas of these vast arenas. It humanized the whole thing. A little burst of irreverent animal energy into a stark, intimidating environment.

It was during the interval that Peggy would really come into her own. Metaphorically, of course, she didn't have some kind of self-revelation suddenly turning into a wolf show-girl. I hated the interval. The adrenaline started to drop, but you knew you had another hour to go. You had the time to feel tired, to question your ability, to fear forgetting what was coming next. What I most needed and found hardest to come by was the chance to switch off a little. And I was given that chance when a little doggy would give me the best welcome ever. It was like she knew how much I needed her. Well, that and the fact that she hated being dumped in soulless dressing rooms and probably felt anxious by osmosis.

I would return, she would bring me a present and leap up at me, I would lie on the sofa, she would run all over me. Sometimes I lay on my stomach and I would love her leaping on my back trying to lick my face, thereby creating a sense of a fresh puppy sniffing at my ear. It was a full-on wordless love-in. The sort of 'animal therapy' that rich people might pay thousands of pounds for in rehab. Calming and funny and loving. I exaggerate not when I say I think I would have sunk into deep anxiety and aloneness if it hadn't been for Peggy at my side on tour (obviously Tour Manager Barry was a delight, but he was extremely professional and absolutely not up for interval ear-sniffing). As the crew embraced her, naturally and without comment, it was no longer strange to have Peggy as my public partner on the road. Peggy and I became used to, and embraced, the post-show screaming and the teenagers and, more to our credit, the screaming teenagers. She would be with me as we signed autographs, people wanting a feel of Peggy.

We knew Peggy was officially a tour success when she started to get fan mail. Yes, you did hear correctly, MDRC. She had been sent the odd thing before but now this was proper Peggy fan-dom. There were drawings of her, a few of which were actually very impressive. Others a bit more disturbing! Mind you, I did try and draw her once myself and created something that looked like a monkey impersonating Hitler so I cannot judge. She was sent leads. Collars. Bowls. A lovely rug with her name on which I still have – thank you, kind Australian. Some very sweet and useful things. Luckily I'm not the jealous kind, because it would certainly feel desperate comparing your own gifts to those your DOG had been given.

It was all good, as they say. Because if fans, tour crew, and kindly strangers were accepting Peggy as part of my life, it was showing me I need have no fear of how it looks, or the label it might give. I stubbornly refused to believe that being publicly, professionally paired off with a dog consigned me to the romantic bargain-bin along with the woman who has forty cockatiels and the woman who knits her own underwear. I continued to believe that through learning to co-exist with Peggy I was learning how to more comfortably co-exist with other humans. Every bump in the road we had I tried to chalk up to experience, to say to myself, 'Live and learn, Hart. One day you'll be glad Peggy put you through that. She's teaching you to chuck out your perfectionism and your daft Prince Charming-ish ideals. People (and dogs) will let you down, and shame you, and embarrass you, but at the end of the day you have to forgive them and go on loving them regardless.'

It's all instructive stuff. Dogs as teachers, forcing us to embrace the ultimate unpredictability of life. I absolutely love that. I couldn't believe how much I'd learnt from her, and how much she'd changed me. My work–life balance was better than ever – perhaps because I'd begun to really love my work, and work is 'life' too, after all – it doesn't do to try and tidy it away too much; and my world was full of joy and fun. The sun had got his hat on and I was out and about again, feeling ready for relationships, and relishing new experiences and new people. And at times I felt – perhaps this is over the top, perhaps not – that it was all because of Peggy. Of course, Peggy alone wasn't enough. As I've said, I needed people. But Peggy had, over the course of a few years, prepared me for my glorious re-entry into the human world. She'd gently ushered me from very dark emotional territory out into happier climes, and she'd given me so much faith in better things yet to come. What more could you ask for from a dog?

I KNEW I WAS A GURU!!!!! *eats foot* *washes bottom, hard* This really really warms the cockles of my lovely beating heart. Because even though Miranda is totes obviously a GIANT meanie who arranges for huge sombrero hats to be put on me when I'm least expecting it, and who feeds me wasabi peas and laughs at me, I do love her more than ANYTHING in the whole wide world. Even more than the Michael Ball dog; even my nightly Dentastix treat; even running back from miles towards her if I have got lost on a walk and her arms are outstretched and I am leaping in a grassy field towards my cuddly mistress. Even that. I just love HER. I mean, sometimes I think I love her so much that I'm going to literally excite myself to death when she comes through the door.

And even though I don't want her attention to be diverted away from me, then well, yes, if she really wants a boyfriend then I suppose she must have one really.

I wonder if I might like to have a boyfriend myself. Hmm. I would have said Michael Sheen, until he helped put the big hat and awful chunky smock on me. And then of course there's Michael Ball. And Michael Bublé. Perhaps I just really like people called Michael. Hmm. Michael Fassbender. Yum, we LOVE him. Miranda says he seems dirty but clean, naughty but nice, and angry but kind. And apparently that's good.

But actually I really really don't think I have the room to love anyone else. I don't even care about any of the show-biz stuff. (OK, I may have gone just a tiny bit starry, paws up.) My heart is just SO SO full of Miranda. *aggressively removes bit of twig from tummy, tumbles over* Sorry slightly ruined the moment there. *farts* Ooops. Tee hee hee.

CHAPTER 11

In Conclusion

MDRC, we are nearing the end of our romp together. I know. Are you feeling horribly sad that the fun times will soon be over? Or perhaps you're feeling relieved because the end of our tome will mean, tragically and painfully, the end of our time together. Of course, I mean the end of your and my time together, not the end for Peggy and me. As I hope you'll have gathered by now, Peggy and I will continue joyfully until death do us part. And, MDRC, I am feeling reflective. The impending ending (RHYME!) of the book has put me in that sort of sad, gentle, end-of-the-summer-holidays mood, a new-school-shoes, blackberry-and-apple-crumble mood, a where-did-it-all-go-right sort of mood, where all I want to do is kick back with a steaming bucket of hot choc and jolly well reflect on things.

So, with hot chocolate in hand, I shall narrow my eyes like a pirate captain and gaze back over the distance travelled.

And I must say, it's been quite a distance. I've come so far and learnt so much in the nine years I've been with Peggy that I look back on my younger self, myself as I was in my pre-Peggy and early Peggy days, with a tiny smidgen of embarrassment. As I skim back through our romp, I am principally ashamed by the way I've talked about pet owners. 'Dog Loonies', 'Crazy Dog People', 'Dog Nutters', 'Crazy Dog Owners' – there's a theme emerging here. I pretty thoroughly and heartily wrote off everyone who dared to display any sort of passion for their hound. I had my reasons – I was in a pretty bleak frame of mind back then; you could have shown me five hundred dancing Father Christmases throwing presents to laughing children and puppies, and I'd simply have shrugged, made a sort of 'bah' noise and thought 'what a bunch of weirdos. Hope they get arrested soon for a public order offence.' But my mental condition notwithstanding, I was so wrong about dog owners. So very, very wrong. Really couldn't have been wronger. I know now that behind what would appear to be eccentricity lies a real, wonderful, enthusiasm. And general passion and commitment and goodness. These people are simply just so enthusiastic and lost in what they're doing that it leaks out in odd ways.

But where would we be without eccentrics, and what I've unfairly called 'nutters'? Obviously, there are some kinds of nutters we could probably do without. The sort who run up to you in the street and set fire to you. The sort who storm your sister's wedding with pants on their head, wielding a pot plant and singing their way through the Susan Boyle back catalogue. They can take a step back, thank you very much. We can get along very nicely without them. But what about the lower-level nutters. The nerds, the obsessives, the people who exist just outside the 'socially acceptable' spectrum, but who so enrich the world with their passions? The people who run model villages, and birds-of-prey centres. I am a sucker for a model village or a bird-of-prey centre, or even a pottery barn or glass-blowing workshop. I literally can't see a brown sign off an A-road without swooping off to have a look. And these places, almost without fail, seem to be run by somewhat eccentric people. See also, gnome competitions. Without the odd, unfashionable people of this world, who would run the garden gnome competitions? Hipsters? Young urban professionals? Rock stars? I think not. There'd simply be no more gnome competitions in the world and the world would be an ever-so-slightly sadder, emptier place.

So if you happen to be someone who feels like an outsider, have been labelled cruelly by yourself or others a freak, then know that you are 100 per cent rock solid OK. Nay brilliant. It's society that's making you feel on the fringes. Which is dull and wrong of it. Because firstly, what is NORMAL? A professional person, with enough money to buy a Land Rover, who looks good in a pair of skinny jeans (whether they're male or female), who eats in moderation but loves a good wine and can name a grape and a vintage they particularly love, who can socially hold their own amongst a raucous group of clever, witty professionals conversationally covering all contemporary cultural bases from *The X Factor*, to where to send the kids to secondary school, to cricket or tennis, to *Question Time*, to Jamie Oliver? Well, if that's normal, then isn't that perhaps bland? Middle of the road? Someone just trying to fit in? Someone scared of who they really are?

And it's not just the model village managers; the celebrated in society, the people who bring us rock 'n' roll, ballet, contemporary dance, comedy, leadership, art, classical music, significant political and sociological change – well, they are the innovators. The 'eccentrics'. The 'nutters'. They are NOT normal. They are thinkers outside of the norm, which is why they do what they do. Anyone who denies themselves to try and be normal, well, THAT'S weird and unhealthy. Surely, we are all nutters. And we are all normal.

I'm thinking back now to the very very first days of Peggy – recorded, I believe, in Chapter Three. Shortly after getting Peg and surviving our first, hideous poocalypse, I felt brave enough to take her to the park. And, you might remember, I was struck dumb by the other dog owners I came across. So taken was I with my impression of them, that in typical comedy-writer style I saw fit to divide them into 'types'. And I'm sorry to say that I was pretty judgemental. Dismissing them as outsiders who I didn't want to be tarnished with by association. Now I think I'm ready to revisit those dog people in the park, and see what I didn't manage to see before.

First up, there were **People Who Talk Through Their Dogs**. These people I wrote off as the weirdos who come up to you uninvited to say things like, 'A hearty WOOF WOOF to you from me and Billy, Miranda and Peggy! We hope you're having the most marvellous of days! WOOF!' while their dog lies on the floor and crosses its paws over its face in shame. I thought these people had lost all sense of perspective, but now I think . . . well, they love their dog so much that they want to give it a voice. They wish it could join in with conversations. A character in a Nancy Mitford

282

novel once wrote that she desperately wished that dogs could talk. Well, so do the **People Who Talk Through Their Dogs**. And so do I. And there's nothing wrong with that, is there?

Next, I was confronted by the **Brisk Posh People Who Ask Lots of Questions**. I believe I made merry with the sight of their cashmere jumpers, husky gilets and bounding Labradors, as well as their habit of charging up to one with terrifying questions about your dog's breeding. In these people, I saw nothing but a bossy obsessive, making me feel rubbish about my own ignorance. But now, when I think of those people, I see the bright-eyed, excited enthusiast behind the bluster, spying a new member of their happy clan, eager to figure out where they might fit into things. And if these particular dog people weren't in the world, there would be no shows, no Crufts. I mean, if you think about it, there is nothing more geeky than Crufts. And nothing more wonderful.

Then there was the **Person With A Problem Dog**. I think I made light of these people for being in charge of a hound which gnaws through its lead, runs off and terrorizes smaller dogs, and causes motorway pile-ups. I thought, 'Ugh, I'll never be *that* person.' But after several incidences of Peggy jumping into rivers, running into traffic, and pooing in hotel rooms, I see this person as nothing more than a reflection of my own helpless self, doing his best and hoping against hope that this time the bloody dog won't ruin everything. Hats off to those carers of the trickier dog (or human) who put themselves to one side to provide love, care and nurture for whoever happens to make up their family.

I no longer feel embarrassment around the **Sweet Teenage Girl With A Puppy**. Nor, astonishingly, any need to please her, or to appear cool around her. The tremendous levelling effect of dog ownership means that I see her as a peer. I look at her and her lovely puppy and simply say to myself, 'There's another woman who has survived a poocalypse. I salute you, fellow poocalypse survivor. I wish all the best to you and your hand sanitizer.' What's more, the gulf between me and the **Scary Youth With A Staffie** has narrowed. Not, I assure you, because I have started to partake of any of his marijuana. No, now as always, I say a polite but firm no to drugs, but because I sense that behind the swagger this young man loves his Staffie more than all the world. The same way that I love Peggy, perhaps. Having her has given me 'compassion goggles'. I can now see a lovely luminous glowy bond between a man and his dog. Which makes it impossible for me to be scared of either of them.

My views on the **Professional Dog Walkers** – those terrifying human spiders who look as if they have been kidnapped by dogs – well, they have not changed at all! I still consider this to be a daunting system, but wish all the very best to those who choose to participate in it. Finally, the **Husband Who's Been Made To Take His Wife's Dog For A Walk.** Here I saw, and laughed at, a man strolling miserably alongside a dog of startling effeminacy, groomed to within an inch of its life, the man looking deeply uncomfortable and as if he'd pay any amount of money for the dog to vanish in a puff of smoke and re-materialize as a German shepherd. But now, I see much more. I see a man doing his bit for his family, exercising a much-loved pet. Or perhaps, I now wonder if the dog was actually *his* dog, and he was miserable for some other reason: perhaps he was heartbroken, or in financial difficulties, and this walk in the park was the only thing standing between him and a breakdown. I know from my own experience that when things feel as bad as they can possibly be, sometimes the only thing to do is snap a lead on the dog and get the hell outside for a big old releasing walk. Yes, I see it all differently now. My eyes have been well and truly opened.

And with that insight comes a fear, MDRC, a real fear of losing my dog. Thinking back to the early days, I wouldn't have been so devastated had Peggy been taken off me – of course, I wanted her to be safe and healthy, just as I would any animal – but had someone said to me, 'sorry, there's been a mistake, you need a special bichon-frise licence to be in charge of Peggy, please return her to sender instantly,' I would have been fine. Now, I don't know what I'll do with myself when she's gone.

I was recently given a hideous run-through of what I might expect when she does go. Just the other day, Peggy broke into my handbag and snaffled a bar of dark chocolate (I'm never without a little bar of chocolate, along with my emergency banana). Unfortunately, this one was a large bar, and Peggy, unbeknownst to me, ate the whole thing overnight. Dark chocolate is completely and utterly lethal to dogs, and the next morning I found her on the floor in a terrible state – imagine the heroine of a tragic opera, somewhere in the middle of Act Five, only with slightly more fur and vomit (one would hope – I don't know much about opera).

I rang the vet, who advised me to get hold of some charcoal tablets 'to help with the wind'. I wasn't entirely sure whether he was referring to me or Peggy (the stress had made me v gassy). Then it was to be a waiting game, pure and simple. The vet had said that the next twenty-four hours would be make or break, and since she had already digested chocolate and it was in her system, there was nothing I or anyone could do to steer things in the right direction. Initially, she was weirdly hyper – the caffeine in the chocolate bar was having an effect. Then she keeled over and slept, ever-so-slightly breathless. I didn't want to leave her but rushed to the nearest chemist to get the charcoal tablets. Despite the round trip being less than an hour, I couldn't help but fear the worse and found myself saying goodbye to Peggy as if it was the last time I'd ever see her. I stumbled to my car, and didn't notice how much I was crying until I was in a queue at the chemist holding some wind relief – what on earth were people wondering was wrong with me?! On return I put my key in the lock, and prayed that she'd bound up to the door, better, and greet me in her merry, healthy, doggy way.

Usually when I return home she'll rush over and spring into my arms, full of pure energy with the excitement of our reunion, before leaping down to rush upstairs, then back down again, find a 'present', leap on to the back of the sofa and present it, then crawl contentedly back into my arms. It's the best thing in the world.

But this time I opened the door and . . . nothing. No greeting, no dog, no sound. My heart sank; she's gone, I thought. I cast about the house, scared and wondering where I'd find her body. Or worse, Peggy on the way out, suffering and frightened and nothing to be done about it. I went upstairs, as prepared as one can ever be, only to find her sitting, very much alive, on the windowsill of my bedroom, looking at me as if to say, 'I'm feeling a tad grim, but hoorah for you being home, is it time for *Strictly*?' She wagged her tail softly and let out a little whimper. A bit of a muted greeting, but I tell you, MDRC, that muted greeting was so so so welcome. She just hadn't had the energy to run down-stairs and greet me. But somehow I knew she was going to be fine. I picked her up and tried not to squeeze her to her death, so relieved was I she was still with me, still mine, still my little dog. I cried as much as I did the first night I got her. But nine years later, life was oh so different.

I had often wondered what Peggy got up to, and how she spent her time when I was out, and now I knew. She sat on my bedroom windowsill, watching the street below, waiting for me to get back. Anxious perhaps, but trusting I'll return. And that's the real joy of a dog – that even when you're out in the hurly-burly of life, stressed-out and miserable, if you've got a dog you're never forgotten. There'll always be a creature at home waiting, who simply can't imagine the world without you. We get to experience the world – whichever bits of it we choose to go to – but our dogs only really experience things when we're around to guide them. They're very much at our mercy. It's not as if when we go out they can pop to the cinema or get on with a tapestry. Their lives begin when we tell them they do. Which is an honour and a huge responsibility.

Oh, PDRC, I really really can't imagine a world without her. Can you? Actually don't answer that. Tee hee.

I would like to say that I don't just hang about waiting for her to get home, that actually I do LOADS of my own stuff and keep really busy, and totally have my own life. But you know me by now, my life is completely and totally and utterly and really really really all about her. Which is why I just love my life so so much.

I do do SOME things when I am home alone. I really like playing Sofa Cushion Safari. It's a game I learned from Miranda, and it's really really fun. And then there's Snack 'n' Forage. That's a really exciting game where I go round every little nook and cranny searching for food that Miranda has dropped, and I eat that food. So you know, I do sometimes snuffle and wuffle about, but basically I just nap. On the windowsill. And either dream of her, or just wait and look at people walking past, hoping it is her coming back.

Despite everything we have been through and, Peggy's dear lovely friendly reader chum, who I love now too, there's really quite a LOT of things I have gone through for this lovely tall lady woman, I am still really committed to making it my sole job and purpose to love her as much as I can.

And it's not a difficult job.

Because it's a rock-solid love now. Not puppyish infatuation, or novelty. But a love based on nine years of shared experience, nine years in which life has changed totally for both of us. We have gone from two anonymous girls in a pen on the floor of the set of Not Going Out, *to ROCK STAR and ROCK STAR'S LAP DOG.*

I have had the BEST TIME with Miranda. I've been to beaches (pebbly and sandy), and moors, and have a really amazing local park where I love to chase ducks, but mainly eat the bread children feed them. I've been to hotels and TV studios, and rehearsal rooms, and film sets, and met some really quite famous film stars and everyone knows my name. I saw myself as chief security guard on her tour and I have been on so many amazing car journeys. I mainly sleep but sometimes I sit on Miranda's lap and look out of the window with her. (I don't like to put my head out, dogs are REALLY brave doing that; I can never breathe if I try it.) And I have been to different houses whilst she has writing 'breakdowns', and I have learnt lots of

*commands and love doing down and high fives with her
and her friends. There has been SO SO SO much we have
done together.*

*And perhaps, just perhaps, all those wonderful changes
happened because – oh, wait, no Peggy, NO CRYING – *big
whiny sniff, which turns into a snort* perhaps it all
happened because we found each other in those studios in
Teddington. Just in time.*

Thank God for Miranda. I love her.

*And I love you, PDRC, and I really really cannot WAIT
to meet you when we are out and about. Please come up
and say hi, just don't scream or do anything to make me
or my owner anxious.*

*Oh bye-bye, Peggy's chum, really miss you already.
*goes all misty eyed, turns and walks off, does a quick
look back, smiles, disappears round the corner**

So, MDRC, we really ought to be bracing ourselves for The
End. With considerable sadness, and also gratitude, because
it really is better to have loved and lost than never to have
loved at all, yes? Another lesson we've learnt from this tome.
And goodness, there have been a few big lessons, haven't
there? It's extraordinary and indeed surprising the wisdom
that's come to me through Peggy. I've learnt that if I trust
Life/God, as Peggy trusts me, then I'll be gently led wherever
I need to go. I've learnt that no matter what's going on, no
matter how tense I am, or neurotic, or worried about something, I can choose to deal with it Peggy-style by letting out
a long breath, bringing myself into the moment and
embracing all the positives around me. I've learnt the joy of
being needed, of being the best and most important person
to another living creature. The importance of community,

fellowship, friendship, relationship. I've finally learnt about the glory of self-acceptance, particularly acceptance of one's own eccentricities and quirks and great huge galloping weirdnesses. And I've realized before the self-approval, before the critical voice has been dampened, relationships will always be like wading through treacle. I've learnt the glorious truth that life and love are messy and unglamorous, and that is a wonderful thing indeed. And I know that, while I hope my life will continue to expand in all sorts of directions, it would be fine, actually, if it was just Peggy and me. There are worse fates that could befall a woman.

Perhaps, MDRC, I'd have reached these conclusions on my own. Eventually. But learning it through dog ownership has been kinder, faster, more positive and more fun than any other method would have been. Through having Peggy, I've shared what I now realize is a genuinely significant life experience, and it's made me more empathetic, more open-minded, and far kinder and more loving.

As regards being more loving, I'd like to share something with you. I try to keep my personal life personal, but I think that you and I trust each other now. For it finally happened, MDRC. All the lessons I had learnt meant I finally opened up the Hart heart again and it led to the most wonderful romance. I found a nice guy – he liked me, he liked Peggy, he even had a dog of his own. I knew it was meant to be because Peggy relaxed her usual regime of scaring the crap out of him the second he came near me. And we fell for each other. There was hope, there was laughter, there was that wonderful early stage of getting to know each other, becoming more and more comfortable, feeling understood and loved. After a few months together we had a week or two in a beautiful country cottage at the height of summer. It was the most perfect, romantic time. Sun-loungers, hammocks, bonfires, walks and all that jazz. Tinged with sadness, though; we knew it would never be this perfect again. For complicated circumstantial issues beyond our control, we both knew that this was probably the end of our romance. We weren't going to be able to make this work long term; it wasn't our time.

At the end of the most perfect holiday, he had to leave first. We said goodbye, knowing it was over but saying nothing, and he drove off down the dusty track (we really should be bringing in some swelling romantic music now, MDRC – feel free to put some on yourself). As he stuck his hand up through the sunroof of his car and waved at me, I cried. A lot. It could have been the start of something so wonderful; but I knew it had to be the end of what was just a beautiful beginning. As his car finally disappeared, I felt terribly alone. More so than ever. I had experienced togetherness and intimacy for the first time in a long time. I now knew what I was missing. And that hurt.

I looked down at Peggy. There she was, sitting loyally beside me, watching what I was watching, checking as ever there was nothing she needed to protect me from. Nine years ago, if I had experienced a painful goodbye, I don't think looking down at my new dog would have made me feel strong again so instantly as I did that day. The love I felt looking at Peggy was so deep my hurt and aloneness vanished. I did feel loved. Content. And I knew there would be time for another beginning. And, more to the point, I would never be alone for as long as my little Pegster lived. It would always be Peggy and me. I wiped away the tears, picked her up, and looked into her eyes:

'It's you and me against the world.'

Acknowledgements

My first big thank you has to go to Hannah Black at Hodder who has guided me through an unusual and stressful publication process with such kindness and patience – from losing the first finished draft three years ago in a burglary to editing this version on my bed whilst I was recovering from an illness. I like to think that was a career high for her! Also thank you Vickie Boff; and to all at Hodder for waiting for and supporting the rewrite.

And following swiftly on to Gordon Wise at Curtis Brown for guiding me through not only the last three years but being a wonderfully supportive agent full stop. And to Rose Heiney for being a genius creative sounding board.

But because this book only came to be due to the existence of the best dog in the world (wholly impartial) my thanks go to all those who have looked after her over the last nine years. Marcia Stanton (who bred her and gave her an amazing start), Sarah and Arun, my sister and her family, Mum and Dad (and Tommy the cat who is scared of Peggy and hides at the end of the garden – what a pussy), DogTown Groomers, Short Bark and Sides (best groomers name ever), Barry and Laura Hilton, Mark Turner, Todd Talbot, Lucy Villiers, Flora Saxby, Lou DiCastiglione, Chris and Nicky Bligh, Beth and Anna

293

Downham, Katie and Philly, Steve Eames, Jools Voce, the cast and crew of *Miranda* (especially Ian Locker) and *Call the Midwife*. Thank you.

And a huge special mention to illustrator and dearest friend Jenny Meldrum who has not only walked Peggy but has captured her in the most beautiful way in her truly wonderful drawings throughout this book. I hope you love them as much as I do.

Peggy would like to thank . . . well, me basically.

Do you wish this wasn't the end?

Join us at www.hodder.co.uk, or follow us on
Twitter @hodderbooks to be a part of our community
of people who love the very best in books and reading.

Whether you want to discover more about a book
or an author, watch trailers and interviews, have the
chance to win early limited editions, or simply browse
our expert readers' selection of the very best books,
we think you'll find what you're looking for.

And if you don't,
that's the place to tell us what's missing.

We love what we do, and we'd love you to be part of it.

www.hodder.co.uk

 @hodderbooks

 HodderBooks

 HodderBooks